STUDIES IN IMPERIALISM

General editors: Andrew S. Thompson and Alan Lester
Founding editor: John M. MacKenzie

When the 'Studies in Imperialism' series was founded by Professor John M. MacKenzie more than thirty years ago, emphasis was laid upon the conviction that 'imperialism as a cultural phenomenon had as significant an effect on the dominant as on the subordinate societies'. With well over a hundred titles now published, this remains the prime concern of the series. Cross-disciplinary work has indeed appeared covering the full spectrum of cultural phenomena, as well as examining aspects of gender and sex, frontiers and law, science and the environment, language and literature, migration and patriotic societies, and much else. Moreover, the series has always wished to present comparative work on European and American imperialism, and particularly welcomes the submission of books in these areas. The fascination with imperialism, in all its aspects, shows no sign of abating, and this series will continue to lead the way in encouraging the widest possible range of studies in the field. 'Studies in Imperialism' is fully organic in its development, always seeking to be at the cutting edge, responding to the latest interests of scholars and the needs of this ever-expanding area of scholarship.

Chosen peoples

Manchester University Press

SELECTED TITLES AVAILABLE IN THE SERIES

WRITING IMPERIAL HISTORIES
ed. Andrew S. Thompson

GENDERED TRANSACTIONS
Indrani Sen

EXHIBITING THE EMPIRE
ed. John M. MacKenzie and John McAleer

BANISHED POTENTATES
Robert Aldrich

MISTRESS OF EVERYTHING
ed. Sarah Carter and Maria Nugent

BRITAIN AND THE FORMATION OF THE GULF STATES
Shohei Sato

CULTURES OF DECOLONISATION
ed. Ruth Craggs and Claire Wintle

HONG KONG AND BRITISH CULTURE, 1945–97
Mark Hampton

Chosen peoples

THE BIBLE, RACE AND EMPIRE IN THE LONG NINETEENTH CENTURY

Edited by
Gareth Atkins, Shinjini Das and Brian H. Murray

MANCHESTER UNIVERSITY PRESS

Copyright © Manchester University Press 2020

While copyright in the volume as a whole is vested in Manchester University Press, copyright in individual chapters belongs to their respective authors, and no chapter may be reproduced wholly or in part without the express permission in writing of both author and publisher.

Published by Manchester University Press
Oxford Road, Manchester M13 9PL
www.manchesteruniversitypress.co.uk

British Library Cataloguing-in-Publication Data
A catalogue record for this book is available from the British Library

ISBN 978 1 5261 4304 4 hardback
ISBN 978 1 5261 6020 1 paperback

First published 2020

The publisher has no responsibility for the persistence or accuracy of URLs for any external or third-party internet websites referred to in this book, and does not guarantee that any content on such websites is, or will remain, accurate or appropriate.

Typeset
by Toppan Best-set Premedia Limited

CONTENTS

List of figures—*page* vii
Contributors—viii
Acknowledgements—x

Introduction — 1
Gareth Atkins, Shinjini Das and Brian H. Murray

Part I: Peoples and lands

1 'A bad and dangerous book'? The biblical identity politics of the Demerara Slave Rebellion — 29
 John Coffey

2 Babylon, the Bible and the Australian Aborigines — 55
 Hilary M. Carey

3 'The Ships of Tarshish': the Bible and British Maritime Empire — 73
 Gareth Atkins

4 Jeremiah in Tara: British Israel and the Irish past — 88
 Brian H. Murray

Part II: The Bible in transit and translation

5 The British and Foreign Bible Society's Arabic Bible translations: a study in language politics — 111
 Heather J. Sharkey

6 Empire and nation in the politics of the Russian Bible — 129
 Stephen K. Batalden

7 Contested identity: the Veda as an alternative to the Bible — 151
 Dorothy Figueira

8 'The Bible makes all nations one': biblical literacy and Khoesan national renewal in the Cape Colony — 167
 Jared McDonald

CONTENTS

9 Distinction and dispersal: the nineteenth-century roots of segregationist folk theology in the American South 186
Stephen R. Haynes

10 Afterword/afterlife: identity, genealogy, legacy 205
David N. Livingstone

Select bibliography—216
Index—222

FIGURES

4.1 *British Israel, and Judah's Prophetic Messenger & Universal News* (2 September 1880). © British Library Board. *page* 103

5.1 'Three Bible Women, Assiut Conference', Assiut, Egypt, 1916. Anna B. Criswell Papers. Courtesy of Presbyterian Historical Society (Philadelphia), PHS RG 184–1–42. 118

CONTRIBUTORS

Gareth Atkins is Bye-Fellow in History at Queens' College, Cambridge. He works on religious culture and politics in eighteenth- and nineteenth-century Britain and the wider Anglophone world, ranging from maritime Christianity to constructions of heroes (and villains) from history: his edited book, *Making and Remaking Saints in Nineteenth-Century Britain*, was published in 2016. He has written widely on Anglican Evangelicalism and his monograph, *Converting Britannia: Anglican Evangelicals and British Public Life, 1770–1840*, was published in August 2019.

Stephen K. Batalden is Professor Emeritus of history at Arizona State University and founding director of the ASU Melikian Center for Russian, Eurasian and East European Studies. A specialist in the field of modern Russian religious and cultural history, his publications include *Russian Bible Wars: Modern Scriptural Translation and Cultural Authority*, winner of the 2014 Reginald Zelnik Book Prize for an outstanding contribution to Russian, Eurasian or East European history.

Hilary M. Carey is Professor of Imperial and Religious History at the University of Bristol. Her books include *Empire of Hell* (2019) and *God's Empire* (2011). She is currently researching a history of religious missions to the Polar North.

John Coffey is Professor of Early Modern History at the University of Leicester. He works on religion, politics and ideas in Britain, the United States and the Atlantic world, and has published extensively on puritanism and dissent, persecution and toleration. His current research is focused on slavery and anti-slavery, and he is the author of *Exodus and Liberation: Deliverance Politics from John Calvin to Martin Luther King Jr* (2014).

Shinjini Das is Lecturer in Modern Extra-European history at the University of East Anglia. She is a historian of the British Empire, with a focus on colonial histories of South Asia, medicine and Christianity; and the author of *Vernacular Medicine in Colonial India: Family, Market and Homoeopathy* (2019).

Dorothy Figueira is a Distinguished Research Professor at the University of Georgia (USA) and an Honorary President of the International Comparative Literature Association. Her scholarly interests include

CONTRIBUTORS

religion and literature, translation theory, exoticism, myth theory and travel narratives. She is the author of *Translating the Orient* (1991), *The Exotic: A Decadent Quest* (1994), *Aryans, Jews and Brahmins* (2002), *Otherwise Occupied: Theories and Pedagogies of Alterity* (2008) and *The Hermeneutics of Suspicion* (2015).

Stephen R. Haynes is Curry Professor of Religious Studies at Rhodes College in Memphis, Tennessee. He is the author or editor of thirteen books, including *Noah's Curse: The Biblical Justification of American Slavery* (2002) and *The Last Segregated Hour: The Memphis Kneel-Ins and the Campaign for Southern Church Desegregation* (2012).

David N. Livingstone is Professor of Geography and Intellectual History at Queen's University Belfast and a Fellow of the British Academy. He is the author of *Nathaniel Southgate Shaler and the Culture of American Science* (1987), *Darwin's Forgotten Defenders* (1987), *The Geographical Tradition* (1993), *Putting Science in its Place* (2003), *Adam's Ancestors* (2008) and *Dealing with Darwin* (2014). He is currently working on an intellectual history of climate determinism to be entitled *The Empire of Climate*.

Jared McDonald is a Senior Lecturer in the Department of History at the University of the Free State, South Africa. He holds a PhD in History from the School of Oriental and African Studies (SOAS), University of London. His research interests include indigenous responses to British colonialism in the Cape Colony during the early nineteenth century, the work of the London Missionary Society in southern Africa, settler-colonialism, and comparative histories of children as victims of genocide.

Brian H. Murray is Senior Lecturer in Nineteenth-Century Literature at King's College London. He is co-editor of *Travel Writing, Visual Culture and Form, 1750–1900* (2015) and *Commodities and Culture in the Colonial World* (2018). He has published articles on Victorian travel writing, nineteenth-century Ireland and the literature of African exploration.

Heather J. Sharkey is a Professor in the Department of Near Eastern Languages and Civilizations at the University of Pennsylvania. She received her PhD from Princeton. Her books include *Living with Colonialism: Nationalism and Culture in the Anglo-Egyptian Sudan* (2003), *American Evangelicals in Egypt: Missionary Encounters in an Age of Empire* (2008) and *A History of Muslims, Christians, and Jews in the Middle East* (2017).

ACKNOWLEDGEMENTS

The idea for this volume, and several of its chapters, emerged out of a workshop organised by *The Bible and Antiquity in Nineteenth-Century Culture*, an interdisciplinary research project funded by the European Research Council (ERC) and hosted by the Centre for Research in the Arts, Social Sciences and Humanities (CRASSH), Cambridge. The editors wish to acknowledge the contribution of all participants and attendees, including Simon Goldhill, Jeremy Morris, Scott Mandelbrote, Janet Soskice, Michael Ledger-Lomas, Alison Knight, Theodor Dunkelgrün, Kate Nichols, Alex Bremner, Halvor Moxnes, Robert D. Priest, Rana Issa, Richa Dwor, Julius Lipner, Andrew Preston, Emma Hunter, Hephzibah Israel, and the late Anthony D. Smith. They would also like, belatedly, to thank the administrative staff at CRASSH for making the practicalities of putting together an event feel so straightforward.

The resulting book is all the more coherent for the painstaking comments and suggestions of two anonymous readers, while its rapid and painless acceleration into print is thanks to the efficiency and attention of Emma Brennan, Alun Richards and the staff of Manchester University Press. Chapter 3 includes material previously published in Gareth Atkins, '"Isaiah's Call to England": Doubts about Prophecy in Nineteenth-Century Britain', *Studies in Church History*, 52 (2016). This material is republished with the permission of the editors of *Studies in Church History*. Chapter 9 includes material previously published in Stephen R. Haynes, 'Distinction and Dispersal: Folk Theology and the Maintenance of White Supremacy', *Journal of Southern Religion*, 7 (2015). This material is republished with the permission of the Association for the Study of Southern Religion.

The research leading to this volume received funding from the European Research Council under the European Union's Seventh Framework Programme (FP7/2007-2013)/ERC grant agreement no. 295463.

Introduction

Gareth Atkins, Shinjini Das and Brian H. Murray

This book will explore how biblical themes, ideas and metaphors shaped narratives of racial, national and imperial identity in the long nineteenth century. It will argue that, far from being a mere relic of a supposed earlier 'age of belief', the Bible supplied languages and frameworks for both interpreting and challenging imperial modernity. In one sense this is a simple claim that rests on the physical ubiquity of Bibles as objects. 'The Bible itself', as the late Christopher Bayly pointed out, 'was, of course, the single most published book in all the Protestant countries of Europe and North America.'[1] But the Bible and the biblical were also omnipresent in subtler, more pervasive ways. Even amid spreading secularism and the development of professionalised science, scriptural notions of lineage, descent and inheritance continued to inform not just popular understandings of race, nation and character but the conceptual scaffolding surrounding them.[2] Although new scientific ideas challenged the historicity of the Bible, high priests of the new discipline often chose to explain their complex and radical ideas through biblical analogy: the emerging 'science of race', for instance, recycled the vocabulary of Genesis.[3] Denizens of the seething industrial cities of America and Europe championed or criticised them as New Jerusalems and Modern Babylons, while modern nation states were contrasted with or likened to Egypt, Greece and of course Israel.[4] Imperial expansion, too, prompted people to draw scriptural parallels. In the self-consciously expanding 'Angloworld', European settler movements portrayed new territories across the seas as lands of Canaan, invoking as they did so the divine injunction to Adam and Eve: 'be fruitful, and multiply, and replenish the earth, and subdue it' (Genesis 1:28).[5]

Yet such language did not just travel in one direction, from centre to periphery; nor did its significance remain the same in new cultural and social contexts. Settlers abroad continually faced the challenge of singing the Lord's song in a strange land, and if many colonised and conquered peoples resisted the imposition of biblical narratives, they also appropriated biblical tropes to their own ends. Across America, Africa, the Middle East and Asia, scriptural stories, scenes and phrases provided ideological ammunition for liberation and nationalist movements; and by the late nineteenth and early twentieth centuries they also fuelled scholarly accounts that challenged the superiority and exceptionalism of Europe and the West, both by advancing alternative understandings of the Bible and by putting forward alternatives to it. If Adam, or Noah, or Jesus were black, what were the implications for white supremacy? And if Indian or Chinese holy books could be seen as alternative Scriptures – Scriptures, moreover, that might boast better-attested claims to antiquity and longer pedigrees than the Judaeo-Christian Bible – how did this in turn affect the authority of Christianity? The answers to these questions, and the tensions that they generated, continue to resonate today. This is reflected in our occasional use of a very long nineteenth century indeed: recognition that 'nineteenth-century' ideas had their roots in earlier thought; and that the theologies, ideas and images we examine did not die out in 1900.

This book, then, starts from the contention that it is impossible to understand empire, nationalism and race in our period without considering the Bible, both as an established source of images, metaphors and political ideas, and as a quarry in which scholars and ordinary readers alike could turn up new and potentially unsettling finds. This is an argument that needs to be made. Classic studies by Elie Kedourie, Ernest Gellner, Tom Nairn, Benedict Anderson, Eric Hobsbawm and John Breuilly continue to propagate the view that nationalism was an offshoot of a secular-minded Enlightenment, meaning that religion has often been dismissed as a 'residual category' in an anti-clerical modernity.[6] Critical theorists of empire and imperialism, from J. A. Hobson to Homi Bhabha, have dismissed the expansion of Christianity as largely a by-product of imperial strategy, seeing the Bible as a weapon deployed in the name of larger political, military or economic ends.[7] While historians of the European missionary project, on the other hand, have added much-needed nuance to such accounts, rightly pointing out the often strained relationship between 'the Bible and the Flag', they have also tended to downplay the extent to which theological justifications were invoked at almost every phase of imperial expansion.[8] And notwithstanding recent work by R. S. Sugirtharajah, Susannah Heschel, Colin Kidd and others, scholars of racial, national and imperial identity in the nineteenth century continue to overlook the prevalence and relevance of Scripture and scriptural language even in secular contexts.[9]

INTRODUCTION

In one recent collection, the Bible did not even make it into the top ten books 'that shaped the British Empire'.[10] Our book insists that biblical narratives and ideas were ubiquitous, albeit in nuanced and problematised forms, and in engagement with other intellectual and cultural currents. Ideas about racial purity, chosenness and sacred genealogy were forged through a ramifying global conversation in which the foundational traditions of Christianity and Judaism developed in dialogue with different cultural traditions, new textual and archaeological discoveries, linguistic study and translation. Taking our lead from wide-ranging studies such as Colin Kidd's pathbreaking *The Forging of Races: Race and Scripture in the Protestant Atlantic World, 1600–2000* (2006), and from James Turner's *Philology: The Forgotten Origins of the Modern Humanities* (2014), this book emphasises the continuing importance of the Bible in a self-consciously 'modern' epoch.

In doing so, though, it underlines in exciting ways the provisional and shifting nature of its significance. Modern scholars have tended to follow either Benedict Anderson in conceiving of 'identity' in national terms as something coeval with the nation state, or Frantz Fanon and others in emphasising a hardening of racial categories with the rise of European overseas empires. We argue decisively that the Bible could at once bolster nationalist and imperial causes and at the same time confront them with uncomfortable counter-narratives. Slaves and their owners, abolitionists and anti-abolitionists alike all returned repeatedly to the proof-texts that justified their views.[11] Bibles shorn of problematic sections were specially produced for distribution in the British West Indies.[12] In Chapter 1 of this volume John Coffey shows how controverted passages from the Book of Joshua and slave congregations' understandings of them were probed in court in the famous trial of their pastor, the Congregationalist missionary John Smith. Biblical stories thus shaped and were in turn shaped by identities and power dynamics. Building on the burgeoning but often disparate scholarships of print culture, translation, biblical scholarship and the institutions that nurtured it, the postcolonial Bible and global religious movements, this book makes an ambitious contribution to a rapidly developing field.

The remainder of this introduction opens up in more detail the main themes of the book. The first section considers how and why missionary organisations and their supporters came to place such weight on the power of the Bible. It shows how a new stress on the agency of an unmediated vernacular text reshaped the metropolitan religious world, creating powerful voluntary agencies whose financial power and cultural reach was founded on the funds they could raise and the supporters they could mobilise through print publicity, lobbying and mass subscriptions. Impelled by millenarian expectation, they deployed the latest technology and organisational innovation to translate and distribute as many Bibles as possible around the globe. The following section examines the myriad ways in which scriptural translation was implicated in processes of European imperial expansion. Briefly touching on what translation meant for the missionary societies, it explicates how translated texts were invoked in justifications of empire as well as the movements and ideologies that resisted it. The final section explores some key developments that shaped understandings of 'race' in the nineteenth century. While acknowledging a shift from paternalistic universalism in the early century to a more rigidly differentiating 'scientific racism' in the second half of the century, it also notes the persistence of the Bible in discussions of ethnic difference during this key period of European imperial expansion.

The power of the word

In the nineteenth century the Bible became for the first time a genuinely global phenomenon. Organised missionary effort was nothing new. But in the sixteenth and seventeenth centuries Catholics led the way, largely in Spanish and Portuguese South America but also in India and China.[13] Protestants had universal aspirations, but these were as yet pipe dreams. For all their success in forging Calvinist or Lutheran 'internationals' based on migration, correspondence and print, these were geared more towards connecting the faithful in the Protestant European heartlands and across the North Atlantic world than to preaching the gospel to the 'heathen'.[14] To be sure, there were attempts to evangelise Caribbean slaves and Native Americans, as well as efforts to proselytise in colonial possessions further afield.[15] But these were sporadic and often resource-starved, depending as they did on over-extended voluntary societies operating within parochially minded early modern state churches.[16] From the late eighteenth century, though, this began to change. In part, as recent revisionism has emphasised, this was an institutional story: of how those churches adapted, creakily at first but with growing success, to territorial expansion, emigration and colonial settlement.[17] But it was also a story of extra-ecclesiastical innovation, as a new generation of evangelical-led missionary societies radically altered the landscape. Prompted in large part by the exploratory voyages of Captain Cook, their ambitious plans bespoke the urgency of their projectors. The Baptist Missionary Society (1792) led the way, being followed by the London Missionary Society (1795), Church Missionary Society (1799), American Board of Commissioners for Foreign Missions

INTRODUCTION

(1810) and, linked to these, the Basel *Evangelische Missionsgesellschaft* (1815).[18] One result was a change in the centre of gravity. Whereas in the eighteenth century globetrotting Danish or German Lutherans trained at the Halle *Frankesche Stiftungen* were employed even by Anglican societies to fill manpower shortages, by the mid-nineteenth century the Protestant world was entrepreneurial, Anglo-American and centred on London as imperial metropolis. Linked to this was theological and organisational change, as predestinarian caution gave way to a more expansive embrace of the 'means' that would translate aspirations into actions.

Undoubtedly the most significant institution in these shifts was the British and Foreign Bible Society (BFBS), founded in 1804.[19] Central to its success was its harnessing of older ideas about Protestant patriotism: the early modern paradigm of the Christian nation as a 'new Israel' remained a powerful one, as Gareth Atkins shows in this volume, and not just in Britain.[20] Yet the rise of the BFBS was also context-specific: amid plunging French fortunes, its skyrocketing receipts in the 1810s were hailed by evangelicals as a divine dividend for Britain's investment in slave-trade abolition and, of course, the Bible Society itself.[21] It thus had immense political and cultural clout. Its leaders hobnobbed with Tsar Alexander, corresponded with Orthodox patriarchs and entertained visiting Persian dignitaries. Infusing its operations was a heady rhetoric that blended together Enlightenment practicality with eschatological triumphalism and a romantic desire to unify the human race. For the objective of the BFBS was at once simple and breathtakingly ambitious. It called on Christians of all denominations to unite in order to provide every inhabitant of the world with a Bible, without note or comment, in his or her language. 'As the influence of the Bible reached every home and heart, it would convert the world's population to a pure, scriptural Christianity, uniting all peoples in a common faith and bringing an end to war, oppression and injustice.'[22] Who, asked its supporters, could baulk at such a prescription? At home, results rapidly surpassed even the most optimistic projections. In war-ravaged Europe, the success of the new endeavour was still more striking. A German Bible Society auxiliary was founded at Nuremburg in 1804; a Prussian Bible Society at Berlin in 1805; Scandinavian societies from 1807. The nationalism that fuelled struggles against French occupation took on a strongly patriotic-religious tone, being actively promoted by rulers such as Frederick William III of Prussia, Francis I of Austria and Tsar Alexander. The latter's foundation of a Russian Bible Society in 1813, influenced by the millenarianism of prominent Pietist mystics in his court, was closely linked to his self-image as leader of what was subsequently to become known as the Holy Alliance.²³ Further afield, Bible Society branches mushroomed across the burgeoning British colonies: the Calcutta auxiliary was founded in 1811 and the Sydney one in 1817.

If the providentialism of the early nineteenth century was fuelled by geopolitical events, it was turbocharged by technology. Evangelicals in particular bought enthusiastically into industrial modernity in this period, believing that the divinely appointed means for bringing about the spread of the gospel across the globe had at last been laid bare.²⁴ Subscription guineas and steam-powered print seemed to be preparing the world for Christ's second coming. Hence pious publicists boasted of printing more Bibles in more languages at lower costs than ever before, driving a cycle in which technological advances and eschatological expectation reinforced one another.²⁵ At the Great Exhibition of 1851 the BFBS stand contained 170 versions of the Scriptures in 127 languages, handsomely bound in red morocco: a greater treasure, some pious visitors averred, than the great Koh-i-Noor diamond.²⁶ Nor did the flow of Bibles slacken off as the century went on: far from it. Even and perhaps especially in the era of higher biblical criticism, there remained a conviction among evangelicals across continental Europe, Britain and North America that the Bible was a stable, reliable set of texts that had not been – and could never be – challenged by textual or archaeological scholarship. Statistics continued to be invoked as evidence of success. Between its foundation in 1816 and 1880 the American Bible Society sold or distributed some 32 million Scriptures, while the price of a standard Bible dropped from 64 cents in 1819 to 2 cents in 1897.²⁷ The BFBS could boast still more impressive figures, having produced 186,680,101 copies by 1904 in 378 languages.²⁸

Underpinning all this was herculean voluntary effort. To dip into local and national publicity literature is to find exhaustive reports of books distributed, subscriptions collected and funds raised, down to the last farthing: the minute ledger-book record of one immense imagined community bent on a common aim. Where the BFBS led, other organisations followed: individual voluntary endeavour along similar lines was the motor for an extraordinary boom in philanthropic receipts. Small wonder that this was hailed as a new Pentecost that would unite not only denominations but races, languages and sexes. One of the features of Bible and missionary endeavours was their involvement of every member as an activist. 'The Hon. Mrs _____', stands for the many women involved in the cause: in 1810–11 she despatched 'to convicts, prisoners of war, cartels, soldiers, and sailors, &c. &c' some '3053 copies of the English Scriptures, 458 of the Spanish, 810 of the Portuguese, 393 of the German, 3118 of the French, 305 of the Italian, 188 of the

INTRODUCTION

Dutch, 92 of the Danish, 25 of the Welsh, and 59 of the Gaelic Scriptures ... [I]n all, 8396 copies.'[29]

Such labour was useful because the Bible was believed to have agency. Sometimes this was conceived in pragmatic terms: texts might travel cheaply and safely into places where missionaries could not – into malarial regions, for instance, or among closeted women in patriarchal cultures – and proselytise in print where preaching for conversion was banned, such as in the Ottoman Empire. Nevertheless, behind evangelical efforts to saturate the world with Scripture lay a deep-seated assumption that salvation came through reading and hearing an unmediated, unadorned text. Hence the division of imperial cities into districts which would then be traversed by distributors and collectors: another widely copied BFBS innovation that was as applicable in Bombay or Cape Town or Toronto as it was in darkest Birmingham. Hence also the establishment of Scripture depots and presses in Malta, Serampore and elsewhere, the spiritual equivalent of the coaling stations that dotted imperial possessions in the age of steam.[30] And hence the often forgotten fact that one of the main foci for Bible organisations was non-Protestant churches. One obvious if well-armoured target was the old enemy, Roman Catholicism. Increasingly, however, mass-produced Bibles were envisaged as a necessary transfusion of gospel life to ailing communions such as the Greek and Russian Orthodox Churches or the multifarious ancient sects of the Middle East, whose moribund state and perceived intellectual backwardness were ascribed to their neglect of the Scriptures.[31]

Yet although the rhetoric was grandiloquent and the statistics impressive, the vernacular Bible project did not always have the desired effect. Dealings with existing churches are a case in point. Despite promising starts in Russia and among the Orthodox ('Greek') church of the Ottoman Empire, relations soured owing to condescension, miscommunication, ignorance regarding ecclesiastical structures and the naïve insistence of the BFBS and ABCFM on using vernacular rather than traditional translations.[32] Testimony to the reach of British and German societies but not to the converting power of their wares were the copies of the Scriptures found everywhere in European Jewish households. Even among Protestant Christians, the ardent conversionism of the Bible Society blurred into broader ideas of what the Bible was and the benefits that it could bring. It should come as little surprise to find cash-strapped colonial authorities taking advantage of the manpower and money that the 'religious public' could mobilise to co-sponsor missionary-led schools, colleges and translation projects.[33] While it would be a mistake to see this as a cynical exercise in every case, teaching people to read using the Bible was undoubtedly part of the inculcation of 'civilisation', loyalty and 'British values' among local elites. White settler movements provide further evidence of a Bible whose importance was as much cultural as it was spiritual. The Bibles that travelled with them were umbilicals linking colonial New Worlds with homelands and histories, being often literally inscribed with family lineages and memories of denominational disagreement in the Old World. It was significant that the English version the BFBS chose to distribute was the King James because, unlike the Geneva or Luther or Douai Bibles favoured by some, it was now widely regarded as transcending denominational strife.[34] Such texts remained prominent even as the frameworks of interpretation and belief that surrounded them crumbled, being celebrated not just by conservative Christians but by liberals and agnostics too as centrepieces in national literary canons.[35]

The progenitors of the nineteenth-century Bible project did not, then, simply sow the Word and then reap the crop, as they hoped. But they did succeed in flooding much of the world with cheap copies of a text made ever more accessible by vernacular translation. That accessibility democratised the Bible but it also decentred its authority. Whether or not one welcomed that development – many did not – it was impossible to ignore the fact that an unmediated text imbued its readers with power. The black American loyalists of the 1780s and 1790s, most of them freed slaves, regarded their journey out of the thirteen colonies as a re-enactment of the Book of Exodus. When they arrived in Sierra Leone, the vaunted 'Province of Freedom', they came to realise that what had been billed as Canaan was in fact a return to Egypt. They flouted the political authority of the English governor ('Pharaoh') in favour of the Moses- and Joshua-like figures who had led them across the Atlantic, worshipping separately in black Methodist congregations, while colonial officials in turn condemned their emotional 'visions' and 'revelations' as unscriptural and presumptuous.[36] A similar story of the Bible as contested cultural and political resource is told by Jared McDonald in this volume. Paradoxically, the power of the Bible was also realised in movements for Hindu and Buddhist reform, many of which stressed the vernacularisation of holy writings and the importance of printed codifications of belief in ways that deliberately emulated those of Protestant missions.[37] Still more unsettling for ecclesiastical authorities was how the vernacular Bible provided raw material for individualistic expressions of belief, ranging from its apotropaic inscription on amulets to its defining role in the thinking of new sects, such as the Mormons or the South African Nazaretha Church.[38] For if the Bible became ubiquitous in our period, both as a text and as a symbol, this ensured that its meaning and significance would become ever more plural.

INTRODUCTION

Translation and the imperial Bible

The great nineteenth-century 'crop of new translations' thus engendered intended and unintended meanings for the Bible.[39] This was because of the many ways in which missionary translation became entangled with the ideologies, practices and institutions associated with European imperial expansion. Since the 1990s, a number of scholars have explored the translation of the Bible and its usefulness to the spread of Christianity. This historiography often shares missionary convictions regarding the translatability of the Word and its universally positive and enabling effects on recipient languages and cultures. Such writers uphold the view that the Bible was translated successfully and seamlessly into the languages of the world, resulting in 'renewing',[40] 'reawakening'[41] and the 'unification'[42] of diverse cultures and languages.[43] Indeed, the rhetoric of 'reawakening' and 'revitalisation' has been invoked recurrently by scholars such as Lamin Sanneh, who have been insistent on the transformative power of the Bible.[44] Rather than missionary imposition, he sees native agency and autonomy as features of the translation movement, suggesting that Africans came to possess their translated Scriptures 'like the ancient Israelites the promised land'.[45] Bible translation, it is held, enabled local cultures around the world to read a universal text and be part of a global community of believers.

Newer research, however, suggests that the process of translation and reading of the Scriptures cannot be studied in isolation from imperial networks. The works of Hilary Carey, Hephzibah Israel, Isabel Hofmeyr, Heather Sharkey, Stephen Batalden, R. S. Sugirtharajah and others, some of them contributors to this book, have opened up important conversations about the reception of the Bible in imperial (and mostly non-western) contexts.[46] In Chapter 6 of this volume, Batalden shows how the Bible Society's presence destabilised the relationship between the Orthodox Church and the Russian Empire, with the translation of the Bible into modern Russian, rather than the traditional Slavonic, becoming a sparkpoint. Here and elsewhere, Protestant insistence on the translatability and accessibility of the Bible collided with the idea that some languages might be more sacred than others; that the language of the everyday was insufficient or inappropriate for the expression of transcendent ideas; and that placing a holy book into the hands of everyone was foolish or even downright dangerous. Such linguistic politics were not unique to Russia. The choice of languages considered as fit vehicles of biblical translations was a contentious issue elsewhere, too. At the heart of the problem was what has been identified by modern translation theorists as the notion of 'equivalence': the presence (or absence) of a corresponding word or idea from the original language in the translated languages.⁴⁷ In late nineteenth-century India, for instance, missionary and educationist James Ballantyne of the Banaras Sanskrit College endorsed the use of Sanskrit as the most appropriate medium of scriptural translation while cautioning that Sanskrit terminologies came 'loaded with layers upon layers of meaning by virtue of the use of specific terms within varying pre-existing, self-referential, Hindu philosophical systems'.⁴⁸ Ballantyne also promoted translation of 'western useful knowledge' in Sanskrit, an effort that gained the support of the English Lieutenant Governor James Thomason, despite being in contrast to the official pedagogical policy of promoting Anglicism.⁴⁹

Missionary scholarship, through acts of representation and classification of the languages and religions of the world, contributed to the discursive formation of the colonised 'other'.⁵⁰ Yet, as Jane Samson has shown, Christian notions of the unity of humanity and the universality of the Gospel meant that the missionary encounter usually involved processes of both 'othering and brothering'.⁵¹ Scholars of missionary science, linguistics and anthropology have argued that many evangelists were torn between their missionary duties and their desire to document and understand host communities.⁵² But even if missionaries were not always conscious agents of empire, and sometimes opposed it, the presence of colonial powers often proved indispensable to the safety and smooth functioning of missionary organisations. Heather Sharkey illustrates how the growing presence of British and French colonial powers in the Middle East contributed towards loosening centuries-old Islamic-state restrictions on Christian conversion. The widespread evangelisation of Christians, Muslims and Jews only began in the late nineteenth century once the colonial powers were firmly entrenched in the region. Others have pointed towards the myriad ways in which missionary linguistics was caught up in how imperial authorities 'ranked' languages into hierarchies.⁵³ Hofmeyr in particular shows how both missionary and imperial efforts to own, classify and codify African languages initiated a complex language politics within which African Christians had to position themselves.⁵⁴

The numerous unnamed indigenous collaborators who aided the missionaries in their language training and translation also indicate the profound power imbalance inherent in acts of translation. It remained customary for translated Bibles to merely mention the role of 'native assistants' in passing.⁵⁵ Aside from Pundit Ramram Basu, an employee of the East India Company's Fort William College who assisted William Carey in his Bible translations, very few native collaborators feature in accounts of the extensive Baptist translation activities in India, for instance.⁵⁶ Basu's proximity to Fort William College and the Baptist missionaries, who were theoretically independent of government, reveal how missionary and imperial networks tended to mesh in practice. The journey of the Australian missionary John Fraser's Australian Awabakal Bible to the World Columbian Exposition of 1893, as shown by Hilary Carey, further illustrates that colonialism often fostered conditions not merely for the translation of Scriptures but also their circulation, preservation and eventual display.[57] Hence, more recently, scholars have been inclined to talk in terms of 'colonial Bibles' or 'imperial bibles' produced through processes of 'political translation'.[58]

It is, however, worth making clear that this volume is methodologically distinct from the strand of literature that labels itself as 'postcolonial biblical criticism'. Led by theologians and deeply steeped in textual studies of the Bible, postcolonial biblical scholarship has recently begun to pose questions of race, ethnicity, empire and liberation of received understandings of the ancient world of the Bible.[59] By contrast, we remain firmly committed to examining the Bible in the context of nineteenth-century empires.

The Bible was frequently invoked in crucial moments of imperial and national crisis. In response to the Indian Mutiny of 1857, British clerics, from London to Calcutta, drew on biblical metaphors to explain the rebellion as an act of divine punishment.[60] When Queen Victoria declared a nationwide 'Day of Humiliation' on 7 October 1857, Anglican and nonconformist sermons invoked Old Testament texts to explain the Mutiny as God's judgement on a sinful British nation. But as Brian Stanley has shown, many of these same preachers derided the East India Company's tolerance of 'Hindu idolatry' and argued that 'mutiny could have been averted if Britain had done more to evangelise India'.[61] Victorian homilies often became a site for articulating British national identity in terms of God's people waging war against God's adversaries. On a more provocative note, a group of theologians including Michael Prior and Mark Brett have claimed that parts of the Bible were invoked in direct justification for settler colonialism.[62] They argue that ideas surrounding the discourse in which a covenanted people receive entitlement to land provided effective justification for settler colonialism and the displacement of indigenous peoples in Latin America, South Africa and Palestine as well as Australia and Ireland.[63] It has been pointed out that specific verses from the Old Testament such as Genesis 1.28 ('subdue the earth') were frequently cited, from the seventeenth century onwards, both as a reason for imperial expansion and as a warrant for linking the cultivation of land to property rights.[64]

Meanwhile, scholars are beginning to appreciate more keenly than ever before how the Bible was appropriated by those on the other side of the colonial divide. For although evangelicals in particular and

Protestants more generally operated with the belief that language was an inert and transparent medium through which God's words could shine, there remained inevitable gaps between mission translations and their reception. Even when they sought to propagate a 'transnationally translatable monoculture', the messages Bibles bore were considerably re-scripted by the recipients.[65] In his study of language and Catholic conversion among the Tagalogs in the Spanish Philippines, Vicent Rafael was one of the earliest scholars to point out that the translated texts opened up spaces for Tagalog resistance to Spanish rule.[66] In the nineteenth century, too, biblical narratives of liberation and exodus were often crucial to anti-imperial resistance. Hence an account of the global Bible in the nineteenth century remains incomplete without understanding the 'intellectual brokerage' that enabled the receiving cultures to associate the Bible with their own aspirations. It is, therefore, imperative to study, as several of our contributors do, how missionaries collaborated and interacted with native people in different contexts. Existing literature offers tantalising hints as to how the Bible may have inspired important anti-colonial movements. Mark Brett mentions the example of Bildad Kaggia, a Gikuyu-speaking trade union leader whose translations of the Bible helped to form the intellectual roots of the Mau Mau rebellion against the British.[67] Mahatma Gandhi found the Sermon on the Mount to be a significant resource, much like the Hindu Gita, in thinking about modes of non-violent agitation. The sermon went 'straight to his heart' and taught him the importance of renunciation.[68] These details call for further exploration of the Bible's role in articulating political identities, movements and self-perceptions in non-Western societies in the long nineteenth century. Indeed, one of the central issues pursued in the volume is to examine the Bible as harbinger of national communities around texts and languages. Whereas Heather Sharkey notes the fault lines created in Arabic nationalism around the publication of an Arabic colloquial Bible, Batalden illustrates the role of the Jewish Bible in strengthening Jewish communities in Russia. Nineteenth-century racial theories of biblical origin continue to cast their long shadow in postcolonial societies. Hilary Carey reminds us that ethnographic and linguistic theories that construed Fijians as descendants of the Lost Tribes of Israel are still relevant in shaping Fijian identity today. These notions resurfaced as recently as the 1987 coup, when claims for biblical ancestry were used to support arguments by Fijian leaders for political and racial ascendancy over Indian and other ethnic emigrants.

Despite significant overlap, then, we should not conflate histories of the Bible's translation and reception entirely with histories of empire.

INTRODUCTION

A number of recent works have been careful in foregrounding contextual factors that shaped particular forms and meanings that the Bible acquired in distinct contexts. In Chapter 5, Heather Sharkey shows how on-the-ground competition between British and Foreign and American Bible societies, coupled with variable levels of language expertise, funding constraints, time and contingent events shaped the circumstances around the publication of Arabic colloquial Bibles. In her work on the Roehl Bible and Swahili language in Tanzania, Emma Hunter too has urged us to go beyond binary understandings of nation and empire.[69] While acknowledging a close relationship between missionary linguistics and the German colonial and postcolonial experience, she emphasises the need to view the missionary Karl Roehl and his collaborators and detractors, both African and European, as constituting a node within wider overlapping networks of Bible translation and the standardisation of Swahili as a written language. Our volume, likewise, pays close attention to the wider transnational and trans-imperial networks that facilitated the global circulation and reading of the Bible. In uncovering the nuances of 'imperial Bible', the chapters together explore the newer layers of meanings acquired by the Bible in course of its extensive transnational travels.

The Bible and race

We cannot understand how the Bible functioned as an imperial (or anti-imperial) text in this period without paying serious attention to the question of 'race'. In the postcolonial era, accounts of nineteenth-century racial thought have tended to trace the emergence of these discourses from the power structures of empire and the slave trade. Postcolonial historians and literary critics have also demonstrated how racist thinkers appropriated the language of science and received sanction from pioneering scholars working in the fields of linguistics, philology, archaeology and history. Recently however, Colin Kidd has suggested that race was also 'a theological construct' and, more provocatively, that 'scripture has been for much of the early modern and modern eras the primary cultural influence on the forging of races'.[70] As Kidd notes, the Bible became a quarry of racial thinking, despite the apparent indifference of biblical authors to questions of ethnicity and skin colour. How could a text that has so little to say about race give rise to so many explicitly racial interpretations? Yet while it would be inaccurate and anachronistic to project a politics of racial difference on to the Bible, both the Hebrew Bible and the New Testament are preoccupied with questions of genealogy, exile, migration, conquest, empire and 'nation'. As 'a source book of evidence for the dispersion of races and the beginnings of racial divisions and patterns', the Bible's silence on the physiological manifestations of ethnicity was an opportunity rather than an obstacle for exegetical ideologues.[71] As Kidd suggests, it is 'this very incongruity between the Bible's significance for an understanding of ethnicity and its silence on matters of race that has tempted theologians and other readers of scripture ... to import racial meanings and categories into the Bible'.[72]

Ethnological accounts of the past could also destabilise biblical chronology. At least one popular strand of scientific racism, polygenesis, was openly heretical in its suggestion that different races did not share a common human ancestor. The most extreme polygenesists denied the Christian principle of the unity of mankind and even regarded some non-white races as separate – usually inferior – species. Like Kidd, David Livingstone sees the origins of the nineteenth-century 'science' of race in the early modern period. While early modern scholars wrestled with newly discovered Egyptian and Chinese chronologies, the 'encounter with the New World threw into yet sharper relief the growing tensions between world geography and the Mosaic record'.[73] In *Adam's Ancestors*, Livingstone explores the long history of the 'Pre-Adamite' thesis: the notion that some form of humanity existed before the arrival of the biblical Adam. As Livingstone demonstrates, in the nineteenth century, the proponents of the pre-Adamite thesis included both monogenesists and polygenesists, Darwinists and religious conservatives.[74] Some even saw Pre-Adamitism as a way to juggle Darwin and Genesis. The Methodist geologist Alexander Winchell admitted that the first men were 'probably black' and originated in Africa. But he was also convinced that the divinely favoured Adam could only have made his appearance once 'under the law of progressive development, a grade had been reached nearly on a level with that of modern civilised man'.[75] Winchell's evolutionary and theological contortions were underpinned by his conviction that 'the black races, which he set out to establish as physically, psychically and socially inferior to whites, were not descended from the biblical Adam but predated him'.[76]

Many of the foremost proponents of scientific racism, particularly in its polygenesist form, attempted to extricate themselves entirely from residual trappings of religion. The Scottish surgeon Robert Knox began his notorious series of lectures on *The Races of Men* with the bald assertion that 'we know nothing correctly' of the origin of man. In an intellectual atmosphere in which 'the present organic world ... can be shown to have an antiquity agreeing ill with human chronologies', Knox would instead excavate the 'zoological history' of man.[77] Convinced that the Christian notion of universal brotherhood was a utopian delusion, Knox cited the history of sectarian conflict as evidence that racial differences could not be glossed over by religion. Modern Christianity itself exhibited 'a variety of forms essentially distinct: with each race its character is altered; Celtic, Saxon, Sarmatian, express in so many words, the Greek, Roman, Lutheran forms of worship'.[78]

The methodological flexibility of racist thinkers who read the Bible through the lens of ethnology was frequently mirrored by their opponents. When the abolitionist and former slave Frederick Douglass was invited to deliver a commencement address to the students of Western Reserve College, Ohio, in 1854, he took the opportunity to refute those who deployed polygenesis in 'denial of the negro's manhood'.[79] In a lecture on 'The Claims of the Negro, Ethnologically Considered', Douglass suggested that polygenesis represented not just an attack on black Americans but a heretical assault on the Gospel's promise of universal salvation and 'the whole account of creation given in early scripture'.[80] Douglass vigorously condemned the 'repeated attempts on the part of Southern pretenders to science, to cast doubt over the Scriptural account of the origin of mankind'. But his own lecture moved fluently from anthropological and geographical evidence to speculations on the complexion of Adam and the Ancient Egyptians, before concluding with a secular appeal to his audience's 'instinctive consciousness of the common brotherhood of man'.[81]

Douglass's speech testifies to the political stakes of racially inflected exegesis in nineteenth-century America. A racialised interpretation of the curses bestowed on Cain and Ham was a standard feature of pro-slavery discourse. In his comprehensive account of the 'perennial American tendency to apply stories from the postdiluvian chapters of Genesis to the problem of "race" relations', Stephen Haynes notes that by the 1830s 'Noah's curse had become a stock weapon in the arsenal of slavery's apologists.'[82] Indeed, as Haynes demonstrates in Chapter 9, these exegetical traditions continued to resonate into the twentieth century. The Mormon prophet Joseph Smith was another enthusiastic supporter of racial interpretations of Genesis. He and his successor Brigham Young put restrictions in place that would prohibit blacks from the lay priesthood until 1978. Smith's own 'translation' of the Bible, begun shortly after the completion of the Book of Mormon in the 1830s, inscribed racist exegesis back onto the text itself and offered 'a providential history in which the God of Genesis took an active interest in dark skin colour as a mark of divinely instituted curses'.[83]

Yet even in the dehumanising context of slavery, the Bible could also provide a site for resistance. If Genesis could be cited in defence of slavery and white supremacy, Exodus simultaneously provided a platform for liberation. As Eddie Glaude has shown, Exodus offered

African Americans a 'model for resistance' and 'a metaphorical framework for understanding the middle passage, enslavement, and quests for emancipation'. 'As time and distance folded in on each other', enslaved Bible readers 'became the children of Israel and the chosen people of God' and 'the sacred history of God's deliverance of his chosen people was transformed into an account of black liberation'.[84]

As many recent commentators have noted, emergent disciplines like ethnography and anthropology played an important role in mapping 'temporal' difference onto geographical distance. Non-European peoples in distant or 'isolated' regions offered potential glimpses of the primitive or savage past.[85] A parallel project subjected the early civilisations recorded in Scripture and ancient history to a distancing anthropological gaze. Suddenly, the rituals and rites described in the Hebrew Bible became grist to the mill of a synthesising anthropological imagination, as thinkers as diverse as J. G. Frazer and Sigmund Freud interrogated the Bible as the product of 'primitive culture'.[86] In his account of 'the impact of racialist analysis on biblical scholarship', Kidd notes a decisive anthropological turn in nineteenth-century biblical criticism: 'ethnology was added to the subjects on which a thorough biblical scholar needed to be expert' and the Holy Land 'became a scene of racialist anthropology'.[87] In works such as *The Races of the Old Testament* (1891), for example, the Anglican cleric and Assyriologist Archibald Sayce promoted the study of modern populations alongside archaeological and literary remains as part of a new discipline of 'biblical ethnology'.[88] At the same time, anthropologically minded missionaries were also keen to find traces of biblical peoples and traditions in the less familiar cultures of Africa, Australasia and the Pacific. In the present volume, for example, Hilary Carey demonstrates how John Fraser drew on a blend of missionary linguistics, ethnography and Darwinian science to argue that Australian aborigines were descended from the biblical Ham.[89]

Even more profound in its impact on the understanding of 'race' was the discovery of Aryan or Indo-European linguistics and consequent readings of the Bible as a product of a 'Semitic race'. As Maurice Olender has argued, although modern philologists and critics 'borrowed the techniques of positivist scholarship ... they continued to be influenced by the biblical presuppositions that defined the ultimate meaning of their work'.[90] In the present volume, Dorothy Figueira suggests that the emergence of the Indo-European thesis offered the possibility of 'a new Eden' for scientific scholars of language – with the Sanskrit Vedas adopted as an 'Aryan Bible'. Tuska Benes likewise argues that 'comparative philology epitomised the nineteenth-century quest for origins ... Philologists ordered languages and ethnic groups based on the model of branching genealogy from a single point of origin.'[91] The persistence of terms like 'Semitic' and 'Japhetic' (a common synonym for Indo-European in the period) indicates the extent to which the Semitic/Aryan opposition relied on a conceptual scaffolding drawn from the Bible.[92]

Olender and Benes also note the important political context. The 'national awakening' across Europe in mid-century intensified 'local rivalries between supposed primordial tongues'.[93] While the search for Aryan origins presented an opportunity to break away from Eurocentric concepts of civilisation, such scholarship always mingled notes of traditional patriotic chauvinism with newer forms of primitivism. As Olender notes, within 'the Aryan universe, the energy and abstract intellectual gifts of the Greeks prefigured the progress of the Indo-European world, while the Vedic pole represented the power of the primitive'.[94] Influential figures like the French philologist and biblical critic Ernest Renan elaborated the Aryan and Semite distinction into a grand set of fixed racial oppositions. Edward Said has famously argued that this manoeuvre was central to the construction of European modernity in opposition to an essentialised Oriental 'Other'.[95] Historians of anti-semitism, such as Léon Poliakov and George Mosse, have even claimed that the genocidal racism of the Nazis had its intellectual roots in the philological distinction between the Semitic and Indo-European tongues.[96]

Some recent scholars, however, have claimed that the historiography of nineteenth-century racism has laid too much emphasis on 'biologically determined racism'. In his study of the English 'national character', for example, Peter Mandler argues that race was relatively insignificant to the definition of Victorian Englishness as a cultural category and performed identity. The Anglo-Saxon 'race', concludes Mandler, was 'one you could join, as well as be born into'.[97] It is important to acknowledge the slippery nature of a category like 'race' in this period. As Robert Priest has shown, while Ernest Renan was committed to the idea that 'the linguistic divergences uncovered by modern philology must simultaneously reflect and shape fundamental ethnic differences between human groups', he was also 'keen to resist any biological explanation of these differences'.[98] Susannah Heschel is, however, more wary. In her study of the Nazi construction of an 'Aryan Jesus', she argues that narrow definitions of racism (as only concerned with immutable biological imperatives) obscure the 'linguistic and cultural genesis' of many forms of modern racism.[99] In a similar vein, Tzvetan Todorov warns that 'linguistic races' can be just as violently exclusionary as their biological equivalents, and that figures like Renan were guilty of 'a cultural determinism at least as rigid' as contemporary scientific racists.[100]

In the nineteenth century, Western European peoples also became increasingly interested in their own ethnicity. Robert Young suggests that the English, for example, were 'far more preoccupied with a complex elaboration of European racial differences and alliances than with what they perceived to be the relatively straightforward task of distinguishing between European and non-European races'.[101] In *The Races of Men*, Robert Knox claimed 'that in human history race is everything', but if race trumped all, then what were imperial nations like Britain, France and Germany to do with the comparatively marginal role afforded to their ancestors in the annals of the classical and biblical past?[102] Why did God lavish so much attention on the Middle East and the Mediterranean while the vigorous Celts, Saxons, Gauls and Teutons – the future inheritors of the Earth – were left to make their way in darkness? In Chapter 4, Brian Murray discusses the eccentric 'British Israel' movement which gained ground in the late nineteenth century. 'British Israelites' explained their nation's imperial triumphs in comfortingly literal terms: the Anglo-Saxons *were* the Chosen People, and the success of the Empire fulfilled the predictions of the Hebrew prophets. A subtler strand of thinking approached this problem through analogies that were nonetheless coloured by the language of race. In late nineteenth-century Britain, the most influential imperial thinkers, including Charles Dilke, J. R. Seeley and Rudyard Kipling, rejected the narrow category of the English Nation in favour of a more expansive 'Greater Britain' peopled by the 'English-speaking peoples' and the 'Anglo-Saxon race'.[103] Imperialist thinkers could point to the facts of recent history to claim that the English had undoubtedly inherited the mantle of both the itinerant Chosen Peoples of Exodus (witness the 'Settler Revolution') and the legacies of the great empires of antiquity.[104] As Gareth Atkins explains in this volume, while these metaphorical arguments did not depend on tracing a bloodline from Surrey to Sinai, they nonetheless supported the idea that Britannia's rule of the waves endorsed its status as a 'chosen' race. The idea of providential chosen-ness (and its attendant responsibilities) was eloquently evoked by Rudyard Kipling in his 'Recessional', composed for Queen Victoria's diamond jubilee in 1897.

> God of our fathers, known of old,
>   Lord of our far-flung battle-line,
> Beneath whose awful Hand we hold
>   Dominion over palm and pine –

Of course, such analogues also suggested the inevitability of imperial decline and fall. In Kipling's poem, triumphalism soon gives way to gloomy Jeremiad: Britain's 'navies melt away' and 'all our pomp of yesterday / Is one with Nineveh and Tyre!' The European nations who elevated themselves to the status of new Chosen Peoples exemplified complacent imperial arrogance. But many of the literary and artistic responses to this notion conclude with melancholic images of the imperial metropolis in ruins, echoing biblical condemnation of Israel's ungodly and decadent tormentors.[105] In this sense, even the hubristic notion of imperial providence anticipates the resistance and revolution of fortunes to follow.

The structure of the book

What follows is organised around two interrelated themes. Part I, 'Peoples and lands', explores biblical ideas of exile, exodus, sacred lands and belonging, all of which informed identities in the modern world. Focusing on travel, geography and racial genealogies, the chapters in this section engage with recent work on encounters and expansion, considering how the Bible infused missionary and nationalist thinking in a variety of contexts. They unravel the specific meanings behind key biblical locations – Israel, Babylon and Tarshish – in the process of examining why Scottish missionaries based in Australia drew the biblical lineages of Aborigines, what missionary preaching signified for colonial authorities facing rebellion in the sugar colony of Demerara, how British maritime empire was slotted into biblical prophecy and how Irish claims to connections with the Old Testament played into the arguments of Anglo-Saxonist racial theorists.

The second group of chapters ('The Bible in transit and translation') engages with questions about language, translation and textual transmission of the Word. It is especially interested in the production of 'cultural Bibles', investigating the local politics of translation and reception against a background of mass global circulation of texts, ideas and people in the nineteenth century. Central to this section is the idea of textual and scholarly encounter, as the Bible was contrasted with Hindu and Islamic religio-linguistic traditions by missionaries but also placed alongside them by comparative scholars; or as mutual ignorance and misunderstanding coloured encounters between Western and Orthodox Christian traditions in Russia. Individual chapters consider the production history of modern Arabic and Russian Bibles, enlightened scholarship and the development of 'segregationist folk theology' to legitimise racial differentiation in America. This last chapter serves also as a reminder that 'nineteenth-century' ideas continued to have purchase well into the twentieth century; and indeed that in some quarters they still do today.

Notes

1. C. A. Bayly, *The Birth of the Modern World, 1780–1914* (Oxford: Blackwell, 2004), p. 357.
2. Colin Kidd, *The Forging of Races: Race and Scripture in the Protestant Atlantic World, 1600–2000* (Cambridge: Cambridge University Press, 2006).
3. David N. Livingstone, *Adam's Ancestors: Race, Religion and the Politics of Human Origins* (Baltimore, MD: Johns Hopkins University Press, 2011). See also e.g. Timothy Larsen, *A People of One Book: the Bible and the Victorians* (Oxford: Oxford University Press, 2011), pp. 195–217.
4. Anthony D. Smith, *Chosen Peoples: Sacred Sources of National Identity* (Oxford: Oxford University Press, 2003); Eitan Bar-Yosef, *The Holy Land in English Culture, 1799–1917* (Oxford: Oxford University Press, 2005); David Gange and Michael Ledger-Lomas, *Cities of God: the Bible and Archaeology in Nineteenth-Century Britain* (Cambridge: Cambridge University Press, 2013).
5. James Belich, *Replenishing the Earth: the Settler Revolution and the Rise of the Angloworld* (Oxford: Oxford University Press, 2009).
6. Elie Kedourie, *Nationalism* (London: Hutchinson, 1960); Ernest Gellner, *Thought and Change* (London: Weidenfeld and Nicolson, 1964); Tom Nairn, *The Break-Up of Britain: Crisis and Neo-Nationalism* (London: NLB, 1977), Benedict Anderson, *Imagined Communities: Reflections on the Origin and Spread of Nationalism* (London: Verso, 1983); Eric Hobsbawm, *Nations and Nationalism since 1780: Programme, Myth, Reality* (Cambridge: Cambridge University Press, 1990); John Breuilly, *Nationalism and the State* (Manchester: Manchester University Press, 1993).
7. J.A. Hobson, *Imperialism: a Study* (London: James Nisbett, 1902), pp. 208–18; Homi K. Bhabha, 'Signs Taken for Wonders: Questions of Ambivalence and Authority under a Tree outside Delhi, May 1817', *Critical Inquiry*, 12 (1985), 144–65.
8. See e.g. Brian Stanley, *The Bible and the Flag: Protestant Mission and British Imperialism in the Nineteenth and Twentieth Centuries* (Leicester: Apollos, 1990); Andrew Porter, *Religion versus Empire? British Protestant Missionaries and Overseas Expansion, 1700–1914* (Manchester: Manchester University Press, 2004); Norman Etherington, ed., *Missions and Empire* (Oxford: Oxford University Press, 2005).
9. R. S. Sugirtharajah, *The Bible and Empire: Postcolonial Explorations* (Cambridge: Cambridge University Press, 2005); Susannah Heschel, *The Aryan Jesus: Christianity, Nazis and the Bible* (Princeton, NJ: Princeton University Press, 2007); Kidd, *Forging of Races*.
10. Antoinette Burton and Isabel Hofmeyr, eds, *Ten Books that Shaped the British Empire: Creating an Imperial Commons* (Durham, NC: Duke University Press, 2014).
11. See e.g. Larry R. Morrison, 'The Religious Defense of American Slavery before 1830', *Journal of Religious Thought*, 37 (1981), 16–29; Michael Taylor, 'British Pro-Slavery Arguments and the Bible, 1832–1833', *Slavery and Abolition*, 37 (2016), 139–58.
12. *Select Parts of the Holy Bible, for the Use of the Negro Slaves, in the British West-India Islands* (London: Law and Gilbert, 1807).
13. Ronnie Po-Chia Hsia, *A Companion to Early Modern Catholic Global Missions* (Leiden: Brill, 2018).
14. Ole Peter Grell, *Brethren in Christ: A Calvinist Network in Reformation Europe* (Oxford: Oxford University Press, 2011); Christopher Clark and Michael Ledger-Lomas, 'The Protestant International', in Abigail Green and Vincent Viaene, eds, *Religious Internationals in the Modern Age: Globalization and Faith Communities since 1750* (Basingstoke: Palgrave Macmillan, 2012), pp. 23–52.
15. J. C. S. Mason, *The Moravian Church and the Missionary Awakening in England, 1760–1800* (Woodbridge: Boydell Press, 2001); Carla Pestana, *Protestant Empire: Religion & the Making of the British Atlantic World* (Philadelphia, PA: University

of Pennsylvania Press, 2009); Travis Glasson, *Mastering Christianity: Missionary Anglicanism and Slavery in the Atlantic World* (New York: Oxford University Press, 2012).

16 See e.g. G. J. Schutte, ed., *Het Indisch Sion: de Gereformeerde kerk onder de Verenigde Oost-Indische Compagnie* (Hilversum: Verloren, 2002); Charles H. Parker, 'Converting Souls across Cultural Borders: Dutch Calvinism and Early Modern Missionary Enterprises', *Journal of Global History*, 8 (2013), 50–71; Jeremy Gregory, ed., *The Oxford History of Anglicanism, Volume II: Establishment and Empire, 1662–1829* (Oxford: Oxford University Press, 2017), pp. 160–252.

17 Rowan Strong, *Anglicanism and the British Empire, c. 1700–1850* (Oxford: Oxford University Press, 2007); Joseph Hardwick, *An Anglican British World: the Church of England and the Expansion of the Settler Empire, c. 1790–1860* (Manchester: Manchester University Press, 2014); Rowan Strong, *Victorian Christianity and Emigrant Voyages to British Colonies, c. 1840–c. 1914* (Oxford: Oxford University Press, 2017).

18 For a superb overview, see Jeffrey Cox, *The British Missionary Enterprise Since 1700* (New York: Routledge, 2008).

19 Stephen Batalden, Kathleen Cann and John Dean, eds, *Sowing the Word: the Cultural Impact of the British and Foreign Bible Society, 1804–2004* (Sheffield: Sheffield Phoenix Press, 2004).

20 See e.g. Theodor W. Dunkelgrün, '"Neerlands Israel": Political Theology, Christian Hebraism, Biblical Antiquarianism and Historical Myth', in Laura Cruz and Willem Frijhoff, eds, *Myth in History, History in Myth* (Leiden: Brill 2009), pp. 201–36.

21 Gareth Atkins, *Converting Britannia: Evangelicals and British Public Life, c. 1770–1840* (Woodbridge: Boydell and Brewer, 2019).

22 Stewart J. Brown, 'Movements of Christian Awakening in Revolutionary Europe, 1790–1815', in Brown and Timothy Tackett, eds, *The Cambridge History of Christianity, Volume VII: Enlightenment, Reawakening and Revolution, 1660–1815* (Cambridge: Cambridge University Press, 2006), p. 587.

23 Stephen K. Batalden, *Russian Bible Wars: Modern Scriptural Translation and Cultural Authority* (Cambridge: Cambridge University Press, 2013), pp. 12–40.

24 Joseph Stubenrauch, *The Evangelical Age of Ingenuity in Industrial Britain* (Oxford: Oxford University Press, 2016).

25 Leslie Howsam, *Cheap Bibles: Nineteenth-Century Publishing and the British and Foreign Bible Society* (Cambridge: Cambridge University Press, 1991).

26 Geoffrey Cantor, *Religion and the Great Exhibition of 1851* (Oxford: Oxford University Press, 2011), pp. 89–100, 116–18.

27 Paul Gutjahr, *An American Bible: the History of the Good Book in the United States* (Stanford, CA: Stanford University Press, 1996), pp. 188–9.

28 William Canton, *The History of the British and Foreign Bible Society*, 5 vols (London: John Murray, 1904–10), V: p. 378.

29 'British and Foreign Bible Society', *Christian Observer*, 11 (1812), 726.

30 Gareth Atkins, 'William Jowett's *Christian Researches*: British Protestants and Religious Plurality in the Mediterranean, Syria and the Holy Land, 1815–30', in Charlotte Methuen, Andrew Spicer and John Wolffe, eds, *Christians and Religious Plurality*, Studies in Church History, 51 (Woodbridge: Boydell and Brewer, 2015), 216–31.

31 Heleen Murre-Van Den Berg, 'The Middle East: Western Missions and Eastern Churches, Islam and Judaism', in Sheridan Gilley and Brian Stanley, eds, *The Cambridge History of Christianity, Volume VIII: World Christianities, c. 1815–c. 1914* (Cambridge: Cambridge University Press, 2006).

32 Canton, *British and Foreign Bible Society*, II: pp. 1–29.

33 Norman Etherington, 'Education and Medicine', in Etherington, *Missions and Empire*.

34 Mark A. Noll, 'The Bible and Scriptural Interpretation', in Timothy Larsen and Michael Ledger-Lomas, eds, *The Oxford History of Protestant Dissenting Traditions, Volume III: the Nineteenth Century* (Oxford: Oxford University Press, 2017).

35 David Norton, *A History of the Bible as Literature*, 2 vols (Cambridge: Cambridge University Press, 1993), II: pp. 176–217, 262–300.
36 Cassandra Pybus, *Epic Journeys of Freedom: Runaway Slaves of the American Revolution and their Global Quest for Liberty* (Boston, MA: Beacon Press, 2006).
37 Bayly, *Modern World*, pp. 330–3, 351.
38 Timothy Willem Jones and Lucinda Matthews-Jones, eds, *Material Religion in Modern Britain: the Spirit of Things* (Basingstoke: Palgrave Macmillan, 2015), p. 1; Joel Cabrita, *Text and Authority in the South African Nazaretha Church* (Cambridge: Cambridge University Press, 2014).
39 Robert Needham Cust, *Linguistic and Oriental Essays, Third Series* (London: Kegan Paul, Trench, Trübner and Co., 1891), pp. 54–5.
40 William Smalley, *Translation as Mission: Bible Translation in the Modern Missionary Movement* (Macon, GA: Mercer University Press, 1991).
41 Robert Frykenberg, 'The Halle Legacy in Modern India: Information and the Spread of Education, Enlightenment and Evangelization', in Michael Bergunder, ed., *Missionsberichte aus Indien im 18. Jahrhundert. Ihre Bedeutung für die europäische Geistesgeschichte und ihr wissenschaftlicher Quellenwert für die Indienkunde* (Halle [Saale]: Verl. der Franckeschen Stiftungen, 1999), pp. 6–29.
42 Philip Stine, ed., *Bible Translation and the Spread of the Church: The Last Two Hundred Years* (Leiden: E. J. Brill, 1990).
43 For a detailed discussion of the earlier historiography of Bible translation see Hephzibah Israel, *Religious Transactions in Colonial South India: Language, Translation and the Making of Protestant Identity* (Basingstoke: Palgrave Macmillan, 2011), pp. 2–4, 10–12.
44 Lamin Sanneh, *Translating the Message: The Missionary Impact on Culture* (Ossining: Orbis, 1989). See also Lamin Sanneh, 'Bible Translation, Culture and Religion', in Michael McClymond, ed, *The Wiley-Blackwell Companion to World Christianity* (Hoboken, NJ: Wiley-Blackwell, 2016), pp. 265–82.
45 Lamin Sanneh, '"They Stooped to Conquer": Cultural Vitality and the Narrative Impulse', in K. E. Yandell, ed., *Faith and Narrative* (Oxford: Oxford University Press, 2001), p. 30.
46 See Isabel Hofmeyr, *The Portable Bunyan: A Transnational History of the Pilgrim's Progress* (Princeton, NJ: Princeton University Press, 2004); Israel, *Religious Transactions*; Sugirtharajah, *Bible and Empire*; Hilary Carey, 'Lancelot Threlkeld, Biraban and the Colonial Bible in Australia', *Comparative Studies in Society and History*, 52 (2010), 447–78; Batalden, *Russian Bible Wars*; Heather Sharkey, 'The Gospel in Arabic Tongues: British Bible Distribution, Evangelical Mission and Language Politics in North Africa', in Sharkey, ed., *Cultural Conversions: Unexpected Consequences of Christian Missions in the Middle East, Africa, and South Asia* (Syracuse, NY: Syracuse University Press, 2013), pp. 203–21.
47 Umberto Eco, *Experiences in Translation*, trans. Alastair McEwen (Toronto: University of Toronto Press, 2001), pp. 3–12.
48 See Michael Dodson, 'Re-presented for the Pandits: James Ballantyne, Useful Knowledge, and Sanskrit Scholarship in Benares College During the Mid-Nineteenth Century', *Modern Asian Studies*, 36 (2002), 287–9.
49 Dodson, 'Re-presented for the Pandits', 263–8; 290–1.
50 Israel, *Religious Transactions*, pp. 7–9.
51 Jane Samson, *Race and Redemption: British Missionaries Encounter Pacific Peoples, 1797–1920* (Grand Rapids, MI: Eerdmans, 2017), pp. 8–9.
52 Patrick Harries and David Maxwell, 'Introduction', in Patrick Harries and David Maxwell, eds, *The Spiritual in the Secular: Missionaries and Knowledge About Africa* (Grand Rapids. MI: Eerdmans, 2012), pp. 6, 25.
53 Sara Pugach, *Africa in Translation: A History of Colonial Linguistics in Germany and Beyond, 1814–1945* (Ann Arbor, MI: University of Michigan Press, 2012).
54 Hofmeyr, *Portable Bunyan*, pp. 16–23.
55 See William Yates and John Wenger, *The Holy Bible containing the Old and New Testaments in the Bengálí Language, Translated out of the Original Tongues by*

INTRODUCTION

     the Calcutta Baptist Missionaries with Native Assistants (Calcutta: Baptist Mission Press, 1845).
56 Sunil Kumar Chatterjee, *Ramram Basu: Munshi of Rev William Carey* (Serampore: Carey Library, 2006).
57 See Carey, 'Lancelot Threlkeld,' 468–70.
58 See Heather Sharkey's Chapter 5 in this volume. See also Israel, *Religious Transactions*, pp. 5–11.
59 For an overview of this agenda see Fernando Segovia and Stephen Moore, 'Introduction', in Segovia and Moore, eds, *Postcolonial Biblical Criticism: Interdisciplinary Intersections* (London: T.&T. Clark, 2005). Also see Fernando F. Segovia and R. S. Sugirtharajah, eds, *A Postcolonial Commentary on the New Testament Writings* (London: T.&T. Clark, 2007).
60 Sugirtharajah, *Bible and Empire*, pp. 60–97.
61 Brian Stanley, 'Christian Responses to the Indian Mutiny of 1857', *Studies in Church History*, 20 (1983), pp. 279–81.
62 See Michael Prior, *The Bible and Colonialism: A Moral Critique* (Sheffield: Sheffield Academic Press, 1997), and Mark Brett, *Decolonizing God: The Bible in the Tides of Empire* (Sheffield: Sheffield Phoenix Press, 2008). Also see Nur Masalha, *The Zionist Bible: Biblical Precedent, Colonialism and the Erasure of Memory* (London and New York: Routledge, 2013).
63 Michael Prior, *Bible and Colonialism*.
64 Mark Brett, *Decolonizing God*, pp. 8–33. Also see Peter Harrison, '"Fill the Earth and Subdue It": Biblical Warrants for Colonization in Seventeenth-Century England', *Journal of Religious History*, 29 (2005), 3–24.
65 Hofmeyr, *Portable Bunyan*, p. 20.
66 Vicente Rafael, *Contracting Colonialism: Translation and Christian Conversion in Tagalog Society under Early Spanish Rule* (Ithaca, NY: Cornell University Press, 1998).
67 Mark Brett, *Decolonizing God*, pp. 24–6. Also see Derek Peterson, 'The Rhetoric of the Word: Bible Translation and Mau Mau in Colonial Central Kenya', in Brian Stanley, ed., *Missions, Nationalism and the End of Empire* (Grand Rapids, MI: Eerdmans, 2004), pp. 165–79.
68 M. K. Gandhi, *An Autobiography, or My Experiments with Truth* (Ahmedabad: Navajiban Publishing House, 1927), pp. 91–3. Also see R. S. Sugirtharajah, *Troublesome Texts: the Bible in Colonial and Contemporary Culture* (Sheffield: Sheffield Phoenix Press, 2008), pp. 44–51.
69 Emma Hunter, 'Language, Empire and the World: Karl Roehl and the History of the Swahili Bible in East Africa', *Journal of Imperial and Commonwealth History*, 41 (2013), 608–9. Also see Nile Green, 'The Transcolonial Opportunities of Bible Translation: Iranian Language Workers between the Russian and British Empires', in Michael S. Dodson and Brian A. Hatcher, eds, *Trans-Colonial Modernities in South Asia* (New York: Routledge, 2012), pp. 116–31.
70 Kidd, *Forging of Races*, p. 19.
71 Kidd, *Forging of Races*, p. 168.
72 Kidd, *Forging of Races*, p. 20.
73 Livingstone, *Adam's Ancestors*, p. 8.
74 Livingstone, *Adam's Ancestors*, pp. 137–200.
75 Winchell, *Adamites and Preadamites*, pp. 26–7. Quoted in Livingstone, *Adam's Ancestors*, p. 147.
76 Livingstone, *Adam's Ancestors*, p. 45.
77 Robert Knox, *The Races of Men*, 2nd edn (London: Henry Renshaw, 1862), pp. 1–2.
78 Knox, *Races of Men*, pp. 4–5.
79 Frederick Douglass, *The Claims of the Negro, Ethnologically Considered. An Address, before the Literary Societies of Western Reserve College* (Rochester, NY: Lee, Man, and Co., 1854), p. 6.
80 Douglass, *Claims of the Negro*, p. 12.

81 Douglass, *Claims of the Negro*, p. 15. For a longer analysis of Douglass's speech in the context of American race science and 'Pre-Adamic Theology' see Livingstone, *Adam's Ancestors*, pp. 180–5.
82 Stephen R. Haynes, *Noah's Curse: The Biblical Justification of American Slavery* (New York: Oxford University Press, 2002), pp. 27–8.
83 Ryan Stuart Bingham, 'Racial Dispensations and Dispensations of Race in Joseph Smith's Bible Revision and the Book of Abraham', *Journal of Mormon History*, 41 (2015), 22. Newell G. Bringhurst, *Saints, Slaves, and Blacks: The Changing Place of Black People within Mormonism* (Westport, CT: Greenwood Press, 1981).
84 Eddie S. Glaude, *Exodus! Religion, Race, and Nation in Early Nineteenth-Century Black America* (Chicago: Chicago University Press, 2000), pp. 3–5. For a longer history see John Coffey, *Exodus and Liberation: Deliverance Politics from John Calvin to Martin Luther King Jr.* (Oxford: Oxford University Press, 2013).
85 Johannes Fabian, *Time and the Other: How Anthropology Makes Its Object* (New York: Columbia University Press, 1983); George Stocking, *Victorian Anthropology* (New York: Free Press, 1987).
86 For Freud's analysis of the Hebrew Bible, see *Totem and Taboo* (1913) and *Moses and Monotheism* (1939). On Frazer and the Bible, see Timothy Larsen, *The Slain God: Anthropologists and the Christian Faith* (Oxford: Oxford University Press, 2014), pp. 37–79.
87 Kidd, *Forging of Races*, p. 168.
88 Kidd, *Forging of Races*, p. 168.
89 See also Peter Clayworth, 'Richard Taylor and the Children of Noah: Race, Science and Religion in the South Seas', in Hilary Carey, ed., *Empires of Religion* (Basingstoke: Palgrave, 2008), pp. 222–42.
90 Maurice Olender, *The Languages of Paradise: Race, Religion, and Philology in the Nineteenth Century* (Cambridge, MA: Harvard University Press, 1992), pp. 19–20.
91 Tuska Benes, *In Babel's Shadow: Philology and the Nation in Nineteenth-Century Germany* (Detroit, MI: Wayne State University Press, 2008), p. 10.
92 Olender, *Languages of Paradise*, p. 8–11.
93 Olender, *Languages of Paradise*, p. 2; Benes, *Babel's Shadow*, pp. 3–4.
94 Olender, *Languages of Paradise*, p. 12.
95 Edward Said, *Orientalism* (New York: Pantheon Books, 1978).
96 Léon Poliakov, *The Aryan Myth: A History of Racist and Nationalist Ideas in Europe*, trans. E. Howard (London: Chatto and Heinemann, 1974); George Mosse, *Toward the Final Solution: A History of European Racism* (New York: Howard Fertig, 1978).
97 Peter Mandler, *The English National Character: The History of an Idea from Edmund Burke to Tony Blair* (New Haven, CT: Yale University Press, 2006), pp. 59–60; Douglas Lorimer, *Science, Race Relations and Resistance: Britain, 1870–1914* (Manchester: Manchester University Press, 2013), pp. 4–5.
98 Robert D. Priest, 'Ernest Renan's Race Problem', *Historical Journal*, 58 (2015), 312. Halvor Moxnes also claims that while Renan's portrait of Jesus was deeply coloured by his own prejudices, the critic frequently draws back from speculating on race in biological terms. Halvor Moxnes, *Jesus and the Rise of Nationalism: A New Quest for the Nineteenth Century Historical Jesus* (London and New York: I. B. Tauris, 2011), p. 138.
99 Heschel, *Aryan Jesus*, p. 29. In an earlier work on the Jewish critic Abraham Geiger, Heschel argues that Geiger's characterisation of 'Jesus as a Pharisee and early Christianity as a paganization and ultimate betrayal of Jesus' Jewish message' constitutes 'one of the earliest examples of postcolonialist writing'. Susannah Heschel, *Abraham Geiger and the Jewish Jesus* (Chicago: Chicago University Press, 1998), pp. 2–3.
100 Tzvetan Todorov, *On Human Diversity: Nationalism, Racism, and Exoticism in French Thought*, trans. Catherine Porter (Cambridge, MA: Harvard University Press, 1993), p. 147.
101 Robert J. C. Young, *The Idea of English Ethnicity* (Oxford: Blackwell, 2008), p. 13.

INTRODUCTION

102 Knox, *Races of Men*, p. 2.
103 Duncan Bell, *The Idea of Greater Britain: Empire and the Future of World Order, 1860–1900* (Princeton, NJ: Princeton University Press, 2007).
104 Belich, *Replenishing the Earth*.
105 The most famous example in the British context is T. B. Macaulay's image of 'some traveller from New Zealand' standing 'on a broken arch of London Bridge to sketch the ruins of St. Paul's'. T. B. Macaulay, 'Von Ranke', *Edinburgh Review*, 72 (October 1840), 258. See also Julia Hell, 'Imperial Ruin Gazing, or Why did Scipio Weep?', in Julia Hell and Andreas Schönle, eds, *Ruins of Modernity* (Durham, NC: Duke University Press, 2010), pp. 169–92 and Rachel Bryant Davies, *Troy, Carthage and the Victorians: The Drama of Classical Ruins in the Nineteenth-Century Imagination* (Cambridge: Cambridge University Press, 2018), pp. 271–338.

PART I

Peoples and lands

CHAPTER ONE

'A bad and dangerous book'?: the biblical identity politics of the Demerara Slave Rebellion
John Coffey

On the evening of Monday 18 August 1823, revolt broke out in the British sugar colony of Demerara. Situated on the north-east coast of South America (in what is now Guyana), Demerara-Essequibo had a small white population of 2,500, vastly outnumbered by 75,000 black and creole slaves (and around 2,500 free blacks). The rising was sparked by rumours of developments in Britain. In May, the abolitionist Thomas Fowell Buxton had introduced a parliamentary resolution calling for the gradual abolition of British Caribbean slavery, and the government responded by issuing instructions to the colonies requiring the amelioration of slavery (including a ban on the use of the whip in the field). In Demerara, Governor Murray chose not to issue a formal proclamation, and garbled reports spread among slaves that he was resisting an emancipation order from King and Parliament. For a tumultuous week, thousands of the colony's enslaved people rose up in a mass protest designed to extract concessions from the authorities. Downing their tools, and arming themselves with cutlasses, cane knives and guns, the insurgents put dozens of overseers and managers in the stocks, demanding either complete emancipation or several days per week without forced labour. They acted with restraint that David Brion Davis finds 'astounding'.[1] Two or three white men lost their lives in skirmishes, but the principal ringleaders made a conscious effort to prevent killing. By contrast, the repression of the revolt was brutal. At least 200 blacks were either killed during clashes with the colony's militia or shot dead following capture; 33 others were executed after trial, ten of these being decapitated. The heads of the leading insurgents were set on spikes and their dead bodies hung on gibbets at the entrance to the plantations.[2]

The colonial authorities were not slow to assign blame. The rebellion had been instigated and orchestrated by the leading men of Bethel

Chapel, pastored since 1817 by the Revd John Smith of the London Missionary Society. In September, his head deacon, Quamina of the Success plantation, was shot dead while on the run; Quamina's son, Jack Gladstone (who bore the surname of the estate's owner, John Gladstone of Liverpool), confessed to leading the plot and implicated the missionary. In October, Smith was put on trial before a court martial, and, after twenty-seven days in the courtroom, found guilty of complicity, and sentenced to death by hanging. The court recommended mercy, but before a reprieve from the king arrived, the missionary died of pulmonary tuberculosis in a damp prison on 6 February 1824.

The prosecution's principal charge against Smith was that for years he had promoted 'discontent and dissatisfaction in the minds of the negro slaves towards their lawful masters, managers, and overseers ... thereby intending to excite the said negroes to break out in such open revolt and rebellion'.[3] As supporting evidence, the authorities cited passages from the missionary's private journal and the testimony of his hearers, some of whom now blamed Smith for their calamitous revolt. The final paragraph of Jack Gladstone's statement alleged that the origin of the revolt lay in Smith's use of the Bible:

> Before this Court, I solemnly avow, that many of the lessons and discourses taught, and the parts of scripture selected for us in chapel, tended to make us dissatisfied with our situation as slaves ... the half sort of instruction we received I now see was highly improper, it put those who could read on examining the Bible, and selecting passages applicable to our situation as slaves ... and served to make us dissatisfied and irritated against our owners, as we were not always able to make out the real meaning of these passages.[4]

The prosecutor concluded:

> though the Prisoner well knew that [the slaves'] minds were thus irritated [by slavery], and though he was well aware that they would pervert, and take as applicable to themselves, any passages which could at all be brought to bear on their situation as slaves, he yet read to them the history of the deliverance of the Israelites from Egypt, and of the wars of the Jews, and explained it to them in words most exactly fitting their own condition.[5]

The missionary, in short, was the real instigator of the revolt. Standing on a tinderbox, he had knowingly risked a conflagration by opening the most incendiary of biblical texts. At every step, the prosecution charged, Smith had been in contact with Quamina and Jack. The revolt had arisen from Bethel Chapel and its biblical identity politics.

THE DEMERARA SLAVE REBELLION

Historiography and sources

The role of the Bible in shaping ethnic and national identities has attracted a growing body of scholarship. Critics of 'modernist' theories of nationalism have argued for 'the sacred sources of national identity', noting that Old Testament themes of election, covenant, deliverance, promised land and sacral kingship were integral to the construction of medieval and post-Reformation national identities.[6] Case studies have shown how emerging Protestant nations were imagined as Old Testament chosen nations.[7] A rich literature explores how post-Reformation England, in particular, was construed as a new Israel.[8] Political readings of the Bible fired the English Revolution of the mid-seventeenth century, but although this provoked a strong reaction against Bible-toting fanatics, political discourse in later Stuart Britain was not descripturalised.[9] The Bible continued to be a potent resource for the Hanoverians, and it was mobilised with new vigour in the American Revolution.[10]

The historiography of the British Empire has been less attuned to this Scriptural turn, though there has been significant work on Bible translation and on the appropriation of Old Testament identities both by the British and by indigenous protest movements.[11] Historians of racial and ethnic identity have alerted us to the fact that the Book of Genesis (alongside other texts) 'played a very large role in the cultural construction of race'.[12] Numerous studies explore how African Americans wrested the biblical text from the hands of white masters, using the Exodus story and 'the Ethiopian prophecy' (Psalms 68:31) to forge their own collective identity.[13] Historians have observed how slave rebellions in the American South had their origins in subversive 'textual communities'.[14]

Work on the British Caribbean has been less attentive to the power of the political Bible and there has been no systematic analysis of the Scriptural politics of the Demerara revolt. Yet no other slave rising generated a body of source material that so richly illuminates the use of the Bible to form collective identities. The official reports on Gabriel's rebellion in Virginia in 1800 record a single tantalising conversation between slaves who cite Exodus and Joshua;[15] the official narrative of the Charleston insurrection of Denmark Vesey in 1822 began with his knowledge of the Scriptures, which he 'could pervert to his purpose', but provided no further analysis;[16] and while Jamaica's 1831 slave rebellion was known as 'the Baptist war' and led by a Baptist deacon, Sam Sharpe, the records are largely silent about the how the Bible was taught and read by missionary congregations.[17] *The Confessions of Nat Turner* (1832), drawn up by a lawyer who interrogated him, are unique in giving a voice to the leader of a slave rebellion, foregrounding his biblically fuelled visions.

But the evidence from Demerara is unparalleled in two respects. First, Smith's dense and vivid journal systematically listed the texts read and preached at Bethel Chapel from March 1817 to July 1823. Although his sermons or outlines do not survive, the journal contains revealing comments on specific texts and their reception, and his listing constitutes an extraordinary record of the biblical diet of an enslaved congregation over the course of six years leading up to the rebellion.[18] Second, the official trial records (of both the insurrectionists and the missionary) contain extensive testimony about Smith's use of the Bible and his congregation's reception of it. These were printed by order of Parliament, together with a set of further papers containing 'documentary evidence' produced by the court martial.[19] The London Missionary Society (LMS) issued its own version of Smith's trial, restoring 'passages erased from the defence' by the court, especially 'citations of Holy Writ ... which formed so powerful an answer to the charges with which he was assailed'.[20] But it was the cross-examination of the witnesses that gave significant insights into how the enslaved themselves heard and responded to the Bible. Here, for example, is a typical set of questions put by the defence and prosecution to a black slave named London: 'Can you read and who taught you? Have you a Bible, and if yea, do you use it in chapel? Can you follow the parson as he reads from the Bible? Do you remember the prisoner reading about Moses delivering the children of Israel from Pharaoh? Did not the prisoner read Exodus to you a few Sundays before the revolt? Did he read Joshua to you? What did you hear read in Joshua?'[21] A rich variety of other materials illuminate the religious culture of Bethel Chapel – missionary correspondence, LMS reports, the church's hymn book, colonial records, newspapers and eyewitness accounts of the rebellion.

This chapter will mine the sources to reconstruct the biblical identity politics of Bethel Chapel and its insurgents. The first section will analyse how John Smith employed the Bible to forge a new identity for his congregation. Section two will turn to the more difficult task of piecing together fragmentary evidence of an interpretive community among the enslaved, a community which, under the leadership of Quamina and other deacons and catechists, would rise up in revolt. The final section will examine the ensuing battle for the Bible between colonial planters and British abolitionists.

The missionary Bible

John Smith was a man of modest social origins. Leaving school at 14, he was apprenticed to a London baker. Around 1810, at the age of 18, his life was radically reoriented by his evangelical conversion, and within a few years he had applied to the London Missionary Society. Trained under the Congregationalist David Bogue at Gosport Academy, and mentored by a minister in Witham, Essex, he was sent (with his wife Jane) to Demerara in 1817.[22] Yet Bogue judged him ill-suited to the challenge of Demerara, and Smith's own pastor, John Angell James, feared that he was 'entirely a novice', lacking in the 'education', 'personal influence', self-confidence and 'wisdom' required to command respect and be 'a repairer of the breach' between the missionaries and the planters.[23]

Smith was one of a new breed of evangelical dissenting missionaries who posed a fresh challenge to the slave colonies.[24] Congregationalists and Baptists were formed by dissenting traditions with strong commitments to 'civil and religious liberty'. As artisans by trade, men like Smith and William Knibb in Jamaica were non-deferential and ill at ease in polite society. As puritanical evangelicals, they deplored the licentiousness and impiety of planter society. As nonconformists raised in a culture of ardent abolitionism, they brought metropolitan antislavery sentiments into the heart of slave societies. Bogue himself had been a keen opponent of the slave trade, and LMS missionaries had direct connections with Wilberforce and his circle. In the 1810s, however, there were no cries for immediate emancipation, and the Society advised its missionaries to be apolitical. Its treasurer, William Hankey, had inherited a slave estate. The short- and medium-term goals of British evangelicals were to promote the Christianisation of the slaves and the amelioration of slavery.[25]

Bethel Chapel had been planted almost a decade earlier by John Wray, another LMS missionary who had relocated to Berbice after conflict with the planters.[26] In Wray's absence it had withered, but Smith's drive and diligence quickly revived it. He held three meetings every Sunday – an early service at 7 a.m., a main service at 11 a.m. or 12 noon (followed by monthly communion or a church meeting), and a final meeting in the early evening (discontinued in 1818). During the week, there was a monthly missionary prayer meeting on Monday, a midweek meeting (usually on Tuesday evening), and a Friday evening meeting. The congregation grew steadily, and raised £190 to build a gallery that increased the Chapel's capacity to around 800. Located on the plantation of Le Resouvenir, the Chapel attracted slaves from across the series of plantations strung along a 20-mile stretch of coastland. In 1817, there were typically forty or fifty at the 7 a.m. service; by the early 1820s this had swelled to three or four hundred. By 1822–23, the building was often overflowing during the main Sunday service, with crowds listening outside. Even midweek meetings could attract several hundred. In his review of 1821 Smith noted that 'the whole year has been a season of great awakening'. In that year alone, he had baptised 390 persons (including 272 adults), married 70 couples, and added 35 new members.[27] By 1823, the mission's register listed some 2,000 baptised adherents, and 200 communicant members.[28]

Yet for all his success, Smith felt surrounded by enemies. At his initial meeting with Governor Murray, he was given an ominous warning: 'If ever you teach a negro to read, and I hear of it, I will banish you from the Colony immediately.'[29] The managers told him that 'the colony is in danger', that teaching slaves was 'impolitic', that 'religion will ruin the slaves', and that missionary work 'will prove subversive of good order, & due subordination'.[30] Already by November 1817 he was writing that 'amongst the Blacks, religion is making rapid progress; but by the Whites it is still violently opposed ... we have only two or three white friends, but a thousand black ones'.[31]

It was hardly surprising, then, that when revolt broke out, Smith fell under suspicion. Having confiscated Smith's private journal, the prosecution used it to argue that he had rashly exposed his congregation to dangerous texts. On the Sunday before the revolt he had preached on Christ weeping over Jerusalem and prophesying its destruction.[32] On the previous Sunday, he had chosen a text for a slave family who faced separation from each other and from the Chapel after being sold at auction ('Remember therefore how thou hast received and heard, and hold fast'; Revelation 3:3).[33] The journal testified to Smith's frustration at the obstructionism of the planters who forced slaves to work in violation of the Sabbath and employed various ruses to prevent their regular attendance at Chapel. And it recorded his detestation of flogging and even of slavery itself. 'O, slavery! Thou offspring of the devil,' he had written in 1817, 'when wilt thou cease to exist!'[34] In 1823, he sided unequivocally with Buxton against Canning: 'The rigors of negro slavery I believe can never be mitigated. The system must be abolished.'[35] With these quotations in hand, it was easy to conclude that the congregation of Bethel Chapel had spent six years under the spell of an abolitionist preacher.

Smith insisted that this charge was false. He was personally opposed to slavery, but scrupulous in keeping this to himself. He had only baptised slaves on receiving references and permissions from their plantation managers.[36] He had never preached against the institution of slavery and repeatedly urged his congregants to obey their masters, even if commanded to work on the Sabbath, against the rules of the colony and the law of God. His sermons were not political, but 'of a moral and religious nature'.[37] He could hardly be condemned for faithfully reading and expounding the Word of God. Nor could he be held responsible for the misapplication of the Scriptures by a minority of his barely literate congregation. On this account, there was a gulf fixed between the spiritual, pietistic and otherworldly Bible of the missionary Smith, and the political, revolutionary Bible of Quamina, Jack and their fellow insurrectionists.

It seems quite clear that Smith had never preached sedition or revolt – as he himself noted, there were usually white witnesses (including 'spies') in his meetings, and he would have been an 'idiot' to select texts that his enemies could turn against him.[38] Yet as we shall see, Jack and Quamina's reading of the Bible was not diametrically opposed to Smith's. Indeed, in various ways, the missionary provided cues that the rebels would follow.

To understand how this was so, we need to examine the evidence of Smith's journal. At the main service on Sunday, the missionary chose a short text – often a single verse, usually from the New Testament – geared towards the evangelistic goal of converting non-members. But the 7 a.m. service, and the midweek and Friday evening meetings, were different. Here Smith was preaching to a committed core and he embarked on an ambitious and systematic programme of Bible reading and Bible teaching. Sunday's 7 a.m. service, as the prosecution noted, was 'when whites never came'.[39] In 1817, there were selected readings from the Psalms and John's Gospel. From July 1817, at least six months were devoted to reading through the Book of Acts, with four or five months in 1818 being given over to Paul's Letter to the Romans. From 'about the middle of 1820' Smith began the consecutive reading of the Old Testament. Although there are some gaps in his record, and some passages were clearly omitted, the congregation appears to have spent around 18 months reading through Genesis, before proceeding to Exodus (by 20 January 1822 they had reached Exodus 19). It seems that Smith then read very selectively in the rest of the Pentateuch, because on 4 August 1822 he 'read and expounded' Joshua chapter 7 (on the sin of Achan) to a congregation numbering three or four hundred people ('as usual'). After readings from Judges and Ruth, he embarked on I Samuel in December 1822, reaching II Kings by the middle of 1823.[40] He would later justify this use of Old Testament history on the grounds that narrative was more accessible and memorable than 'didactic discourses', while character studies provided 'striking examples of virtue and vice ... more efficacious than mere abstract lessons'. As for the Exodus, it was an indispensable part of 'sacred history'.[41] On midweek and Friday evenings, the Sunday diet was supplemented by further mammoth series on Genesis (18 months from March 1817), Ephesians (16 months from March 1817), I Peter (15 months from July 1818), Matthew (two years from early 1820) and Acts (around 18 months in 1822–23). Altogether, this was an immersive course of Bible study that matched the expositional feats of England's leading nonconformist preachers.

Smith's choices and omissions, and his comments on specific texts, are very revealing. The LMS instructions were quite clear that its missionaries must teach slaves to be a *subject* people. In emphatic terms, missionaries were warned against stirring unrest: 'Not a word must escape you, in public or in private which might render the slaves displeased with their masters, or dissatisfied with their station.' The Gospel preached should 'render the slaves who receive it the most diligent, faithful, patient, and useful servants'. The LMS cited the classic texts on political submission, Romans chapter 13 and I Peter 2, where Christians are taught to submit themselves to the governing authorities, for the powers that be are ordained of God.[42]

Smith claimed to have observed these instructions, and he did omit biblical passages that might be readily politicised. As the prosecution observed, he had 'passed over' the latter part of Genesis 13 where Abraham is promised the land of Canaan – 'I was apprehensive the negroes might put such a construction upon it as I would not wish.'[43] According to John Wray, 'in publishing the Ten Commandments for slaves' Smith 'left out' the prologue: 'I am the Lord thy God, who brought thee out of the land of Egypt, out of the house of bondage.'[44] The congregation heard little from the Hebrew prophets, whose vehement denunciations of injustice were hard to avoid. Nor did Smith preach on other texts beloved by anti-slavery activists – Mary's Magnificat in Luke chapter 1, or Christ's sermon at Nazareth in chapter 4 ('to preach deliverance to the captive'). He expounded almost every verse of Ephesians, but not the duties of masters in chapter 5, verse 9, which instructed them to forbear 'threatening: knowing that your Master also is in heaven; neither is there respect of persons with him'. And Smith rarely turned to the inflammatory Book of Revelation.

His omission of such passages shows that he had paid attention to the LMS instructions; he was not an innocent abroad. Indeed, in June 1817 he recorded that Thomas Talboys, the Methodist missionary in Georgetown, 'was taken before the Governor for circulating [quarterly membership] tickets with Matt. 11.12 on them' ('The kingdom of God suffereth violence').[45] That text had long perplexed interpreters – was it condemning the persecution of John the Baptist, or commending his fiery zeal? Either way, it unnerved the authorities. Talboys fled the colony after a campaign of intimidation, noting that 'We dare not use some passages of Scripture in the pulpit such as "If the Son shall make you free, ye shall be free indeed."'[46] (In the wake of the revolt, John Wray 'felt much flurry' in the pulpit as he stumbled on the same text when reading John chapter 8).[47] With the example of Talboys before him, and white spies at his main services, Smith knew that he had to tread carefully.

All the stranger, then, that he omitted passages inculcating submission, obedience and reverence for masters. Most notably, in March 1819, when preaching verse-by-verse through I Peter, he took the unusual step of passing over four verses on submission to governors (I Peter 2:13–16: 'Submit yourselves to every ordinance of man for the Lord's sake: whether it be to the king, as supreme; Or unto governors, as unto them that are sent by him for the punishment of evildoers'). This omission was overlooked by the prosecution, but it suggests that Smith was reluctant to press home the necessity of subjection, either because he feared the congregation's reaction, or because he was sickened by the victimisation of slaves by masters. He probably did preach on Romans 13 as part of his series on the letter in 1818, but there are gaps in the journal, and the specific passage is not recorded. He skipped over the latter part of Genesis 9 and 10, describing the curse of Ham and the Table of the Nations, passages that had been used by Christians since the early modern era to justify the enslavement of Africans. There can be little doubt that Smith abhorred this exploitation of the text. There is little evidence in his journal that he used the Bible to teach subjection.

He was much more eager to get his hearers to see themselves as sinners in need of redemption. Smith was a pastor-evangelist. If he saw his people as victims of oppression, he also saw them as sinners – in the hands of an angry God – who urgently needed to repent, believe in Christ, receive forgiveness and live holy lives by the power of God's Spirit. He warned the congregation of eternal hell, and directed them on 'the way to heaven'.[48] This was the Gospel taught in Watts's Catechism, whose questions and answers were memorised by hundreds of adults and children connected to Bethel Chapel. Even when preaching on Old Testament narrative, the lessons he drew in his sermons were almost certainly personal rather than political. But his preaching was as much about collective identity as about individual salvation. During their 16-month immersion in Ephesians, his congregation would have learned to think of themselves as God's adopted children, the body of Christ, seated 'in heavenly places', 'fellow citizens with the saints, and of the household of God' (Eph. 1–2).

Smith also used Scripture to construct his congregation's identity as a persecuted people. In June 1818, having completed Ephesians, he decided to begin a series on I Peter, because it was 'very suitable in their present circumstances' – the apostle had written to 'Christians, who were scattered and persecuted, which is the case with our people'.[49] Three weeks later, after listening to 'one of the negroes', who 'breathed out a pious complaint' in prayer against the opposition of the planters, Smith 'could not help thinking that the time is not far distant when the Lord will make it manifest by some signal judgment that he hath heard the cry of the oppressed. Exodus, iii. 7 and 8.'[50] That text must have seemed all the more pertinent, given the daily floggings that punctuated plantation life; on Le Resouvenir, they were so prolonged that Smith took to counting the number of blows. Even during evening services, he complained, 'we are much annoyed ... by the flogging the negroes, the cracking the whip & the cries of the people', a soundscape unlike that of any English nonconformist chapel.[51] For the prosecution, Smith's mental association of the planters with Egyptian taskmasters was evidence of a seditious mind, and the journal's comments on Exodus 3 and 1 Peter were accordingly deployed in court. They showed that Smith's reading of the Bible was not so far removed from the politicised 'misinterpretation' of the insurgents. He saw his flock as the Hebrews in Pharaoh's Egypt, and the persecuted Christians of Nero's empire. The prosecution thought it 'ridiculous to say that he did not teach them to consider themselves oppressed and persecuted'.[52]

Indeed, when it came to the planters' violation of the Sabbath, Smith did not hide his disapproval. Smith admitted that in speaking to slaves, he had contrasted the slave colony to England, a 'free country', in which people were not forced to work on the Lord's Day.[53] Here he was transgressing the boundary line between the internal, 'spiritual' liberty of the believer, and the external 'religious liberty' to worship publicly without hindrance, a freedom dear to English nonconformists. While he instructed slaves to submit even when ordered to work on Sundays, he seems to have advised some to tell their masters that Sabbath labour was against the law of God.[54] When his deacons or members complained and prayed about their sufferings, the missionary did not intervene to check them. In December 1817, he even forwarded a letter to the LMS from four leading men of the church – Quamina, Satin (Seaton), Bristol and Azaar (Azor) – in which they complained that the planters 'are watching for us as a Cat would for a mouse'.[55] Understandably, Smith did not want this made public.[56]

While Smith's sermons had to pass muster with white hearers, on at least one occasion, his preaching provoked a stormy reaction. Expounding Christ's parable of the unmerciful servant (Matthew 18:21–35), before a 'pretty large' congregation on Friday evening, Smith 'felt considerable liberty in speaking and in applying the conduct of the unmerciful servant'. Among the hearers was the plantation manager, John Hamilton, whose brutal floggings of slaves had appalled the missionary. The sermon 'touched the conscience of Mr H— too closely, for he started up and hurried out banging the door after him, evidently in a rage. These men don't like plain truth. He stood outside till the service closed.'[57]

The prosecution overlooked this passage, and had no knowledge of the deacons' letter to England, but even without that evidence, it still had good grounds for its charge that Smith 'did promote ... discontent and dissatisfaction in the minds of the negro slaves towards their lawful masters, managers, and overseers'. When Smith read the story of the exodus from Egypt or the conquest of Canaan, he may never have told them 'Go ye and do likewise'; but the texts did 'the business' – 'and he knew and felt this'. At this point, the prosecution overreached, for it had no compelling evidence for the charge that the missionary was 'thereby intending to excite the said negroes to break out in such open revolt and rebellion'.[58] Smith had used Scripture to forge his congregation's identity as the persecuted people of God, but we can be confident that he never intended them to arm themselves with cutlasses and cane knives and to put the planters in the stocks.

The insurrectionist Bible

Nevertheless, the rebellion was instigated by men associated with Bethel Chapel. In an attempt at damage limitation, the LMS published a report claiming that only five or six of those executed had been among the congregation's 2,000 baptised adherents; and only one of these was among its 200 communicant members (Telemachus).[59] But Smith and his wife admitted that 'many' of their members were 'implicated', and Jack's letter conveying plans for the rising was written on behalf of himself 'and the rest of the brethren of Bethel Chapel'.[60] The prosecution maintained that 'being attendants at Bethel Chapel' was 'almost the only bond of connexion to be found among the leaders of the rebellion'.[61] Jack Gladstone and his father Quamina were at the heart of the revolt, though Smith suspected that Jack was the villain of the piece, and one later report claimed that Quamina had got on his knees to beg Jack to hold off.[62] Jack's testimony implicated all four of the deacons who had signed the 1817 letter to the LMS: Quamina, Seaton, Bristol and Azor.[63] But the Chapel's younger teachers seem to have been the real ringleaders: Jack himself, Joseph and Telemachus of Bachelor's Adventure, Sandy of Non Pareil, Paul of Friendship and Jack of Vigilance.[64] They were, as the prosecution noted, 'the principal tradesmen on their estates, men in the confidence and favour of their masters'.[65] On Success, Jack was the head cooper; his father the head carpenter.[66] Quamina was shot, and Telemachus, Sandy, Paul and Jack Gladstone were condemned to death, though Jack was eventually banished to St Lucia.[67] One key witness, the Anglican minister, W. S. Austin, had talked with the rebels, and found 'in no one instance among my numerous inquiries, did it appear, or was it stated, that Mr Smith had been in any degree instrumental to the insurrection'. However, the rebels 'very generally' had complained that they were prevented from attending 'Mr Smith's Chapel' and holding evening meetings on the estates; one leading insurgent, Sandy, alleged that the estate manager had confiscated his Bible.[68]

Given the limitations of the source material, we will never understand the mind of the insurgents as clearly as we can grasp the thinking of Smith, but it does seem that they came to form a distinct interpretive community, within and beyond the Chapel, one that arrived at a more militant reading of Scripture. Jack himself had a strong streak of independence. He was not a full member of the congregation with access to the Lord's Supper, and he had a reputation as 'a wild fellow'.[69] However, his father was the congregation's chief and 'most active' deacon, and Jack himself enjoyed informal status as a teacher or catechist on the plantation.[70] Smith recorded a number of personal conversations with him.[71] Jack's estranged wife, Susannah, had been 'one of our most sensible, active and in every respect most promising members' until she was excommunicated in June 1821 after becoming the concubine of her master, John Hamilton – the manager of Le Resouvenir, who had stormed out of Smith's sermon a few months before. According to Susannah, the relationship had begun when Hamilton raped her. When she was excluded from membership, Jack's 'brother-in-law' Bristol, one of the deacons, openly wept.[72] Thereafter, Jack himself cohabited with a number of women, including a church member, Gracey, something that vexed his father.[73] In short, Jack had multiple strong ties to the Chapel, but was firmly inclined to think and act for himself.

While Smith presided over the congregation as its patriarch, he had (whether deliberately or inadvertently) created an indigenous leadership cadre. As a Congregationalist, Smith believed strongly in the priesthood of all believers. Church members voted on the admission of new members, and deliberated together when agonising over excommunications.[74] His deacons prayed aloud at the 7 a.m. service, distributed the bread and wine at communion, catechised, prepared candidates for baptism, took up collections for the London Missionary Society, and visited the sick. Quamina even officiated at a funeral.[75] While the intensive catechising programme entailed rote learning, Smith was prepared to adopt more active methods of teaching. At the 7 a.m. services, he asked for questions after the Bible reading, provoking lively discussions on such topics as the Israelites in the Wilderness (a 'mutual conversation' that 'discovered a deal of good sense among the members'); and marriage regulations (a discussion on Exodus 18, which elicited 'many interesting questions', with Smith refusing to answer 'improper' ones).[76] Even during his evening homilies, he would stop to ask questions. Speaking to a 'large congregation' on a Friday, he records that 'the negroes answered the questions which I put to them during my discourse, with more judgment & propriety than usual'.[77] Interactive discussion with the congregation seems to have been Smith's common practice.

It was enhanced by the access to the Bible enjoyed by literate slaves. Already in 1817, Smith had received a shipment of 50 Bibles and 100 Testaments from the Bible Society,[78] selling them at reduced rates on the grounds that a book paid for was more likely to be valued that something given away.[79] By 1823, Smith could report that 'A great proportion' of the congregation 'are furnished with Bibles, Testaments, Dr Watts' First or Second Catechism, and a hymn-book; and these, being their whole library, they usually bring to chapel every Sunday'.[80]

Smith had little control over how these Bibles were read and discussed beyond the Chapel. He did not appoint the 'teachers' or catechists on each estate; these were chosen by the deacons, and were not necessarily members (thus it was that Jack could do some catechising). Indeed, Smith described the teachers as 'wholly unconnected with the church'.[81] It is clear from their testimony that deacons and local teachers went beyond catechising; they glossed Smith's sermons or commented on passages of Scripture.[82] Inevitably, then, the biblical text was explained and applied in ways that Smith had never authorised. In particular, slaves latched onto the dramatic Old Testament narratives that had been read on Sunday mornings, identifying themselves with the oppressed Hebrews in Pharaoh's Egypt, or imagining themselves as the victorious Israelites conquering Canaan under Joshua. Listening to the witnesses for the prosecution, Smith admitted to being struck that their 'memories were so very tenacious on the subject of Moses and Pharaoh, and the children of Israel, though it is two years since I have read to them about these persons'.[83] According to Smith's journal, Quamina was overcome by emotion after hearing the reading of Exodus 14 in December 1821. The chapter told the story of the Hebrews being pursued by the Egyptians, and being delivered across the Red Sea. 'Quamina was so much affected in prayer that he could not proceed for some time.' Smith 'envied the devotion of his mind', but this may have been a naively pietistic reading of the chief deacon's reaction.[84]

Bristol and Azor, senior figures in the Chapel, agreed that Smith had never been heard to 'apply the history of the Israelites to the condition of the negroes', and they emphasised that some of the slaves had done this for themselves.[85] As the prosecution shrewdly observed, the witnesses unwittingly testified to a striking case of semantic slippage. The translators of the King James Bible had translated the Hebrew term *ebed* and the Greek word *doulos* not as 'slave' but as 'servant', making the text more relevant to early modern English society.[86] Yet when Smith's congregation told the story, they departed from the Authorised Version, and 'we find them talk of slaves and slavery'. The prosecution alleged that Smith himself must have 'represented' the Exodus 'as a struggle between the slaves and the soldiers, in which the former were victorious and the latter destroyed'. Smith denied this, and it seems more likely that it was the slaves themselves who retold the story as an anti-slavery narrative.[87] Indeed, some of his congregation were frustrated at his diplomatic reserve, complaining that 'Mr Smith was making them fools' and 'would not deny his own colour for the sake of black people'.[88] Bristol maintained that it was the younger men ('the boys'), who had spoken most eagerly about 'the fighting of the Israelites', including Jack and his key collaborators. They and 'the people' read and 'discoursed' about Moses and Joshua, and 'applied ... and put it on themselves ... they said that this thing in the Bible applied to us just as well as to the people of Israel'.[89]

Jack's militant reading of Scripture did not go unchallenged in the interpretive community of the enslaved. In a conversation with the Governor's servant, Daniel, who belonged to the Methodist chapel in Georgetown, they turned to the Bible, swapping texts as they debated resistance as a case of conscience. Jack read a passage from Romans, probably chapter six: its promise that 'if we be dead with Christ ... we shall also live with him' (v. 8) seems to have been adopted as an oath by the insurgents, though rendered in various forms: 'as we live in Christ, so we must die in Christ'; 'By Christ we live, and by Christ we die'; 'I live in Christ, and I die in Christ'; 'we are to die by Christ, as we live by Christ'.[90] Daniel tried to curb Jack's rashness by citing the 'foolish war' slaves had fought in Barbados, and by reading II Timothy 3, a character sketch of false teachers that he probably applied to Jack himself. Jack had a reputation as one of those who 'creep into houses, and lead captive silly women ... with divers lusts' (verse 6), and Daniel may have compared him to Jannes and Jambres who rebelled against Moses (i.e. Smith?), and whose 'folly shall be manifest unto all men' (verses 8–9). Jack retorted by citing the promise of Romans 8:28 on which Smith had recently preached ('All things work together for good to those who love God').[91]

Other slaves were more receptive than Daniel to Jack's interpretations of the text. At the trials of the insurrectionists, witnesses testified that on the eve of the revolt Jack and other leaders made them swear on the Bible.[92] These testimonies were inconsistent, but all confirmed the talismanic role of Scripture in the rising. And those who encountered the rebels during the week of 18 August recalled their appeal to the

Bible. On the Clonbrook plantation, a slave seized the proprietor by the ear and called him 'a second Pharaoh'.[93] The Scots minister in Georgetown, Archibald Browne, was convinced from reports he had heard that 'a parallel drawn by their Religious Instructors, between the slaves of this Colony and the Israelites in Egypt, was the primary cause of the late Insurrection'. Browne suspected that the rebels saw 'the bush of Demerara' as the Wilderness, and the planters as the Canaanites. The fact that witnesses spoke of the fugitive King David and Quamina hiding in 'the bush' suggests that they did map biblical narrative onto local geography.[94] Browne also claimed that the insurgents had told one manager to read Psalm 120, David's cry of complaint against his oppressor. Even more provocatively, they were alleged to have quoted the last four verses of Psalm 149: 'To bind the kings with chains, and their nobles with fetters of iron; to execute upon them the judgment written: this honour have all his saints.'[95] This had been a favourite text of the English regicides in 1649; now, allegedly, it was used by rebels who bound their masters in the stocks.

When the encampment of the fugitives Jack and Quamina was discovered on 13 September, it contained '7 books – being 2 Bibles, 1 Testament, 1 Wesley's Hymn-book, 1 Watts' do., Spelling-book, and Sunday Tracts'.[96] A report sent from Demerara on the day before Smith's trial began informed the British public that Quamina was found dead with a Bible in his pocket, 'with the leaf doubled down which contains the 8th chapter of the book of Joshua' (describing the biblical hero's conquest of the city of Ai); one British reader thought this 'a fable, intended to cast reproach upon the Scriptures and Missionaries', though its idiosyncratic specificity is arguably a mark of authenticity.[97] Archibald Browne claimed that Smith himself had confessed to reading this chapter repeatedly in the Chapel, alongside more pacific texts, but the witnesses had no recollection of this.[98] Yet Smith did concede the textual sources of the insurgency. On the one hand, the Christian rebels had apparently misapplied Scripture, foolishly attempting to recapitulate the march from Egyptian bondage and the wars of the Jews. On the other hand, the 'mildness and forbearance' shown by 'the Christian negroes' during the revolt was a sign that the Gospel had 'produced a material alteration for the better' in their minds. It was the heathen blacks who had advocated violence, as in 'former revolts' in the colonies. In Demerara, however, Christian slaves had said, 'We will shed no blood, for it is contrary to the religion we have been taught.'[99] Even as he disowned the rebellion, the missionary praised its Christian ringleaders for heeding the pacific teachings of the Gospel.[100]

In the light of the evidence, it is possible, however tentatively, to reconstruct the Scriptural politics of Jack Gladstone and the other rebel leaders from Bethel Chapel. They read themselves into biblical narrative, inhabiting biblical identities. Taking cues from Smith himself, they identified with the persecuted people of God in the New Testament, but also with the Children of Israel in their exodus from Egypt and their conquest of Canaan. Having located themselves within this biblical frame, they appear to have drawn a number of conclusions. First, that God was on the side of the oppressed. The 'boys' fascination with the deliverance of the Jews, together with Jack's use of Romans 8:28, suggest a providentialist confidence that God would deliver the enslaved. It was a confidence that helped to overcome well-justified fears of repeating the fiasco of 'the Barbadoes business' in 1816.[101] A second conclusion was that God helped those who helped themselves. The Exodus story was filled with divine intervention, but even the Hebrews had to march for their freedom; the walls of Jericho collapsed on the mere blast of trumpets, but the Israelites had to march around the city seven times. Divine and human agency worked together. Nothing would happen if Demerara's slaves failed to 'make a push for it'.[102] The rebels had to be willing to 'die in Christ' (Romans 6:8). Finally, Jack and his principal assistants seem to have concluded that godly rebels should be reluctant to destroy human life. Smith had emphasised this in teaching about Saul and David, and in preaching through the Sermon on the Mount.[103] It is notable that on various occasions during the insurrection, ringleaders from Bethel Chapel intervened to prevent bloodshed. Jack's revolt, like Smith's preaching, was devoid of the apocalypticism that made Nat Turner's rebellion so violent.

The pro-slavery Bible

The trial of the missionary and the interrogation of his congregation prompted a battle for the Bible that reached all the way to the House of Commons. The planters sought to turn the rebellion against evangelical missionaries and metropolitan abolitionists. They depicted Smith as a subversive fanatic, seizing on his cryptic remark that 'much blood had been shed at different periods in religious wars, or on account of religion'.[104] As a Congregationalist taught by David Bogue, it is quite possible that Smith saw an analogy between the slave rebellion and the seventeenth-century civil war fought by persecuted Puritans against their Laudian and Royalist enemies.[105] Whatever Smith meant by this remark, he was certainly depicted as a neo-Cromwellian. And in the fierce backlash against the 'Sectarian' and 'Methodist' missionaries, Wray's chapel in Berbice was destroyed by arsonists, while a Methodist chapel in Barbados was burned to the ground by a white mob.[106]

In their struggle to regain the moral high ground, violence was less helpful than argument. In particular, it was necessary to reclaim the Scriptures. Scripture had long been cited to reinforce the hierarchical domination of white masters over black slaves, but with the conversion and baptism of the enslaved, it became harder to justify such domination by reference to the Israelites' enslavement of heathens. Appeals to the so-called 'curse of Ham' (Genesis 9:20–5) had some purchase, but the use of that obscure text was often dismissed as tendentious. Slavery had to be legitimised in New Testament terms, as the rule of benevolent Christian masters over obedient Christian slaves. However, Caribbean planters had been notoriously lukewarm in their Christianity, and half-hearted (at best) in their mobilisation of the Bible. They had little appetite for the strict, pious and assertive Christian paternalism that was already becoming entrenched in the American South. But stigmatising Smith's abuse of the Bible was not enough; colonists had to recapture it. It did not help that Georgetown's Anglican minister, Austin, bravely defended the missionary's use of the Bible against the prosecution.

The colonists' counterattack was launched by Archibald Browne, minister of the Scots' Church in Georgetown, whose arrival in the colony Smith had welcomed in 1818.[107] In *Three Discourses* preached in St Andrew's Church in Georgetown, Browne returned to the very texts that the LMS had urged upon Smith in 1817. One sermon was on Romans 13, another on I Peter 2. Browne endeavoured to revivify pro-slavery identities, addressing himself to idealised Christian masters and submissive Christian slaves. On the one hand, he sought to reassure the planter elite. He feared that by misrepresenting the Bible as an anti-slavery text, abolitionists had created 'a secret misgiving' among slaveholders 'on this tender point'. This was 'one of the reasons why the sacred volume is so generally and habitually neglected' by white colonists – 'a fear that in the course of reading, something might turn up to warn, or reprove, or admonish them'. Browne insisted that the Bible was the friend of slaveholders, not their enemy. Abolitionists 'employ Religion as the foremost of their arguments', but 'they fight in Achilles' armour'; Buxton had no biblical grounds for 'his favourite doctrine' that 'Slavery is inconsistent with Christianity'. The 'brave defenders of our Colony' should be saluted for 'putting down a rebellious and daring Insurrection'.[108]

In his sermon on II Peter 2, Browne directly addressed the slaves, drawing their attention to a series of New Testament texts commanding submission to masters. Such was the abundance of texts on this topic that one might almost think that 'the Scriptures were mainly intended for the use of Slaves'. Slavery in antiquity was 'in a much worse form' than in modern times, yet 'in spite of all its horrors', the Bible sought to reconcile slaves 'to their unhappy condition'. Browne assured his enslaved audience that 'your condition is greatly preferable to that of the Christian slaves' of the apostolic age. The late rebellion had been inspired by 'the perversion of Scripture'. But the Bible, properly read and applied 'by well-educated and regularly ordained Ministers', was on the side of civil authority.[109]

This kind of unapologetic pro-slavery reading of the Bible would flourish in the antebellum United States, and initially, there were signs that it might gain traction in Britain too, given the reaction against the revolt.[110] John Gladstone lamented that Smith had 'corrupted and inflamed' the minds of the slaves with 'the doctrines of emancipation'. When his abolitionist critic, James Cropper, mocked the idea of a planter belonging to the Bible Society and 'promoting the circulation of the Sacred Volume', Gladstone was undeterred. He remained wholly committed to the religious instruction of the negroes, 'but from pure sources, not such as the emancipators have hitherto forced upon the Planters'.[111] The Liverpool clergyman, Robert Buddicom, who had supported the Anti-Slavery Society, now turned his back on the cause, and Zachary Macaulay complained that many other Anglican Evangelical clergy in Bristol and London were under the sway of the planters.[112]

The abolitionist Bible

Yet over the course of 1824, it became evident that the West Indian account of Smith and his congregation would not prevail. The trial record, designed in Demerara as a devastating indictment of the missionary, was read quite differently in Britain. Evangelicals and abolitionists declared Smith innocent, proclaimed him a martyr for the Gospel, and bombarded Parliament with 200 petitions. The *Christian Observer* charged the colony with using the missionary's trial to 'discredit the Bible, as a bad and dangerous book'. Wilberforce, Smith and the Bible had been incriminated as 'the three great incendiaries that lighted the flame of insurrection'.[113] In the *Edinburgh Review*, Sydney Smith declared the legal proceedings a travesty and praised 'this martyred teacher'. And he seized on a statement in the *Demerara Journal*: 'If we expect to create a community of reading, moral, church-going slaves, we are woefully mistaken.' In a prophetic concluding remark, Smith wrote: 'If [the West Indian system] cannot exist together with Christianity, then is it indeed condemned to swift destruction!'[114]

In June 1824, the Whig MP Henry Brougham brought a motion of censure against the colonists to the House of Commons, introduced with an eloquent four-hour oration (followed up by Wilberforce in one of the final speeches of his long parliamentary career). Brougham hailed Smith as an heir of 'the Independents', the Cromwellian champions of 'civil and religious liberty', who 'with the zeal of martyrs, the purity of the early Christians, the skill and courage of the most renowned warriors, gloriously suffered and fought and conquered for England the free constitution which she now enjoys'. This sounded like an endorsement of religiously inspired wars of liberation, but Brougham mocked the Court Martial for accusing Smith of fomenting insurrection. Reading potentially inflammatory passages of Scripture was not a crime; if it was, all clergy would be guilty. Supposedly seditious Scriptures like Christ's weeping over Jerusalem had been described by W.S. Austin as 'a text of singular beauty', and the Church of England's own lectionary required clergy to read provocative chapters like Ezekiel 14 ('the land shall be desolate'). Wilmot Horton retorted that Smith was an enthusiast, not a respectable clergyman. He should have stuck to New Testament doctrines of 'fidelity, patience, and obedience', instead of reading Old Testament passages 'calculated to excite dangerous impressions'.[115] The censure of the planters was voted down, but Smith's status as 'the Demerara martyr' was secured. At the Annual General Meeting of the Anti-Slavery Society in July, Thomas Babington Macaulay denounced 'those wretched islands', and praised 'this traduced and persecuted missionary'.[116] In response to these developments, the LMS planned to publish and circulate Smith's journal; when John Gladstone caught wind of this, he rushed off a letter to the missionary society's treasurer, William Hankey, refuting the 'slanders' of harsh treatment on Success. He was determined to clear 'this stain upon my name': 'my instructions have ever been to treat my people with kindness'.[117] In the court of public opinion, however, it was hard for an ameliorationist planter to compete with a missionary martyr.

Not only was Smith rehabilitated; so was his congregation. As Catherine Hall has shown, missionaries and planters in the Caribbean fought a 'war of representation', presenting rival accounts of 'the disputed figure of the African', with the missionaries endeavouring 'to construct new Christian subjects'.[118] The trial records served their purpose. The British religious public was familiar with missionary reports, but never before had it been exposed to such a chorus of voices from an enslaved congregation. Large portions of the proceedings were reprinted in newspapers and periodicals, notably *The Anti-Slavery Magazine*. The witness testimony, designed to incriminate the missionary, had incidentally provided a vivid account of the religious culture of Bethel Chapel, and the biblical piety of its people. Some, like Jack, had misinterpreted the Scriptures, but even they had shown admirable restraint in their rising, after years of intolerable provocation. Observers noted with disapproval that Jack's wife had been stolen from him by a white planter.[119] The extracts from Smith's journal were now read as an eloquent record of the horrors and injustice of the slave system. For the Leicester Quaker, Elizabeth Heyrick, writing a series of seminal pamphlets on 'immediate emancipation', the blacks of Demerara had proved themselves 'fit' for freedom, thus refuting the pessimism of gradualists. The stark contrast between their restraint and the violence of the slaveholder 'mob of Barbados' was 'the practical illustration of BLACK and of WHITE principle'. The masters had acted like barbarous heathen; the slaves as true Christians.[120] As Seymour Drescher notes, the revolt was a major turning point:

> Missionary Smith was the abolitionists' Archimedian fulcrum ... His death allowed the rebels to be identified not just as fellow men and brothers, but as fellow freedom-loving Christians ... the most important step in the 'Anglicisation' of the slaves and the detoxification of slave insurgencies occurred within the cycle of the Demerara revolt.[121]

Slaves were indeed acquiring a new identity, but it was the result of scripturalisation as much as Anglicisation, and owed something to the Hebrew Bible as well as to Christianity. In particular, Britain's Caribbean slaves were being reimagined as the oppressed Israelites suffering under heathen taskmasters. Smith himself made that identification, as he heard the whips and cries on Le Resouvenir. Elizabeth Heyrick made it too as she reminded her readers of the Old Testament God: 'who "will deliver the poor that crieth and him that hath no helper;" – will "take the prey out of the hands of the mighty" – "will execute judgment upon the oppressor, and justice for the oppressed"'.[122] In the wake of the rebellion, Wilberforce's close associate, James Stephen, declared that there was a 'striking resemblance' between the Hebrews in Egypt, forced to make bricks without straw, and 'the grass picking drudgeries of the sugar colonies'. Like Pharaoh's taskmasters, British planters were involved in 'oeconomical oppression'. 'The prayer of every petition', he advised, 'should be as simple as the demand of [Moses] to the Egyptian monarch, LET THE PEOPLE GO.'[123] Wilberforce himself applied Exodus to the case of the West Indian slaves, noting in his Bible that 'yellow fever attacking whites only' in the Caribbean was analogous to the Ten Plagues visited on the slaveholding Egyptians.[124] The medal struck to celebrate the abolition of the slave trade in 1807 had borne the words of God in Exodus: 'I have heard their cry.' With Wilberforce on one side, and Britannia on the other, it implied that abolitionists might play the part of Moses, crying 'Let my people Go'.[125] By the 1820s, with calls for gradual emancipation being matched by demands for immediate emancipation, that biblical role-play took on a new urgency.

Conclusion

The Demerara revolt exposed a crisis of biblical identity politics in Britain's West Indian colonies. Archibald Browne's pro-slavery Bible squared up against John Smith's missionary Bible and Wilberforce's abolitionist Bible.[126] The balance of power and prestige here would prove very different than in the battle over the Bible in antebellum America, where abolitionists arguably 'lost the exegetical war'.[127] But without Jack Gladstone's insurrectionist Bible, the course of events could have been quite different. The rebellion ended with Quamina's body hanging in chains from a gibbet in front of Success, the plantation owned by John Gladstone, evangelical MP and father of a future Prime Minister. Jack was transported to St Lucia, unaware that his revolt had been transformed into a *cause célèbre* in the metropolis.[128] When Wilberforce heard of Smith's death, he felt Britain's 'day of reckoning' approaching.[129] The crisis of British Caribbean slavery had been hastened by 'a community of reading, moral, church-going slaves'.

Notes

I am grateful to Clare Anderson and Trevor Burnard for comments on this chapter. The research was made possible by the generosity of the Leverhulme Trust, whose award of a Research Fellowship in 2012–13 enabled me to read my way into a new field of historical enquiry.

1. David Brion Davis, *Inhuman Bondage: The Rise and Fall of New World Slavery* (New York: Oxford University Press, 2006), p. 217.
2. The finest study of the revolt is Emilia Viotta Da Costa, *Crowns of Glory, Tears of Blood: The Demerara Slave Rebellion of 1823* (New York: Oxford University Press, 1997). Other modern accounts include Stiv Jakobssen, *Am I not a Man and a Brother? British Missions and the Abolition of the Slave Trade and Slavery in West Africa and the West Indies, 1786–1838* (Uppsala: Almquist and Wiksell, 1972), pp. 298–369; Cecil Northcott, *Slavery's Martyr: John Smith of Demerara and the Emancipation Movement, 1817–24* (London: Epworth Press, 1976); Michael Craton, *Testing the Chains: Resistance to Slavery in the British West Indies* (Ithaca, NY: Cornell University Press, 1982), pp. 267–90; Noel Titus, 'Reassessing John Smith's Influence on the Demerara Slave Revolt of 1823', in Alvin O. Thompson, ed., *In the Shadow of the Plantation: Caribbean History and Legacy* (Kingston, Jamaica: Ian Randle Publishers, 2002), pp. 223–45; Michael A. Rutz, *The British Zion: Congregationalism, Politics and Empire, 1790–1850* (Waco, TX: Baylor University Press, 2011), pp. 53–74; Anthony E. Kaye, 'Spaces of Rebellion: Plantations, Farms and Churches in Demerara and Southampton, Virginia', in Dale Tomich, ed., *The Politics of Second Slavery* (Albany: State University of New York Press, 2016), pp. 199–228.
3. *Proceedings of a Court Martial in Demerara, on Trial of John Smith, Missionary* (London: House of Commons, 1824), p. 3.

4 *Further Papers Relating to Insurrection of Slaves in Demarara* (London: House of Commons, 1824), pp. 78–9; Most of Jack's statement had been 'dictated' to the barrister, but this final paragraph was added by the Georgetown merchant, Robert Edmonstone, who claimed to be paraphrasing what he had heard from Jack: *Further Papers*, p. 74.

5 *Proceedings*, p. 84.

6 Adrian Hastings, *The Construction of Nationhood: Ethnicity, Religion and Nationalism* (Cambridge: Cambridge University Press, 1997); Anthony D. Smith, *Chosen Peoples: Sacred Sources of National Identity* (Oxford: Oxford University Press, 2003).

7 See Paul Regan, 'Calvinism and the Dutch Israel Thesis', in Bruce Gordon, ed., *Protestant History and Identity in Sixteenth-Century Europe*, 2 vols (Aldershot: Scolar Press, 1996), II: pp. 91–107; Graeme Murdock, 'Magyar Judah: Constructing a New Canaan in Eastern Europe', *Studies in Church History*, 36 (2000), 264–9.

8 See Achsah Guibbory, *Christian Identity, Jews and Israel in Seventeenth-Century England* (Oxford: Oxford University Press, 2010).

9 Christopher Hill, *The English Bible and the Seventeenth-Century Revolution* (London: Allen Lane, 1993); Kevin Killeen, Helen Smith and Rachel Willie, eds, *The Oxford Handbook of the Bible in Early Modern England, c. 1530–1700* (Oxford: Oxford University Press, 2015), part IV: 'The Political Bible'; Kevin Killeen, *The Political Bible in Early Modern England* (Cambridge: Cambridge University Press, 2016).

10 Ruth Smith, *Handel's Oratorios and Eighteenth-Century Thought* (Cambridge: Cambridge University Press, 1995), part II; Pasi Ihalainen, *Protestant Nations Redefined: Changing Perceptions of National Identity in the Rhetoric of the English, Dutch and Swedish Public Churches, 1685–1772* (Leiden: Brill, 2005); James P. Byrd, *Sacred Scripture, Sacred War: The Bible and the American Revolution* (New York: Oxford University Press, 2013); Mark Noll, *In the Beginning was the Word: The Bible in American Public Life, 1492–1783* (New York: Oxford University Press, 2016).

11 See Norman Etherington, ed., *Missions and Empire* (Oxford: Oxford University Press, 2005),

12 Colin Kidd, *The Forging of Races: Race and Scripture in the Protestant Atlantic World, 1600–2000* (Cambridge: Cambridge University Press, 2006), p. 19. See also David Mark Whitford, *The Curse of Ham in the Early Modern Era* (Farnham: Ashgate, 2009); Stephen R. Haynes, *Noah's Curse: The Biblical Justification of American Slavery* (New York: Oxford University Press, 2002); Travis Glasson, *Mastering Christianity: Missionary Anglicanism and Slavery in the Atlantic World* (New York: Oxford University Press, 2012), pp. 44–7, 63–6; Davis, *Inhuman Bondage*, pp. 60, 64–9, 187–8.

13 From a copious recent literature see Eddie Glaude, Jr, *Exodus! Religion, Race and Nation in Early Nineteenth-Century Black America* (Chicago: University of Chicago Press, 2000); Allen Dwight Callahan, *The Talking Book: African Americans and the Bible* (New Haven, CT: Yale University Press, 2006); Roy Kay, *The Ethiopian Prophecy in Black American Letters* (Gainesville, FL: University Press of Florida, 2011); Vincent Wimbush, *White Men's Magic: Scripturalization as Slavery* (New York: Oxford University Press, 2012); John Coffey, *Exodus and Liberation: Deliverance Politics from John Calvin to Martin Luther King Jr.* (New York; Oxford University Press, 2014); Emerson B. Powery and Rodney S. Sadler, Jr, *The Genesis of Liberation: Biblical Interpretation in the Antebellum Narratives of the Enslaved* (Louisville, KY: Westminster/John Knox Press, 2016).

14 The biblical framing of these revolts is often noted in passing, but for deeper analysis see James Sidbury, 'Reading, Revelation, and Rebellion: The Textual Communities of Gabriel, Denmark Vesey, and Nat Turner', in Kenneth S. Greenberg, ed., *Nat Turner: A Slave Rebellion in History and Memory* (New York: Oxford University Press, 2003), pp. 119–33.

15 Sidbury, 'Reading, Revelation, and Rebellion', pp. 119–23.
16 *An Official Report of the Trials of Sundry Negroes charged with an Attempt to Raise an Insurrection* (Charleston, SC: James R. Schenck, 1822), pp. 17–18.
17 See e.g. *Facts and Documents connected with the Late Insurrection in Jamaica* (London: Baptist Missionary Society, 1832).
18 School of Oriental and African Studies (SOAS), CWM/LMS/12/05/02, 'Journal of John Smith, 1817–1823'. A basic transcription of the diary is available online: http://www.vc.id.au/fh/jsmith.html (accessed 18 March 2017).
19 I. *Proceedings of a Court Martial in Demerara, on Trial of John Smith, Missionary*; II. *Further Papers relating to Insurrection of Slaves in Demarara*; III. *Documentary Papers produced at the Trial of Mr. John Smith, Missionary* (London: House of Commons, 1824). In line with Da Costa, I refer to these as *Proceedings*, *Further Papers Relating to Insurrection*, and *Further Papers: Documentary Evidence*. The parliamentary report on Smith's trial was made available to a wider public in *An Authentic Copy of the Minutes of Evidence on the Trial of John Smith, a Missionary, in Demerara* (London: Samuel Burton, 1824), while the trials of the insurgents were published in Demerara as *Report of the Trials of the Insurgent Negroes* (Demerara: A. Stevenson, 1824).
20 *The London Missionary's Society's Report of the Proceedings against the Late Rev. J. Smith, of Demerara ... From a Full and Correct Copy transmitted to England by Mr. Smith's Counsel* (London: F. Westley, 1824), p. vi.
21 *Proceedings*, pp. 62–4.
22 On Bogue's missionary training see Christopher Daily, *Robert Morrison and the Protestant Plan for China* (New York: Columbia University Press, 2013), pp. 37–82.
23 Letter dated 23 February 1816 in *The Life and Letters of John Angell James*, ed. R. W. Dale (London: James Nisbet, 1821), pp. 137–42.
24 The most perceptive characterisation of this new cohort is in Catherine Hall, *Civilising Subjects: Metropole and Colony in the English Imagination, 1830–1867* (Cambridge: Polity Press, 2002), pp. 84–139.
25 See Rutz, *British Zion*, pp. 57–62.
26 See Thomas Rain, *The Life and Labours of John Wray, Pioneer Missionary in British Guiana* (London: John Snow, 1892).
27 'Journal', 31 December 1821.
28 *The Missionary Smith: Substance of the Debate in the House of Commons on Tuesday the 1st and on Friday the 11th June, 1824* (London: Hatchard and Son, 1824), p. xviii.
29 SOAS, CWM/LMS/12/Box 2, John Smith to the LMS, 4 March 1817.
30 SOAS, CWM/LMS/12/Box 2, John Smith to the LMS, 18 March 1818.
31 SOAS, CWM/LMS/12/Box 2, John Smith to the LMS, 27 November 1817.
32 *Proceedings*, pp. 7, 9–11, 14, 76.
33 *Proceedings*, p. 40.
34 'Journal', 3 September 1817.
35 'Journal', 15 July 1823.
36 See *Further Papers: Documentary Evidence*, pp. 21–7, 30–5. The prosecution used this evidence to argue that the planters were not enemies of Christian mission.
37 *Proceedings*, p. 34.
38 *Proceedings*, pp. 7, 34, 41.
39 *Proceedings*, p. 79.
40 'Journal'; *Proceedings*, pp. 9, 12, 63.
41 *Proceedings*, p. 33.
42 *Further Papers: Documentary Evidence*, pp. 27–9.
43 'Journal', 8 August 1817; *Proceedings*, p. 5.
44 Rain, *Life and Labours of John Wray*, p. 236.
45 'Journal', 12 June 1817; John Smith to George Burder of the LMS, 10 July 1817 (SOAS). Talboys had previously been accused of 'exciting the negroes to disaffection and revolt' in Trinidad. Richard Watson, *A Defence of the Wesleyan Methodist Missions in the West Indies* (London: Thomas Cordeux, 1817), pp. 36, 82–95.

46 G. G. Findlay and W. W. Holdsworth, *The History of the Wesleyan Missionary Society*, 5 vols (London: Epworth Press, 1921), II: pp. 275–7.
47 SOAS, CWM/LMS/12/05/05, 'Journal of John Wray, 1824–37', 45, 15 August 1824.
48 SOAS, CWM/LMS/12/Box 2, John Smith to the LMS, 10 July 1817.
49 'Journal', 30 June 1818; *Proceedings*, pp. 5–6.
50 'Journal', 19 July 1818; *Proceedings*, p. 6.
51 'Journal', 24 November 1821.
52 *Proceedings*, p. 78.
53 *Proceedings*, pp. 36; 14, 77.
54 *Proceedings*, p. 36.
55 SOAS, CWM/LMS/12/Box 2, Letter from the Negroes to the Missionary Society, 14 December 1817.
56 SOAS, CWM/LMS/12/Box 2, John Smith to the LMS, 15 December 1817.
57 'Journal', 17 March 1821, referring to his Friday evening sermon. The journal mentions 'Mr H', but in context this is almost certainly Hamilton, the plantation manager.
58 *Proceedings*, pp. 3, 79.
59 *The Missionary Smith: Substance of the Debate*, pp. xviii, xx–xxi.
60 Northcott, *Slavery's Martyr*, p. 108; *Proceedings*, pp. 26–7, 71, 82.
61 *Proceedings*, p. 82.
62 *Proceedings*, pp. 43–4; SOAS, CWM/LMS/12/05/05, 'Journal of John Wray, 1824–37', p. 48.
63 *Further Papers Relating to Insurrection*, p. 41.
64 *Further Papers Relating to Insurrection*, p. 76, passim; *Proceedings*, p. 82.
65 *Proceedings*, p. 82.
66 *Proceedings*, p. 49.
67 *Further Papers: Documentary Evidence*, pp. 36–8; Da Costa, *Crowns of Glory*, p. 244.
68 *Proceedings*, p. 53. For Sandy's complaint see also *Report of the Trials of the Insurgent Negroes*, p. 69.
69 *Proceedings*, p. 9.
70 'Journal', 17 January 1819; *Proceedings*, pp. 9, 11, 13, 24.
71 Smith's journal records several conversations with Jack on Sundays (12 September 1819; 17 December 1820; 24 June 1821).
72 'Journal', 15 April, 29 April, 3 June 1821; *Further Papers Relating to Insurrection*, p. 79. On the missionary critique of concubinage and the sexual economy of the plantations see Katherine Paugh, *The Politics of Reproduction: Race, Medicine, and Fertility in the Age of Abolition* (Oxford, 2017), pp. 190–231.
73 *Further Papers: Documentary Evidence*, pp. 8, 22.
74 *Proceedings*, pp. 13, 73–4; 'Journal', 3 June 1821.
75 'Journal', 28 May 1821.
76 'Journal', 31 December 1821; 13 January 1822.
77 'Journal', 12 March 1819.
78 *Further Papers: Documentary Evidence*, p. 10.
79 *Proceedings*, pp. 35, 16.
80 London Missionary Society, *29th Report* (1823), p. 118.
81 *Proceedings*, pp. 13, 16, 32.
82 *Proceedings*, pp. 10, 12, 13, 16, 18.
83 *Proceedings*, p. 34. See also pp. 58, 62, 72.
84 'Journal', 16 December 1821.
85 *Proceedings*, pp. 15, 17, 34.
86 Naomi Tadmor, *The Social Universe of the English Bible* (Cambridge: Cambridge University Press, 2010), pp. 82–118.
87 *Proceedings*, pp. 79, 34.
88 *Proceedings*, p. 10.
89 *Proceedings*, pp. 15, 17.

THE DEMERARA SLAVE REBELLION

90 *Further Papers Relating to Insurrection*, pp. 43–4. The trial record specifies Romans 5 ('about the first ten verses'), but this must be an error of transcription or a failure of memory, since it is hard to see how that passage could be applied to a slave rising. By contrast, Romans 6 (especially verse 8) keeps recurring in the testimony of witnesses: see *Further Papers Relating to Insurrection*, pp. 41, 45, 54; *Report of the Trials of the Insurgent Negroes*, pp. 147–50; see also *Proceedings*, p. 79.
91 *Further Papers Relating to Insurrection*, pp. 43–4, 74–5; 'Journal', 25 May 1823.
92 *Further Papers Relating to Insurrection*, pp. 12, 45, 48; *Report of the Trials of the Insurgent Negroes*, pp. 14, 24, 32, 49, 66, 146–51, 159.
93 *Further Papers Relating to Insurrection*, p. 84.
94 Archibald Browne, *Three Discourses ... on the Duty of Subjects ... on the Duty of Slaves ... Preached in St Andrew's Church, Georgetown, Demerara, in Consequence of the Insurrection* (Demerara: A Stevenson, 1824), p. 37n; *Proceedings*, pp. 11, 15, 79.
95 Browne, *Three Discourses*, 5n. Another report claimed that Psalm 149 had been read out by a missionary 'on the night preceding the insurrection' (*Liverpool Mercury*, 12 December 1823).
96 Bryant, *Account of an Insurrection*, p. 86.
97 See *Caledonian Mercury*, 27 November 1823; *Liverpool Mercury*, 28 November 1823; *Bristol Mercury*, 1 December 1823; Viscountess Knutsford, *Life and Letters of Zachary Macaulay* (London: Edward Arnold, 1900), pp. 417–18.
98 Browne, *Three Discourses*, p. 5n; *Proceedings*, p. 63.
99 *Proceedings*, p. 45.
100 Browne, *Three Discourses*, p. 5n.
101 *Further Papers Relating to Insurrection*, pp. 26, 29, 44, 69, 75.
102 *Proceedings*, p. 11.
103 *Proceedings*, p. 59; Browne, *Three Discourses*, p. 5n.
104 *Proceedings*, pp. 26, 78.
105 See David Bogue and James Bennett, *History of Dissenters from the Revolution in 1688 to the Year 1808*, 4 vols (London: printed for the authors, 1808–12), I: pp. 77–84. The long struggle against persecution and for 'religious liberty' was a major theme of this work. It should be noted that Bogue was a pacifist whose lecture on 'Universal Peace', first published in *Discourses on the Millennium* (London: T. Hamilton, 1818), was republished a year later by the London Peace Society.
106 On anti-Methodism in Barbados see David Lambert, *White Creole Culture, Politics and the Identity during the Age of Abolition* (Cambridge: Cambridge University Press, 2005), Ch. 5.
107 'Journal', 28–9 September, 6 October 1818.
108 Browne, *Three Discourses*, pp. v–viii, 21.
109 Browne, *Three Discourses*, pp. 23–5, 29, 37, 31.
110 Although see Michael Taylor, 'British Pro-Slavery Arguments and the Bible, 1832–1833', *Slavery and Abolition*, 37 (2016), 139–58.
111 *The Correspondence between John Gladstone, Esq., M.P., and James Cropper, Esq.* (Liverpool: West India Association, 1824), p. 67. On Gladstone's sophisticated case for pro-slavery amelioration see Christa Dierksheide, *Amelioration and Empire: Progress and Slavery in the Plantation Americas* (Charlottesville: University of Virginia Press, 2014), Ch. 6; Trevor Burnard and Kit Candlin, 'Sir John Gladstone and the Debate over the Amelioration of Slavery in the British West Indies in the 1820s', *Journal of British Studies*, 57 (2018), 760–82.
112 Zachary Macaulay to Thomas Chalmers, 13 September 1827, New College, Edinburgh, Chalmers MSS, 4.79.8–9. I am grateful to Gareth Atkins for supplying this reference.
113 'Insurrections of Slaves in the West Indies', *Christian Observer*, 24 (March 1824), 162.
114 'West Indian Missions', *Edinburgh Review*, 40 (March 1824), 270.
115 *The Missionary Smith: Substance of the Debate*, pp. 3, 31–3, 53–5.

116 *Anti-Slavery Magazine*, 31 July 1824, 118–19.
117 John Gladstone to William Hankey, 21 December 1824, cited in Dierksheide, *Amelioration and Empire*, p. 196.
118 Hall, *Civilising Subjects*, pp. 107–20.
119 *Christian Observer*, 24 (1824), 21.
120 [Elizabeth Heyrick], *An Enquiry: Which of the Two Parties is Best Entitled to Freedom? The Slave or the Slave Holder* (London: Baldwin, Cradock, and Joy, 1824), pp. 5, 16–19. See also Heyrick, *Immediate, not Gradual Abolition* (London: Hatchard and Son, 1824), pp. 30–2.
121 Drescher, *Abolition*, p. 257.
122 [Heyrick], *An Enquiry*, pp. 20–1.
123 James Stephen, *The Slavery of the British West India Colonies Delineated*, 2 vols (London: Joseph Butterworth, 1824), I: p. 127; II: pp. 325–6.
124 Comment on Exodus 8:22 in 'Annotated extracts from Wilberforce's copy of the Bible', British Library, Western Manuscripts, RP 9120. The same linkage between yellow fever in the Caribbean and the plagues of Egypt is made in James Stephen, *England Enslaved by her own Slavery Colonies* (London: Hatchard and Son, 1826), p. 55. For other uses of Exodus in the Wilberforce circle see Coffey, *Exodus and Liberation*, pp. 105, 111.
125 See Coffey, *Exodus and Liberation*, pp. 105–6.
126 See also Michael Taylor, 'British Pro-Slavery Arguments and the Bible, 1832–1833', *Slavery and Abolition*, 37 (2016), 139–58.
127 See Mark Noll, 'The Bible and Slavery', in Randall Miller, Harry Stout and Charles Wilson, eds, *Religion and the American Civil War* (New York: Oxford University Press, 1998), pp. 43–73, quotation at p. 66; Molly Oshatz, *Slavery and Sin: The Fight against Slavery and the Rise of Liberal Protestantism* (New York: Oxford University Press, 2012), pp. 61–80.
128 Drescher, *Abolition*, p. 256.
129 Robert Isaac and Samuel Wilberforce, *The Life of William Wilberforce*, 5 vols (London: John Murray, 1838), V: p. 221.

CHAPTER TWO

Babylon, the Bible and the Australian Aborigines
Hilary M. Carey

> [God] hath made of one blood all nations of men for to dwell on all the face of the earth, and hath determined the times before appointed, and the bounds of their habitation. (Acts 17:26)

'One blood': John Fraser and the origins of the Aborigines

In 1892 Dr John Fraser (1834–1904), a schoolteacher from Maitland, New South Wales, published *An Australian Language*, a work commissioned by the government of New South Wales for display in Chicago at the World's Columbian Exposition (1893).[1] Fraser's edition was just one of a range of exhibits selected to represent the products, industries and native cultures of the colony to the eyes of the world.[2] But it was much more than a showpiece or a simple reprinting of the collected works of Lancelot Threlkeld (1788–1859), the missionary linguist who had first published these same translations and grammatical works some fifty years earlier.[3] Besides delivering a serviceable edition of some rare grammatical texts, Fraser provided an extensive introduction which promoted his own theories about the peopling of the Australian continent.[4] After an intricate argument covering issues of comparative philology, ethnology and religion, he concluded that the Aborigines of Australia were not only kin to the Dravidian peoples of southern India but that both had their origins in biblical lands: 'In my opinion,' he concluded, 'the ultimate home of origin of the negroid population of Australia is Babylonia.'[5] It was a theory he had been promoting since at least 1882, a late flowering in the long tradition of biblically sourced narratives of the peopling of the world which is the focus of this book.

Fraser's ideas may seem strange to modern ears but they emerged naturally out of a nineteenth-century worldview in which race, religion and language were inextricably bound together. Babylonian Aborigines form part of what Colin Kidd has called the 'Aryan moment' in the nineteenth century, when a mutual obsession with religion and race gave rise to numerous racialist – and frequently racist – theories of the origins of the peoples of the known world.[6] Kidd was primarily concerned in his study with the Protestant Atlantic world, but similar ideas and theories were current well beyond the northern hemisphere. Fraser's writing on the Australian Aborigines is a good example of the way biblical theories of race, language and descent were expounded in the southern British colonies and Oceania. These lands included Australia, New Zealand, Papua New Guinea and Oceania, regions which had been mapped during James Cook's voyages of exploration in the eighteenth century and which were swiftly infiltrated by British colonial forces including their dynamic, mostly Protestant, missionary societies. This chapter will seek to place the particular views of John Fraser within this wider frame, analysing the contemporary and more recent reception of biblical narratives of race, language and migration in the southern world.

Fraser and the missionaries

In Australia, missionaries laid the way for the Christian ethnography promoted by Fraser by preparing grammars, word lists and sample sentences and prayers of the various indigenous peoples among whom they were stationed. Fraser explains the trouble he took to gather materials together and that he intended his book to be a record of the languages fast disappearing from eastern Australia.[7] To identify his sources he made good use of the work of the distinguished Prussian linguist, Wilhelm Bleek (1827–75), who had curated the philological collections of the colonial administrator, Sir George Grey (1812–98), one-time lieutenant governor of South Australia, then governor of Cape Colony and New Zealand.[8] Besides the various published works of the missionary linguist Lancelot Threlkeld (1788–1859), Fraser had tracked down a holograph of Threlkeld's Gospel of St Luke which had been deposited by Sir George Grey in the Public Library of Auckland (where it remains). Fraser transcribed this unique text into an orthography of his own devising and created a new name for the Aboriginal language in which it was written which he called 'Awabakal'. What Fraser aimed to do was to pledge these and other vestiges of the failed missionary efforts to convert and civilise the Australian Aborigines to a new purpose – that of demonstrating the place of the Aborigines in the biblical sequence of the settlement of the Earth.

Fraser's methods were scientific by the standards of his day, and his Australian study cites both Franz Bopp (1791–1867), who had demonstrated the common origin of languages of the Indo-European group, and Max Müller (1823–1900), though his reference to Bopp appears to have been acquired second-hand.[9] In his study of the 'Oceanic' languages, published in the same year as his study of Aboriginal languages, Fraser displays his learning with citations of German, French and English authorities, including Wilhelm von Humboldt, Franz Bopp, Hans Conon von der Gabelentz, A. B. Lesson and A. B. Meyer.[10] He was well aware of anthropological criticism of linguistic arguments of racial origin, noting: 'Some anthropologists, especially when they are not linguists themselves, sneer at the labours of philology as deceptive and liable to serious error.'[11] Yet, Fraser claimed, an understanding of the Sanskrit and 'the Hindu race' had been achieved by means of philology; he was determined to do the same for the languages of the Australian Aborigines.

Fraser's most important innovation was the claim that he had demonstrated beyond doubt the existence of linguistic and ethnic connections between the Aborigines of Australia and the Dravidians of southern India. This was not an original idea, and the substance of his argument was derived from Robert Caldwell (1814–91), bishop of Tirunelveli (from 1877) in the southern Indian province of Tamil Nadu, specifically the second edition of Caldwell's *Comparative Dictionary of the Dravidian Languages*, which appeared in 1875.[12] Caldwell, regarded as the 'father of Dravidian linguistics' by contemporary linguists, published the first edition of his comparative grammar of the languages of southern India in 1856.[13] While a much better linguist than Fraser, Caldwell shared a similar biblically inspired worldview. He explained that his research on the Dravidian languages had a dual purpose; first, to be kind of a treasure house for the Dravidian peoples who wished to know more about their own culture and civilisation, and secondly to provide evidence of their origins and migrations back to a putative biblical point of origin.[14] Caldwell did not see the matter as proven, only suggesting, tantalisingly, that a solution to the question of Dravidian origins would one day be found: 'My own theory', he hazarded, 'is that the Dravidian languages occupy a position of their own between the languages of the Indo-European family and those of the Turanian or Scythian group – not quite a midway position, but one considerably nearer the latter than the former.'[15]

Caldwell aimed to distinguish the Dravidians as a group, unlike Max Müller, who had proposed that the 'Turanians' of Central Asia constituted, with the Aryans and Semites, one of only three major ethnographic and linguistic groupings of the Old World.[16] Caldwell extended his speculations further in a chapter which sought to identify which other groups of languages were related to the Dravidian group. It is here that he proposed a number of links between the languages of India and Australia. Caldwell cited Müller, along with other authorities, in order to assert that the 'Turanian' languages (a group which includes Turkish, Finnish, Hungarian and Japanese) had a common origin, which Müller linked to nomadism.[17] Caldwell went on to suggest that the resemblance between the pronouns in Dravidian and those of the Australian Aborigines suggested historical links between the two races.[18]

For his knowledge of Australian languages, Caldwell was indebted to a paper which Wilhelm Bleek read to the Anthropological Society in London in 1871, which was also known to Fraser.[19] Bleek seems to be responsible for promoting the idea that the hypothetical linguistic affinities between the Dravidian languages and the (very scanty) records of Australian Aboriginal languages should be taken to imply direct historical and ethnic connections as well. Bleek's original research was involved with the complex clicking languages of the Khoesan peoples of southern Africa, but he acquired considerable knowledge of Australian Aboriginal languages while serving as librarian to Sir George Grey.[20] Like Caldwell, whose work he also knew, Bleek favoured the theory of linguistic connections between Turanian, Dravidian and Australian languages, postulating that they constituted a language family which united all nomadic peoples from the steppes of Asia to those of Africa, India and, ultimately, Australia. Bleek and Caldwell supported the theory of a common 'nomadic' or 'Scythian' language.[21] However, Bleek goes much further than Caldwell in assuming that language provided direct insights into other, cultural and ethnographic features of human societies. In particular he accepted the view, also proposed by Max Müller, that nomadism was a kind of function of language and that culture and languages might degenerate from a higher order of organisation. For example, the evidence of a Dravidian connection to the Australian peoples was further proof, in his view, that the Australian Aborigines had declined from a higher state of civilisation (with the Dravidians higher up the scale).[22] In a final flourish, Bleek concluded his paper by suggesting that the differences between prefix- and suffix-forming languages were also reflected in their mythology, with the prefix-forming peoples adhering to what he called 'ancestor worship', whereas the suffix-forming nomads (who included Turanians/Scythians such as the Dravidians and Australians) practised 'worship'.[23] Fraser also believed that religion and language were reflections of a common racial heritage, favouring a fourfold division into Aryan, Shemitic, Turanian and Hamite, each with their own religious traditions.[24] Suffice it to say that the linguistic and cultural speculations of Bleek and Fraser have not weathered the test of time. Their views reflect the deeply held assumptions of the age and the drive to classify and categorise peoples, languages and religious beliefs into a single racially determined hierarchy.

Fraser was convinced of his own authority and made no concessions to potential critics. That his work was never cited beyond the circle of missionary admirers suggests that this confidence was misplaced; however, he does make a number of distinctive, albeit unjustifiable, claims. Building on his earlier essay on the same subject,[25] the introduction to *An Australian Language* has eleven sections, beginning with a review of grammatical principles and a biographical account of his hero Threlkeld. The remaining sections comprise a comprehensive, if erratic, comparative linguistics of what he assumes to be a single Australian language (in fact over 200 are known), focusing on a series of test words, especially pronouns, numerals and prepositions. Section five looks at the Australian numerals one, two and three; section six at the test words for water, blind and eye; section seven at an assortment of other test words (louse, shit, sun, bad, good, dead, the negative, to speak, to strike, woman); section eight at pronouns; section nine at word formation and section ten at grammatical form and syntax. In this tenth section there are over 30 examples, of which the first eight are 'general', while the rest compare Australian with Dravidian. Section eleven, the last, is the most speculative and concerns the origins of the Australian race from the point of view of the Book of Genesis.

To justify his flights of logical fancy, Fraser makes the bold claim that 'all languages have one common, although ancient, origin, and that, in the essential words of these languages, there are proofs of that common origin'.[26] The problem with this assumption is that it is so loosely configured that any linguistic element from any language could be cited to demonstrate a particular linguistic genealogy. In his discussion of the number one, for example, Fraser had no intellectual qualms in comparing *pir* (one) in 'Australian', to terms plucked, in turn, from languages he terms 'Aryan' (including Lithuanian, Greek, Gothic and Keltic [sic], Dravidian and Sanskrit), as well as others taken from Malay, Melanesian and Polynesian languages, including Ancityum ('a Papuan island of the New Hebrides'), Samoan, the Aroma dialect of New Guinea, Motu, the Efate language of the New Hebrides, the languages of New Britain and Duke of York Island, a language of 'the negroes to the west of Khartoum', Hebrew and 'Shemitic'.[27] At the end of this confection he concludes: 'I cannot see how it is possible for anyone to avoid the force of the argument from this that our Australian indigenes have a share in a common ancestry, and that, in language, their immediate ancestors are the Dravidians of India.'[28] In fact, it was only possible to do so if you shared Fraser's underlying religious convictions.

Where Fraser differs from more eminent philological authorities was not so much in his methods, which would have been recognisable, if open to criticism, but in the final section, where he extended the linguistic evidence by means of the mythic and historical narratives of the Book of Genesis. Here he asserted that the linguistic evidence demonstrated that the Australian Aborigines were descendants of the Hamites, whom he calls 'progenitors of the negro races'.[29] To his own satisfaction, Fraser then transforms this argument, based largely on words collected in the nineteenth century, into claims for a geographical journey by historical peoples: first the confusion of tongues in Babylonia, then the spread of 'the black races' (i.e. the Hamites) from Central Asia via the mountains of southern India and an onward migration by sea and land until they eventually arrived in Australia. Fraser does provide some additional layers of complexity to the narrative by suggesting that that there were two migrations to Australia, one from the north and another from the south of India, and that these migrations correspond to divisions between 'Hamites' and fairer-skinned 'Kushites' in pre-Aryan India. Yet his credulity in assembling cultural assemblages to demonstrate the links he proposed knew few bounds. For example, in a list of supposed cultural affinities between Australia and India he asserts an Egyptian origin, via India, for the Australian boomerang: 'The native boomerang of Australia is used on [sic] the south-east of India, and can be traced to Egypt – both of them Hamite regions.'[30] Other highly malleable arguments could be made by referring to variations in physical appearance: the Aborigines look like certain Dravidian peoples in terms of their skin colour, height, gait and other physical attributes.[31]

Fraser's biography and reception

A study of Fraser's biography reveals that, far from being an isolated crank, he was well connected to intellectual circles in the rising colony of New South Wales as well as its missionary outposts in the Pacific and his Scottish homeland. Fraser was born in Perth in Scotland and might have been destined for the ministry had he not been diverted by the lure of emigration and a career as a colonial schoolteacher. He studied Classics at the University of Edinburgh and graduated with a BA in 1852 when he was still in his teens.[32] In New South Wales he headed to West Maitland in the Hunter Valley, where he built and founded Sauchie House, a Presbyterian college which was later incorporated into Maitland High School.[33] Fraser was also an ardent amateur linguist and ethnographer, corresponding and disputing with better connected figures such as Lorimer Fison (1832–1907), the

BABYLON, THE BIBLE AND THE AUSTRALIAN ABORIGINES

Wesleyan missionary and pioneer anthropologist of Fiji and Tonga, and the eccentric Daisy Bates (1859–1951).[34] Beyond the schoolroom Fraser regarded himself as a serious rather than a speculative thinker: for the Polynesian Society, he published articles on the Malay and Polynesian languages;[35] and his essay on the Australian Aborigines was awarded the 1882 Prize of the Royal Society of New South Wales, the oldest learned society in any of the southern colonies.[36] This essay, entitled 'The Aborigines of New South Wales', provides the first version of his biblical ethnography of the Aborigines from a displacement of the Kushite tribes from old Babylonia into the remote parts of the world, and it is worth summarising. Fraser provided eleven points which, he states, supported his theory of the global movement of the Hamitic tribes from Babylon via India and Melanesia and Polynesia to Australia:

1. Ethnologists recognise two pre-Aryan races in India, of which the 'noseless' people of the Vedas are 'our aboriginals'.
2. The Kolarian and Dravidian languages have inclusive and exclusive forms for the plural of the first person – as do 'many of the languages of Melanesia and Polynesia' and 'probably' the dialects of the north-west of Australia, through Fraser admits he does not have any evidence of this.
3. The Aborigines of the south and west of Australia use the same words for I, thou, he, we, you as the natives of the Madras coasts of India.
4. The native boomerang of Australia is used on [sic] the south-east of India, and can be traced to Egypt – both Hamite regions.
5. Among the red races of America 'who are Turanian', four is a sacred number. In Egypt the pyramids have square bases; the castes of India are four, and the 'universal' division of the native tribes in Australia is also four.
6. The class names form their feminines in tha, a 'peculiarly Shemitic inflexion'.
7. Several tribes practise circumcision – another Shemitic feature. The Aborigines also look like Hamites (Africans); others look like Kushites.
8. In some parts of Australia, the Aborigines erect stages to expose the dead, just like the Parsee. In other places, they place them in a hollow tree, just like the Persians.
9. 'There is nothing improbable in the supposition that the first inhabitants of Australia came from the north-west, that is, from Hindustan or 'Further India', because native Polynesians all point to the west as the source for their ancestors.

10. The kinship system among the Tamil and Telugu is 'the same essentially' as that of the Australian Aborigines.
11. Identity of language is strong evidence of identity of origin and therefore all the Australian tribes speak the same languages, with phonetic variations.[37]

Hence, he concludes, '[these] eleven points are the main points of an argument by which I would maintain that our black people came originally from the shores of the Persian Gulf, and that they came to us through India'.[38] None of these points was provable or scientific and several, such as the link between the four sides of an Egyptian pyramid and the number of division in Aboriginal tribes, are decidedly implausible, but Fraser was undeterred by logic or criticism. He continued to repeat the same basic thesis in all his subsequent studies of Aboriginal linguistics, culminating in *An Australian Language*.

Despite his intellectual limitations, Fraser shared his passions with a close circle of like-minded religious friends. Niel Gunson sees him as the prime mover in a circle of missionary ethnographers active in the Pacific region corresponding with agents in the field, as well as with those who had retired to Sydney.[39] Besides his work for the Royal Society of New South Wales, Fraser was a founder of the Australasian Society for the Advancement of Science (AAAS) and the Polynesian Society. With other missionaries he presented papers to the early meetings of the AAAS, which D. J. Mulvaney has suggested 'skirted the lunatic fringe' and were little more than religious propaganda.[40] His most ardent scholarly research was in the field of comparative linguistics, using the erratic methods we have already observed for other creative exercises in historical ethnography.[41] In 1879 he published his first book-length work of linguistic archaeology, entitled *The Etruscans: Were they Celts?*, which attempted to demonstrate, from an analysis of forty Etruscan 'fossil words', that the Etruscans were not only Celts but the first of the 'Japhetian' tribes to populate Europe.[42] This curious study, referred to as 'a monument to his linguistic attainments and intellectual power', was the foundation for the award of the degree of Doctor of Laws from the Queen's University of Kingston, Canada, in 1887, at which stage he was still living in Maitland, New South Wales.[43] The citation also refers to his work on the ethnology of the Australian Aborigines and 'his character of singular modesty and worth'.[44] The modesty seems to have been genuine; after his retirement as Principal in 1884, he refused any ceremony but accepted a testimonial of appreciation put together by his former pupils.[45] He then devoted the years of his retirement to the huge project of editing the works of Lancelot Threlkeld, which finally appeared in 1892, as well as publishing the works of Presbyterian missionary comrades in the New Hebrides.[46] His linguistic studies of the languages of the Pacific were, like his work on the Australian languages, spiced with speculative genealogies of origin; a good example of this is his study of the links between Malay and Polynesian languages.[47]

Unfortunately, Fraser's philological and historical theories were not welcomed either by contemporary or modern scholars. According to his most sympathetic modern critic, Neil Gunson, Fraser's edition of the work of Lancelot Threlkeld was significantly damaged by the racial and linguistic assumptions of the introduction, which severely limited the quality of his analysis.[48] With a number of other missionary ethnographers, including Daniel MacDonald (1846–1927) of the New Hebrides, Gunson sees Fraser as regrettably attached to what he calls 'exotic and bizarre theories'.[49] In his own day Fraser was enmeshed in trench warfare which pitted Darwinian evolutionists of human society, such as the Wesleyan missionary ethnographer Lorimer Fison (1832–1907) and Sir Walter Baldwin Spencer (1860–1929), whose photographs and fieldwork in Central Australia make him the founding father of Australian anthropology, against Christian evolutionists who continued to use Scriptural narratives to support racial and social speculation about indigenous societies. Fison referred to him in a letter to Spencer as 'that ass Fraser', decrying both his academic credentials and those of fellow Scottish Presbyterian, the Revd John Mathew (1849–1929):[50] 'it will be a be a lasting disgrace to our University [i.e. the University of Sydney] if the authorities give him a degree for that rubbish'.[51] The 'rubbish' which won for Mathew the prize and medal of the Royal Society of New South Wales shared Fraser's assumptions. Mathew thought that the Aboriginal people were formed as a result of three successive invasions, by Papuans, Dravidians and Malays, and that each wave was culturally superior to the one which preceded it. He likened the process to the formation of the United Kingdom of Great Britain and Ireland, with the British Celts likened to the Papuans in Australia, the Saxons to the Dravidians and the Normans to the Malays: 'In each case,' he explained, 'from the first two races the bulk of the people is sprung and the vocabulary and grammar are inherited, while the third race sprinkled here and there over the land has left the slightest lingual traces of its presence.'[52]

In the wake of the popularisation of the work of Charles Darwin after the publication of *The Origin of Species* (1859), it is sometimes suggested that secular evolutionists and Christians divided into mutually warring camps. The Darwinians might be presented as the successors and rivals to the missionary linguists who preceded them and for whom language was a tool for the Christianisation of the heathen; who saw it as a means to mediate from a lower to a higher spiritual condition.[53] Modern postcolonial critics have continued to reach harsh conclusions about scripturally driven narratives of missionary linguists and anthropologists, such as those of the Scottish Presbyterians Fraser, MacDonald and Mathew.[54] Such views, they argue, reflect racial anxieties about the legitimacy of the ongoing conquests of subject peoples (including the Australian Aborigines), and settler colonial fears of racial mixing leading to degeneration and national decline. Yet there is another view, which sees biblical theories of race as an integral part of the colonising worldview of Victorian Christians, one which allowed adjustment to be made for the shock of new discoveries and the expansion of the human family. Christian evolutionists also acted as a bulwark against harsher, more hierarchical forms of racism that suggested that the races and languages of the world were evidence of separate species. It is also important to recognise that native peoples themselves frequently embraced Scriptural interpretations of their origins, reclaiming Christian myths of origin as part of postcolonial self-fashioning. This was particularly the case for theories which linked the various peoples of the Pacific with remnants of the Lost Tribes of Israel, as we will now see.

The Lost Tribes in the Pacific

As part of the discourse of the Lost Tribes, claims have been made for the Semitic origins of Pacific peoples since at least the seventeenth century when the author of a map of the journeys of the English adventurer William Dampier claimed that he had detected members of the Lost Tribes in Papua New Guinea.[55] They continued unabated in missionary writing, such as in the works of the founder of the Baptist Missionary Society, William Carey (1761–1834). As part of the Enlightenment project of naming and describing the world's peoples, missionaries and government agencies collaborated in describing new territories for European exploitation while seeking to explain and integrate the extraordinary people, languages and cultures they encountered in the Pacific.[56] While missionaries led the way, they were not isolated in their support of the Bible as a source for historical and linguistic truths about the world. Timothy Larsen has argued that the Bible retained its primacy for people across the reading classes throughout the Victorian age and that its imprint is as clear on those who decried its truths as for its more overt adherents.[57] This meant that for both Christian and 'secular' Victorians, it was not ridiculous to suppose that Aborigines were, ultimately, migrants from Babylon or that Pacific Islanders were Jews.

To briefly recap the main outline of the Lost Tribes as recounted in the Book of Genesis, Noah had three sons, Shem ('dark'), Ham ('black') and Japheth ('wide'/'fair'), who were traditionally seen as progenitors of the peoples of Asia, Africa and Europe, although earlier people had given birth to other children and giants.[58] Fifteen generations later, Shem's descendants, the twelve sons of Jacob (Israel) – Reuben, Simeon, Levi, Judah, Dan, Naphtali, Gad, Asher, Issachar, Zebulun, Joseph and Benjamin – were said to have taken possession of the Promised Land of Canaan.[59] However, the tribes did not enjoy their possession of the Promised Land for long. In 722 BCE, the northern Kingdom of Israel – made up of ten tribes, with the exception of the tribes of Judah and Benjamin – was conquered by the Assyrians, after which the ten tribes fall from knowledge.[60] The legend of what eventually became of the 'lost' tribes constitutes one of the most fascinating elements in the diasporic history of the Jewish people. As the *Encyclopaedia Judaica* puts it, there is hardly a place or a people from across the globe, from the Japanese to the Native Americans, which has not been associated with one of the Lost Tribes.[61] In Chapter 4 of this volume, Brian Murray explains how the British Israelites, a religious movement that began in the mid-nineteenth century, traced the British themselves to the Lost Tribes.[62] What is significant, therefore, is not so much the claim that the Maori or the Aborigines were members of the Lost Tribes, but the particular shape that this origin narrative takes in different colonial contexts. It is also critical to recognise that the Semitic Lost Tribes were regarded as people of Asia; the Hamites were peoples of Africa, and in the race-obsessed context of the later nineteenth century this implied different orders of civilisation.

Along with Cook's voyages, the potential existence of lost Judaic peoples in the Pacific acted as a spur to those ardent Christians who preached in favour of missionary societies in the late eighteenth and early nineteenth centuries.[63] William Carey's widely read tract, *An Enquiry into the Obligation of Christians to Use Means for the Conversion of the Heathens* (1792), makes a particular point of referring to the South Seas.[64] Carey used tables to lay out the world like a scene for Christian battle with Pagans, Muslims, Jews and other kinds of Christians ('Papists' and 'Greek Christians' chief among them) waiting in their millions for the arrival of suitable missionaries. Carey felt a particular urgency for the 'new' lands of New Holland, New Guinea and New Zealand, inhabited as they were by 'savages' and 'cannibals': 'They are in general poor, barbarous, naked pagans,' Carey wrote, 'as destitute of civilisation, as they are of true religion.'[65] It was therefore essential that Christian missionaries be sent to enlighten, educate and Christianise these new regions.

Missionary rhetoric was soon followed by the arrival of missionary agents. The missionary voyages of the *Duff* in 1796, 1797 and 1798 were the immediate response of the London Missionary Society (LMS, founded in 1795) to Cook's discoveries in the South Seas.[66] The official account of these voyages, including the published journals of the missionaries, is full of Enlightenment enthusiasm for the promotion of knowledge. This encompassed both the advance of scientific information about the geography, languages, physical composition, politics and cultural habits of the natives, and the nobler object, as the Society put it in their dedication to the King, of communicating the message of Christianity to these unenlightened regions.[67] When Fraser proposed a biblical narrative for the peopling of the Pacific, he was the heir to two centuries of Christian speculation, Enlightenment enthusiasm and missionary endeavour.

While many peoples claimed to be descendants of the Lost Tribes, in the Pacific the most highly developed version of this mythic history focused on the Maori of New Zealand.[68] Steeped in biblical history, the first missionaries to New Zealand had speculated on different explanations for the racial origins of the Maori. It was natural for them to attempt to connect the peoples they observed with descendants of one or other of the three sons of Noah, usually the Hamites, or, more prestigiously, with the wanderings of the Semitic Lost Tribes. The theory was elaborated by the missionary Richard Taylor (1805–73) in his history of New Zealand, which came complete with explanations for the Semitic features of the Maori language, customs and physical appearance.[69] But the Maori were not alone: other missionaries speculated on the Semitic origins of peoples scattered throughout Polynesia and Melanesia and the route of their journeys from Bible lands to the South Seas.[70] According to the academic anthropologist Edward Tylor, the Aryan progenitors of the Sanskrit language were also the ancestors of the peoples and languages of the Malayan and Polynesian islands which included, at the far west of the migration, the New Zealand Maori.[71] Daniel MacDonald (1846–1927), the first Presbyterian missionary to the New Hebrides, argued that all the Oceanic languages were Semitic in origin, a theory he promoted in a series of books.[72] In *The Asiatic Origin of the Oceanic Languages*, McDonald prepared a lengthy etymological dictionary of Efate, a language of the New Hebrides, in which he proposed parallels between words in Efate with Hebrew.[73] It was therefore inevitable that the Australian Aborigines would be given a scriptural makeover of the kind provided by Fraser which would unite them to tribal remnants dotted throughout the Christian world.

Despite their relative ubiquity, speculative scriptural theories of racial origin were not acceptable to all Christian scholars, many of whom were convinced by more rigorous critical standards in the rising sciences of philology, history and ethnography. Critics included the Cornish missionary to New Zealand, William Colenso (1811–99), who noted that in the rush to establish European and/or Indian roots for the native people of New Zealand many neglected to understand the Maori language: 'some Europeans have ventured to write "learnedly" upon it! using (without acknowledgement) the material obtained by others and racking and distorting by turns Hebrew, Sanskrit, Arabic, Greek, Coptic, Spanish, and many others; never once suspecting their ignorance of that of New Zealand'.[74] There was also controversy over particular versions of the theory: whether, for example the Maori were properly numbered among the Hamitic descendants of Noah in Africa, or were one of the later, Semitic, Lost Tribes.

Importantly, many Pacific people still accept the legitimacy of the theory of the Lost Tribes. For example, the notion of the Aryan Maori was an attractive one to Maori, who favoured the Aryans as a warrior people like themselves with a capacity for seafaring and dominance over other races.[75] Lynda Newland has argued that Fijians routinely assumed and deeply felt their descent from the Lost Tribes in the late nineteenth century.[76] These scriptural notions resurfaced as recently as the 1987 coup, when claims for biblical ancestry were used to support arguments for political and racial ascendancy by Fijian leaders over Indian and other ethnic emigrants.[77] In these and other ways, it is evident that Christian narratives of origin were not displaced by 'secular' anthropology, philology and history in the late nineteenth century, but were adapted to new visions of the past.

Conclusion

Finally, we need to return to John Fraser and the Babylonian Aborigines. Fraser's ethno-linguistics of the Australian Aborigines reveals the persistence of scriptural and racial ideas, which continued to flower in the era of Darwinian evolutionism, driven as they were by missionary ideals. These include the need to justify scriptural narratives about the source and origin of human races ('one blood'), historical patterns of global emigration ('inheriting the earth') and millennial excitement about the coming end. These notions were important for missionaries and their supporters in the Pacific, Australia and New Zealand, agents for whom John Fraser was a central and significant intellectual advocate. Despite what might appear to be derogatory comments about the place of the Aborigines in the hierarchy of the races, Fraser was a consistent and humane advocate for the Aboriginal people of Australia, being opposed to any suggestion that they were not human or had evolved separately to other peoples of the word: the Aborigines were 'an integral portion of the human race'.[78] Fraser's Babylonian Aborigines ultimately demonstrated the spiritual as well as the linguistic and racial identity of the people of the world, that God, as the author of the Book of Acts made plain, 'hath made of one blood all nations of men for to dwell on all the face of the earth' (Acts 17:26).

It is clear that these ideas were not particularly new or original and that Fraser was simply following the model of other respectable writers who used linguistic and other comparative evidence to create a racial history which would connect known to unknown peoples. In able hands the science of linguistics had yielded up what appeared to be extraordinary evidence of hitherto unknown relationships between languages. While this in fact said very little about the physical migration history of the contemporary people who spoke those languages, there were few who resisted the temptation to extend the linguistic evidence well beyond what it revealed. Scientific linguists were attempting to move the study of ancient people beyond the mythical domain of Scripture which postulated that all peoples were descended from the three sons of Noah or, as we have seen, might be related to one or other of the Lost Tribes of Israel.

In suggesting that the languages of the Australian Aborigines, which he edited with such care, could be linked first to southern India and then to Babylon, Fraser was following the precedent of some of the most distinguished linguists of his own day, including Max Müller, who dreamed of demonstrating through grammar 'that men are brethren ... – the children of the same father – whatever their country, their colour, their language and their faith'.[79] While always presented as scientific and detached, all theories which attempted to link the races of mankind to some putative ancestral home in and around Mesopotamia were following a much older narrative of origins. These theories carried with them the assumption of a single creation myth, a homeland and a proto-language out of which all the peoples of the world had subsequently dispersed. It implied a lost Garden of Eden, an Ark and a flood, a Tower of Babel and a multiplication of languages from a pre-lapsarian universal tongue. In such a world, the Lost Tribes of Israel continued to wander, the Dravidian people of India travelled across seas and islands to colonise Australia – or, in an alternative scenario, they were defeated by the triumphant Aryans who eventually travelled as far as New Zealand. These were all assumptions made by people with an intimate knowledge of the Bible. John Fraser was part of this speculative bubble and the Babylonian Aborigines are only understandable within this context.

Notes

1. L. E. Threlkeld, *An Australian Language as Spoken by the Awabakal the People of Awaba or Lake Macquarie*, ed. John Fraser (Sydney: Government Printer, 1892).
2. David J. Bertuca, Donald K. Hartman and Susan M. Neumeister, *The World's Columbian Exposition* (Westport, CT: Greenwood Press, 1996).
3. For studies of Threlkeld's missionary linguistics see Hilary M. Carey, 'Lancelot Threlkeld and Missionary Linguistics in Australia to 1850', in Otto Zwartjes and Even Hovdhaugen, eds, *Missionary Linguistics* (Amsterdam: John Benjamins, 2004), pp. 253–75; David A. Roberts, '"Language to Save the Innocent": Reverend L. Threlkeld's Linguistic Mission', *Journal of the Royal Australian Historical Society*, 94 (2008), 107–25; Anne Keary, 'Christianity, Colonialism, and Cross-Cultural Translation: Lancelot Threlkeld, Biraban and the Awabakal', *Aboriginal History*, 33 (2009), 117–56; Hilary M. Carey, 'Lancelot Threlkeld, Biraban and the Colonial Bible in Australia', *Comparative Studies in Society and History*, 52 (2010), 447–78; James Wafer and Hilary M. Carey, 'Waiting for Biraban: Lancelot Threlkeld and the "Chibcha Phenomenon" in Australian Missionary Linguistics', *Language and History*, 54 (2011), 112–39. For biographical studies of Threlkeld see Niel Gunson, 'Threlkeld, Lancelot Edward (1788–1859)', in *Australian Dictionary of Biography* (Melbourne: Melbourne University Press, 1967), pp. 528–30; Niel Gunson, ed., *Australian Reminiscences and Papers of L. E. Threlkeld*, 2 vols (Canberra: Australian Institute of Aboriginal Studies, 1974); Anna Johnston, 'A Blister on the Imperial Antipodes: Lancelot Threlkeld in Polynesia and Australia', in David Lambert and Alan Lester, eds, *Imperial Careering in the Long Nineteenth Century* (Cambridge: Cambridge University Press, 2006), pp. 58–87; Anna Johnston, *The Paper War: Morality, Print Culture and Power in Colonial New South Wales* (Perth: UWA Press, 2011).
4. Fraser's pamphlets and articles on the Australian Aborigines include 'The Aborigines of New South Wales', *Journal and Proceedings of the Royal Society of New South Wales*, 16 (1882), 193–233; *The Aborigines of Australia: Their Ethnic Position and Relations* (London: Victoria Institute, 1888), pp. 1–36; 'Some Remarks on the Australian Languages', *Journal and Proceedings of the Royal Society of New South Wales*, 24 (1890), 231–53; 'On the Languages of Oceania', *Journal and Proceedings of the Royal Society of New South Wales*, 26 (1892), 342–67; 'The Woddowro Pronouns', *The Wombat* (1902), 1–12; 'Linguistic Evidence and Archaeological and Ethnological Facts (the Sir John Rhys Memorial Lecture)', *Proceedings of the British Academy*, 12 (1926), 257–72.
5. Threlkeld, *Australian Language*, ed. Fraser, p. lviii.
6. Colin Kidd, *The Forging of Races: Race and Scripture in the Protestant Atlantic World, 1600–2000* (Cambridge: Cambridge University Press, 2006), p. 168.
7. 'Editor's Preface', in Threlkeld, *Australian Language*, ed. Fraser.
8. W. H. I. Bleek and James Cameron, *The Library of His Excellency Sir George Grey*, 3 vols (London: Trübner, 1858).
9. Threlkeld, *Australian Language*, ed. Fraser, p. xviii: 'Bopp says that the lowest numerals can never be introduced into any country by foreigners.' This comment was probably adopted from Robert Caldwell, *A Comparative Grammar of the Dravidian or South-Indian Family of Languages*, 2nd edn (London: Trübner, 1875), pp. 24–5.
10. Fraser, 'Languages of Oceania', 344.
11. Threlkeld, *Australian Language*, ed. Fraser, pp. xviii–xix. Fraser revisited this theme for his John Rhys lecture for the British Academy, 'Linguistic Evidence', 257–72.
12. Caldwell, *Comparative Grammar*.

13 For example, Guglielmo Cinque and Richard S. Kayne, eds, *The Oxford Handbook of Comparative Syntax* (Oxford: Oxford University Press, 2005), p. 213.
14 Caldwell, *Comparative Grammar*, p. x.
15 Caldwell, *Comparative Grammar*, p. vii.
16 See Max Müller, *Letter to Chevalier Bunsen on the Classification of the Turanian Languages* (London: Spottiswoode, 1854), pp. 153–6 for Müller's consideration of Humboldt's and Crawford's views on the languages of Polynesia, Malaya, India and New Holland (Australia): the latter, for Humboldt, having the 'lowest grade of civilisation which has ever been occupied by mankind'.
17 Caldwell, *Comparative Grammar*, p. 67. See Müller, *Letter to Chevalier Bunsen*, p. 21: 'Turanian languages may be characterised as *nomadic*, in opposition to the *Arian* languages, which ... may be called *political*.'
18 Caldwell, *Comparative Grammar*, p. 78.
19 W. H. I. Bleek, 'On the Position of the Australian Languages', *Journal of the Anthropological Institute of Great Britain and Ireland*, 1 (1872), xi.
20 Bleek, 'Position of the Australian Languages', 89–104.
21 Bleek, 'Position of the Australian Languages', 90, citing Caldwell, *Comparative Grammar*, pp. 51–3.
22 Bleek, 'Position of the Australian Languages', 102.
23 Bleek, 'Position of the Australian Languages', 101.
24 Fraser, *Aborigines of Australia*, p. 2.
25 See Fraser, 'Aborigines of New South Wales'.
26 Threlkeld, *Australian Language*, ed. Fraser, pp. xx–xxi; Müller, *Letter to Chevalier Bunsen*, 213.
27 Threlkeld, *Australian Language*, ed. Fraser, pp. xx–xxi.
28 Threlkeld, *Australian Language*, ed. Fraser, p. xxii.
29 Threlkeld, *Australian Language*, ed. Fraser, p. lxi.
30 Threlkeld, *Australian Language*, ed. Fraser, p. lxii.
31 Threlkeld, *Australian Language*, ed. Fraser, p. lxii.
32 *A Catalogue of the Graduates in the Faculties of Arts, Divinity and Law of the University of Edinburgh* (Edinburgh: Neill, 1858), p. 234.
33 David Roberts, 'John Fraser', *Awaba*, accessed 19 December 2016, https://downloads.newcastle.edu.au/library/cultural%20collections/awaba/people/fraserjohn.html.
34 For Lorimer Fison's connections, see for example his correspondence with Walter Baldwin Spencer, held in the Pitt Rivers Museum, Oxford, accessed 19 December 2016, http://web.prm.ox.ac.uk/sma/index.php/primary-documents/primary-documents-index/489-spencer-box-1-fison-letter-1-on.html.
35 John Fraser, 'The Malayo-Polynesian Theory', *Journal of the Polynesian Society* 4–5 (1895–96), 241–55, 92–107.
36 Fraser, 'Aborigines of New South Wales', 193–233.
37 Fraser, 'Aborigines of New South Wales', 196–9.
38 Fraser, 'Aborigines of New South Wales', 199.
39 Niel Gunson, 'British Missionaries and Their Contribution to Science in the Pacific Islands', in Roy MacLeod and Philip F. Rehbock, eds, *Darwin's Laboratory: Evolutionary Theory and Natural History in the Pacific* (Honolulu, HI: University of Hawai'i Press, 1994), p. 303.
40 Gunson, 'British Missionaries', p. 316, citing D. J. Mulvaney, 'Australian Anthropology and ANZAAS', in Roy MacLeod, ed., *The Commonwealth of Science: ANZAAS and the Scientific Enterprise in Australasia, 1888–1988* (Melbourne: Oxford University Press, 1988), pp. 199–200.
41 Gunson, 'British Missionaries', p. 304.
42 John Fraser, *The Etruscans: Were They Celts?* (Edinburgh: Machlachlan and Stewart, 1879), p. 3.
43 *Calendar of Queen's College and University at Kingston, Canada* (1898–9), 213.
44 *Toronto Daily Mail*, quoted in *Maitland Mercury and Hunter River General Advertiser*, 30 June 1887, p. 5.

45 'Testimonial to Mr John Fraser', *Maitland Mercury and Hunter River General Advertiser*, 29 January 1884, p. 5.
46 Sydney H. Ray, 'The Languages of the New Hebrides, Ed. By John Fraser', *Journal and Proceedings of the Royal Society of New South Wales*, 22 (1893), 101–67, 469–70.
47 Fraser, 'Malayo-Polynesian Theory'.
48 Gunson, ed., *Australian Reminiscences*, I: p. 1.
49 Gunson, 'British Missionaries', p. 304.
50 For John Mathew and his major work, *Eaglehawk and Crow* (1899), see Malcolm Prentis, *Science, Race and Faith: A Life of John Mathew, 1849–1929* (Sydney: Centre for the Study of Australian Christianity, 1998).
51 Fison to Spencer, letter 2, 1899 or 1900: Spencer Papers, Pitt Rivers Museum, Oxford. Transcribed for Pitt Rivers Virtual Collections, accessed 8 November 2014, http://web.prm.ox.ac.uk/sma/index.php/primary-documents/primary-documents-index/489-spencer-box-1-fison-letter-1-on.html.
52 Mathew, *Eaglehawk and Crow*, p. 383. Cited by Ian J. McNiven and Lynette Russell, *Appropriated Pasts: Indigenous Peoples and the Colonial Culture of Archaeology* (Lanham, MD: AltaMira Press, 2005), p. 127.
53 E.g. Rachael Gilmour, 'Missionaries, Colonialism and Language in Nineteenth-Century South Africa', *History Compass*, 5 (2007), 1761–77; Gilmour, *Grammars of Colonialism: Representing Languages in Colonial South Africa* (Basingstoke: Palgrave, 2006); Johannes Fabian, *Language and Colonial Power: The Appropriation of Swahili in the Former Belgian Congo, 1880–1938* (Cambridge: Cambridge University Press, 1986); Fabian, 'Missions and the Colonization of African Languages: Developments in the Former Belgian Congo', *Canadian Journal of African Studies*, 17 (1983), 165–87.
54 McNiven and Russell, *Appropriated Pasts*; Lynda Newland, 'The Lost Tribes of Israel – and the Genesis of Christianity in Fiji: Missionary Notions of Fijian Origin from 1835 to Cession and Beyond', *Oceania*, 85 (2015), 256–70; Matt Tomlinson, 'Efficacy, Truth, and Silence: Language Ideologies in Fijian Christian Conversions', *Comparative Studies in Society and History*, 51 (2009), 64–90.
55 See 'Map of the Discoveries made by Captain William Dampier in the Roebuck in 1699', in John Harris, *Complete Collection of Voyages and Travels* (London: T. Woodward, etc., 1744). For discussion, see Ivan Davidson Kalmar and Derek Jonathan Penslar, eds., *Orientalism and the Jews* (Waltham, MA: Brandeis University Press, 2005), p. 61.
56 Newland, 'Lost Tribes', 251–5.
57 Timothy Larsen, *A People of One Book: The Bible and the Victorians* (Oxford: Oxford University Press, 2011), pp. 1–7.
58 Genesis 6:4.
59 Genesis 29:5–33.
60 Though see also Isaiah 11:11, Jeremiah 31:8 and Ezekiel 37:19–24 for prophecies that they would return.
61 Louis Isaac Rabinowitz, 'Ten Lost Tribes', in Michael Berenbaum and Fred Skolnik, eds, *Encyclopaedia Judaica*, 2nd edn (Detroit, MI: Macmillan Reference USA, 2007), XIX: pp. 639–40.
62 Kidd, *Forging of Races*, p. 210.
63 For the impact of Cook's voyages on missionary advocates, see Elizabeth Elbourne, *Blood Ground* (Montreal: McGill-Queens' University Press, 2002), p. 51.
64 William Carey, *An Enquiry into the Obligations of Christians, to Use Means for the Conversion of the Heathens* (Leicester: Ann Ireland, 1792), p. 67.
65 Carey, *Enquiry into the Obligations of Christians*, p. 67.
66 London Missionary Society, *A Missionary Voyage to the Southern Pacific Ocean ... in the Ship Duff* (London: T. Chapman, 1799).
67 *Missionary Voyage*, a2.
68 Tudor Parfit and Emanuela Trevisan Semi, *Judaising Movements: Studies in the Margins of Judaism in Modern Times* (London: Routledge, 2002), pp. 9–10. For an introduction to debates about the Semitic Maori, see M. P. K. Sorrenson, *Maori*

Origins and Migrations: The Genesis of Some Pakeha Myths and Legends (Auckland: Auckland University Press, 1979).
69 Richard Taylor, *Te Ika a Maui, or, New Zealand and Its Inhabitants*, 2nd edn (London: William Macintosh, 1870).
70 K. R. Howe, 'Ideas of Maori Origins –1770s–1840s: Early Ideas', *Te Ara – the Encyclopedia of New Zealand*. Last updated 22 September 2012, accessed 13 July 2019, http://www.TeAra.govt.nz/en/ideas-of-maori-origins/page-1.
71 Howe, 'Maori Origins'.
72 J. Graham Miller, 'Daniel MacDonald (1846–1927)', *Australian Dictionary of Evangelical Biography*, Southern Cross College, 2004, accessed 11 January 2017, http://webjournals.ac.edu.au/ojs/index.php/ADEB/article/view/958/955.
73 Donald McDonald, *The Asiatic Origin of the Oceanic Languages* (London: Melville, 1894).
74 Quoted by Sorrenson, *Maori Origins and Migrations*, p. 19.
75 For Maori adaption of Christian origin theories, see Tony Ballantyne, *Webs of Empire: Locating New Zealand's Colonial Past* (Vancouver: UBC Press, 2012), pp. 139–60.
76 Newland, 'Lost Tribes', 256–70.
77 Newland, 'Lost Tribes', 256–70.
78 Threlkeld, *Australian Language*, ed. Fraser, p. lix.
79 Müller, *Letter to Chevalier Bunsen*, p. 226.

CHAPTER THREE

'The Ships of Tarshish': the Bible and British Maritime Empire

Gareth Atkins

In January 1860, the Bolton clergyman Walter Chamberlain completed his latest book. In 424 closely wrought pages, *Isaiah's Call to England* sought to expose how 'Isa[iah] xviii is an unfulfilled prophecy, foretelling the ingathering of all Israel to Zion; ... and that, for such purpose of ingathering, Isaiah hails a people friendly to Israel, and to be renowned for their ships and maritime power.' That power, Chamberlain revealed triumphantly, was 'ENGLAND'.[1] If this was not immediately obvious from the passage, which talked in vague terms of woe to a land beyond the rivers of Ethiopia, and of vessels of bulrushes sent to a scattered people, Chamberlain maintained that this was because commentators had wrongly assumed Isaiah 18 to be ancient history. In applying it to events as yet unfulfilled, Chamberlain starts with tame exposition, but begins before long to pull exegetical rabbits out of the hat: the apparent 'woe' in verse one of the chapter is in fact Isaiah's favourable 'ho!'; the lions on the English and Scottish arms match references culled from Ezekiel; and the events Isaiah foretold are imminent, to take place between 1864 and 1914.[2] Layers of ancient Scripture are stripped back to reveal modern visions: a prophesied highway translates into a railway from the Euphrates to the Mediterranean, while in the most bizarre passage, 'vessels of bulrushes' become, through process of philological scrutiny, 'steam-packet boats'.[3] Even Chamberlain realised that this was a bit much – 'I have halted here a little while just to give the reader time to laugh' – but he believed it all the same.[4] He concludes with a seventeen-point prognostication concerning the likely steps towards Israel's restoration, encompassing the machinations of France under Napoleon III, the collapse of the Ottoman Empire, a Russian invasion of the Middle East and, lastly, the preservation of England – 'TARSHISH' – as fulcrum of the divine plan.[5]

One way of dealing with *Isaiah's Call to England* is to pigeonhole it as a throwback to the chiliastic jeremiads that had proliferated between 1820 and 1840 and still littered the British religious publishing landscape.[6] While historicist premillennialists like Chamberlain continued to treat the apocalyptic books of the Bible and current events as mutually reinforcing interpretative keys, others were doubtful about the utility of this method. The ecclesiastical tattler W. J. Conybeare was one of them, his famous *Edinburgh Review* article of 1855 on 'Church Parties' lampooning those obsessed with 'the Red Dragon', 'Gog and Magog', the ten Lost Tribes of Israel and the location of Armageddon.[7] Yet Chamberlain was by no means the outré fanatic Conybeare had in mind. 'Should any one suspect me of being a dreamer or an enthusiast', he remarked drily, they ought to try moving to Bolton, where 'the cooling sedative of six months' residence in a manufacturing town' would soon put paid to flights of fancy.[8] Nor was Chamberlain uneducated. A graduate of Corpus Christi College, Cambridge,[9] his career was punctuated by publications not just on prophecy but on questions that were of more general concern to Anglican clergymen. He wrote in 1863 against Bishop Colenso's critical account of the Pentateuch, for example, and fought Irish disestablishment later in the decade.[10] If the apocalyptic writing and painting that had so thrilled audiences in earlier decades no longer appealed to such a broad audience, prophetic books and periodicals still found a ready readership, in evangelical circles especially.[11] The *Quarterly Journal of Prophecy*, edited by the Free Church of Scotland minister Horatius Bonar, was among several publications that noticed *Isaiah's Call* favourably.[12] Only two years later, in 1862, one of the classics of the genre, Edward Bishop Elliott's *Horae Apocalypticae*, went into its fifth edition.[13] Recent scholarship suggests that apocalyptic language continued to appeal to politicians, preachers and activists for much of the nineteenth century.[14]

Nevertheless, Chamberlain was speaking to an intellectual subculture that, while still viable, was coming to look old-fashioned. There were a variety of reasons for this. As W. H. Oliver suggested, in what remains the best survey of the subject, 'few parts of the Bible were as vulnerable to modern critical scholarship as those dwelt upon by prophetical exegetes': the books of Daniel and Revelation, and (to a lesser extent) Isaiah, Jeremiah and Ezekiel.[15] Just as important as higher criticism was a growing sense among liberal thinkers inside and outside the Churches that the historicity of the Bible was less important than the eternal truths it contained. Instead of warping recent history and ancient texts to fit one another, maintained Thomas Arnold of Rugby, commentators would be better employed in applying the timeless moral lessons articulated by biblical prophets to present-day ills.[16] And there was also the problem of dates.

For those who had followed Elliott in predicting on the basis of the 'Year-Day Theory' that the millennium would take place in 1866, the non-event necessitated an embarrassing climbdown.[17] 'Recent events have fully confirmed the belief that the 1260 years of Papal Supremacy were to close', insisted Revd Samuel Minton of Eaton Chapel. 'But the discovery of a strange, though very general, oversight in the application of Daniel's supplemental period of 75 years, has revealed the truth that the overthrow of Papal rule, is not the overthrow of the Papacy itself.'[18] While many simply altered their calculations, for hostile observers it served to underline the futility of the exercise *tout court*.

What follows charts the rise and fall of the providentialist readings of Britain's maritime empire that Chamberlain found so seductive. Tempting though it is to assume that the sidelining of such ideas took place against an increasingly secular backdrop, it should already be clear that changing conceptions of the Bible, prophecy and providence necessitated a constantly shifting reassessment of what belief and doubt meant, and how they fitted together. To say one 'believed' in a prophetic passage in around 1800 was different from saying the same thing in 1850 or 1900, and this chapter seeks to examine why. Prophetic topoi did not trace a course of linear decline; nor were they the preserve of evangelical literalists, as readers of much of the existing work on the subject might conclude. We cannot assume that there was ever general agreement as to what prophecies meant and that people then 'doubted' that meaning. Rather, the potency of prophecy was dependent on 'current affairs' and a host of other scholarly and cultural influences that rendered them applicable and doubtful by turns, and that altered how such passages were to be read, understood and applied. This chapter reflects on how inherited strands of prophetic thought did not fray entirely in the nineteenth century but were repeatedly respun for new purposes. In doing so, it emphasises how countering one form of doubt could leave the way open for new uncertainties in other areas. Protestant scholars continued, as they always had done, to deploy discoveries about the texts, biblical geography and linguistics in order to underline the Bible's coherence and bolster its authority. As we will see, however, those tools were two-edged, encouraging the sort of historical contextualisation that made Scripture appear chronologically remote and culturally strange, and rendering hitherto accepted typological and prophetic readings inadmissible or just plain wrong.[19]

The Bible and British naval power

Chamberlain was far from being the first to associate Old Testament passages with British maritime ventures. Ever since the early modern period, Protestants had used scriptural passages pertaining to Israel to frame interpretations of military victories and defeats, sudden deaths, harvests, famines and extreme weather, interpretations which continued to echo in the nineteenth century.[20] They still saw in the defeat of the Spanish Armada parallels with the Israelite escape through the Red Sea ('God blew and they were scattered'), while from 1690 until its pruning in 1859 the Book of Common Prayer enshrined memories of another Protestant wind in its service for 5 November, which, as well as commemorating the Gunpowder Plot, celebrated William of Orange's landing at Torbay in 1688.[21] The eighteenth century added further layers of naval-providential rhetoric. 'The Wrecks of our Navies and Fleets Preach to us, that 'tis in vain we pretend to be Wall'd about by the Ocean, and ride Masters of the Sea', Daniel Defoe had written after the Great Storm of 1703, warning that God was punishing Britain by the obliteration of her ships and commerce.[22] Annual 'storm sermons', endowed to impress the message on future generations, were still being preached in the 1780s, while Defoe continued to be read long after that.[23] In the 1790s the ex-slaver turned clergyman John Newton glumly likened Britain to her Old Testament counterpart both in her divinely conferred advantages and in her flagrant disregard for the obligations this entailed, embodied most glaringly, Newton thought, in the triangular trade.[24] Abolition (1807) and emancipation (1833) would thus provide Victorian sermonisers with a satisfying narrative of national redemption. Typology and prophetic fulfilment were part of an apologetic edifice developed to show both the applicability of the Bible and the continuing intervention of the Almighty in human affairs.[25]

Yet if posing as a 'new Israel' had worked well for embattled states like sixteenth-century England, such language had less to offer for a global power whose sway depended on naval hegemony. Scriptural references to maritime trade supplied a rich alternative vocabulary for those keen to celebrate commercial success or to condemn its demoralising effects.[26]

> Since the first dominion of men was asserted over the ocean, three thrones, of mark beyond all others, have been set upon its sands: the thrones of Tyre, Venice, and England. Of the First of these great powers only the memory remains; of the Second, the ruin; the Third, which inherits their greatness, if it forget their example, may be led through prouder eminence to less pitied destruction.[27]

These sermonic cadences were those of John Ruskin in the celebrated opening to *Stones of Venice* (3 vols, 1851–53), but his message would have been recognisable to many a seventeenth- and eighteenth-century congregation. It was not just a poignant image. Commentators had long sought to counter doubts about the inspiration of the Bible by demonstrating the accuracy of the prophecies it contained, and the recorded facts of Tyre's destruction by Nebuchadnezzar and its fall to Alexander the Great in the great siege of 332 BCE made this a straightforward but resonant example of how Old Testament predictions had been fulfilled. Travellers' morbid accounts of the ruins were read both literally, as confirmatory evidence, and figuratively, as warnings to modern nations tempted to pursue profit at the expense of virtue.[28]

Rhetorically useful in a different way was Tarshish, with which Tyre was often associated. The prophet Jonah sought to flee there, explains Father Mapple in *Moby Dick*, because it was modern-day Cadiz, 'as far by water, from Joppa, as Jonah could possibly have sailed in those ancient days, when the Atlantic was an almost unknown sea'.[29] Mapple was certainly up to date with modern scholarship; but although the French geographer Samuel Bochart had convincingly identified Tarshish with Strabo's Tartessus, in south-western Spain, as long ago as 1646, this did not prevent its typological appropriation.[30] It appears twenty-one times in the King James Bible, but aside from obscure references in genealogy and geography, what really excited prophetic commentators was the relationship of Tarshish with Israel. It crops up repeatedly as a source of wealth, most significantly in 1 Kings 10:22, in connection with the legendary golden age of Solomon: 'once in three years came the navy of Tharshish [sic], bringing gold, and silver, ivory, and apes, and peacocks'.[31] Yet there was also a sense in which Tarshish was associated with prophecies unfulfilled. Could it be that it referred to shores beyond those of Spain? George Horne's much reprinted *Commentary on the Psalms* (1776) offered a multi-layered reading of the appearance of Tarshish in Psalm 72, encompassing the treasures of Solomon; the queen of Sheba; the gifts of the Magi, 'the first-fruits of the Gentiles'; and 'lastly, the accession of the nations to the faith' – 'even these "isles of the Gentiles"', he ventured.[32] Isaiah, which Horne cross-referenced, provided the most tantalising passages of all. Isaiah 60:9 evokes a future time when from the 'isles', the 'ships of Tarshish' will 'bring thy sons from afar', restoring the exiles of Israel to the Promised Land, while Isaiah 66:19 prophesies how 'the isles afar off' would declare God's glory among the Gentiles. If Chamberlain was unusual in his focus on Isaiah 18, the quotation of Isaiah 60:9 on his title page placed him among numerous others who had considered its implications.

The idea that Britain's destiny and the fate of the Jews were peculiarly intertwined was not, then, a new one.[33] But in the 1790s shadowy aspirations came to look like concrete certainties.[34] The outbreak of revolution in 1789, the execution of Louis XVI in 1793, the expulsion of Pope Pius VI from the papal states in 1798 and the invasion of Egypt by Napoleon the same year each prompted commentators to revise their eschatological timetables.[35] French defeats in the Middle East at the hands of Nelson and Sidney Smith, in particular, sparked an orgy of prophetic speculation about Britain's place in the divine plan, not just from wild-eyed enthusiasts but also from cultured high churchmen like the bishop of Rochester, Samuel Horsley, and from the respectable evangelical commentators G. S. Faber, James Bicheno and James Hatley Frere.[36] 'Is it an improbable conjecture', asked Henry Kett, 'that *this maritime, commercial, Protestant* kingdom should take the lead in executing the Divine will?'[37] Ralph Wedgwood was more bullish, his discovery that 'Brit' was the Hebrew word for 'covenant' acting as springboard for the extravagant theory that Scripture prophecies did not in fact refer to the Jews at all: *'the British Empire is the peculiar possession of Messiah, and his promised Naval Dominion'*.[38] Frere, likewise, thought that to oppose Britain was to oppose 'the Israelitish Nation', the new chosen people of God, an idea given added credence by Napoleon's attempts to align himself with Catholicism and Islam.[39] Others were more pessimistic. Bicheno coupled Bonaparte's success with his overtures to the Jews, warning that this showed France, not Britain, to be Tarshish and that to oppose her was to risk being crushed under the inexorable wheels of providence.[40] The Unitarian Ebenezer Aldred went further, mocking loyalist attempts to read Jacobins into the book of Revelation and inverting Protestant typology to argue that not Rome but Britain was the whore of Babylon. His language deliberately echoed the denunciations of Isaiah and Ezekiel: 'we make gold our God, commerce our God, our navy our God'.[41] Yet even this frenzy of predictive writing was not as certain as it seemed. Each new event prompted scholars and savants to elaborate further their road-maps of the route to Armageddon, drawing caustic commentary from sceptics.

Prophecy and providential optimism in post-war Britain

Doubt cannot have been further from the minds of patriotic sermonisers in the aftermath of Waterloo.[42] The victory seemed to vindicate claims about Britain's special providential status, fostering a consensus that British philanthropy, wafted around the world on maritime trade routes, now had a special part to play in the global spread of Christianity. Thus the missionary publicist Edward Bickersteth cited the 'vessels of bulrushes' in Isaiah 18 in equating maritime power with the despatch of 'Christian ambassadors to all the inhabitants of the world'; the Methodist scholar Adam Clarke wondered whether the angel of

Revelation 14:6 might in fact be the British and Foreign Bible Society; and two of the most ambitious works, Alexander Keith's *Signs of the Times* (1832) and Elliott's *Horae Apocalypticae* (1844), interpreted British naval victories as the second vial poured out in Revelation 16:3, the turning of the waters into blood denoting extensive casualty lists and the deaths of 'every living creature' being tenuously applied to the cessation of trade brought about by British wartime blockades.[43]

Although ingenious manipulation of Scripture texts was not always married to self-awareness, it emphasises how demonstrations of the predictive precision of the Bible could be used to buttress believers against doubt, and illustrates the intense interest among evangelicals both in the conversion and the restoration of the Jews.[44] Enthusiasts were predictably thrilled by the installation of Michael Solomon Alexander, a Jew by birth, as first Anglican-Lutheran bishop of Jerusalem in 1841. Here too the participation of Britain's vaunted navy was a key piece in the symbolic jigsaw. 'Wonderfully surprised', gushed the future earl of Shaftesbury in his diary. 'Received yesterday a short note from Peel, stating that "orders would be given for an Admiralty steamboat to carry out the Bishop to Syria"!' '"Surely the Isles shall wait for thee and the ships of Tarshish first, to bring thy sons from afar and thy daughters from the ends of the earth"', he marvelled.[45] 'He will go out and disembark under the British flag', reported Bickersteth joyfully. 'Hail to the ships of Tarshish! We have here sanctified our national standard.'[46] The prophetic writer William Cuningname of Lainshaw went so far as to maintain that the ship assigned, the unfortunately named *HMS Devastation*, was literally that prophesied in Isaiah 60, 'devastation', he claimed, being equivalent to the Hebrew word Tarshish: 'to reduce' or 'to be reduced to poverty'.[47]

Linguistic contortions aside, reactions to the new bishopric serve also to emphasise the perils of hitching one's prophetic cart too closely to current affairs. If wars and rumours of wars in the 1790s and 1800s had encouraged prophetic commentators to construct ever more detailed timelines, the long-running boom in such works gave hostile commentators plenty of ammunition. As mentioned earlier, even the most painstaking apocalyptic number-crunchers might be sent back to the drawing board, as in 1866. There was a growing division between the mostly evangelical constituencies who looked for the literal fulfilment of prophecy, and those who did not, although the line between them was not always clear. British geopolitical interest in the decaying Ottoman Empire continued to provide reassuring portents for 'Christian Zionists' right up until the First World War, but it also attracted scriptural and quasi-scriptural language from those who did not believe in the predictive potency of Scripture.[48] This division was further problematised by a growing ambivalence at mid-century about the part Britain was destined to play in global evangelisation. For although 'Commerce and Christianity' provided mid-Victorian missionaries with a catchy slogan, booming trade was not matched by mass conversions. 'We know not how long it may please God to uphold the mighty fabric of the British Empire', mused the bishop of Llandaff, Alfred Ollivant, in an 1850 sermon before the University of Cambridge. Christ's promise to be with his disciples, he pointed out, was 'inseparably connected' with the fulfilment of the Great Commission, a burden that some, he averred, were reluctant to take up.[49] Britain's privileged status, Ollivant warned, was provisional.

It may be significant that Ollivant avoided referring to the literal fulfilment of Old Testament prophecy, which was becoming a niche interest. A very different brand of providentialism was in evidence in the annual sermons given before the Master and Brethren of Trinity House, effectively the British lighthouse authority. This was a set-piece occasion, the sermon being in the gift of the Master, who was usually a high-ranking politician, and the polished offerings published as a result evince a gradual shift away from earlier certainties among establishment thinkers.[50] To trace the series through its heyday in the 1820s, 1830s and 1840s is to find preachers playing safe, extolling the corporation's protection of British seafarers but steering clear of direct prophetic application in favour of moral and metaphorical parallels drawn from the usual maritime-themed texts. The Claphamite evangelical, C. R. Sumner, hit a familiar-sounding note in 1824, warning how 'the navies that were of old [had] perished' and that the commerce of Tyre and Tarshish had failed to preserve them: 'if we would secure to our own maritime eminence a more abiding inheritance, we must range ourselves on the side of the Lord'.[51] Nevertheless, it was a far cry from the full-blown prophetic mode. Perhaps in the optimistic early 1820s the Old Testament was less relevant for those, like Sumner, who held that missions were effectively writing new chapters in the book of Acts instead. Others, such as the up-and-coming high churchman Richard Mant (1818) and the Cambridge scientist William Whewell (1835), avoided even veiled references to catastrophic judgements, opting instead to outline the 'great machinery' of trade, enterprise and civilisation benevolently ushering humanity towards more perfect knowledge of God.[52]

Contextualising prophetic passages

If Trinity House preachers offered broad brushstrokes rather than detailed blueprints, it was partly because it was becoming harder to read Britain into the Bible. The emphasis was shifting, from using current events to defend the predictive accuracy of prophetic passages to using past events to reinforce the integrity and historicity of the Bible as a whole. Even among evangelicals there were those such as Samuel Lee, Regius Professor of Hebrew at Cambridge, who maintained that Old Testament prophecies concerning Israel had already been fulfilled.[53] One did not have to be learned to appreciate the point: readers of the evangelistic *Sailor's Magazine and Naval Journal* in 1837 were informed that 'Ships of Tarshish' was a generic phrase for large, seagoing merchant ships.[54] E. B. Pusey was making much the same point in a Bible commentary of 1860 when he equated 'Tarshish-ships' with 'the East-Indiamen which some of us remember': it was a label, not a place of origin.[55] It was possible, of course, for inherited providentialist interpretations to coexist with scholarly ideas. After all, if Mediterranean seafarers were capable of getting to Tartessus, they were surely also capable of visiting Britain. 'We know that the Phoenicians did come to the British Isles for tin, why not Jews also? The islands were well known to Herodotus.'[56] The idea that the products of Cornish mines might have adorned the Solomonic Temple remained seductive.[57] So too did the recurring Protestant fantasy that Paul had visited Britain to impart Christianity direct from the fountainhead, which theory avoided embarrassing concessions about the role of papal missionaries in her conversion.[58] When the Oxford philologist Max Müller asked in an 1867 essay 'Are there Jews in Cornwall?', his answer – no – prompted a lengthy and learned reply from the Cornish clergyman-scholar Dr John Bannister.[59] By the later nineteenth century, however, such ideas were becoming the preserve of writers on the wilder fringes of evangelicalism, and of British Israelites, whose racially tinged ideas drew eclectically on evangelical philosemitism, antiquarian texts and cod linguistics to argue that the British – or, more precisely, the Anglo-Saxon race – were literally descended from the ten Lost Tribes.[60] In Chapter 4 of this volume, Brian Murray explores the details of a particularly outlandish strand of such thinking regarding the descent of the Irish and Scottish monarchs from the daughters of King Zedekiah of Judah.

The eclipse of prophetic literalism bespoke changing priorities among the British clerical scholarly establishment. In the decade after *Essays and Reviews* (1860), their main concern was to defend the historical truth and textual integrity of the Bible against German 'higher critics' such as De Wette and Wellhausen, whose questioning of traditional assumptions about authorship, canonicity, textual integrity and supernatural inspiration were regarded with suspicion. Prophecy was still useful in countering doubt, but not for what it said about the future. Instead it was the scientific recording by archaeologists of predictions long fulfilled – the fall of Jerusalem, say, or the destruction of Babylon – that provided extra-biblical evidence to support beleaguered advocates of the Bible's historical accuracy. William Smith's *Dictionary of the Bible* (3 vols, 1860–63) was a case in point. Its mostly Anglican contributors sought to use archaeology, travel literature and natural science to throw new light on Middle Eastern life, languages, flora and fauna, and in so doing to show that it was a creation of its times and culture. Facts were what mattered. Thus entries for 'Metals', 'Ship', 'Solomon' and 'Tarshish' elucidated the place of Tarshish in Israel's economy and diplomacy, but gave no hint that it was or ever had been linked with Britain, save possibly via Phoenician tin merchants.[61] Believers could thus guard against doubt by reassuring themselves that the biblical books were backed up by other forms of evidence.

This did not prevent speculation about the location of Tarshish; but the arguments adduced drew not on recent events but on philology and ancient geography. In 1859 the statesman and littérateur George Cornewall Lewis rehearsed in *Notes and Queries* the argument from classical literature for its being in Spain, but by the time his friend Edward Twisleton came to write the *Bible Dictionary* entry, another scholar-cum-civil servant, Sir James Edward Tennent, was championing a fresh theory.[62] Tarshish, he argued, was not one place but two. Most Old Testament references were to a source of silver and lead in the extreme west of the ancient world – Tartessus – while those in Chronicles must refer to another, accessible through Ezion-Geber – Idumea – on the Red Sea, and thus far to the east. The peacocks were the clincher: while the gold of 2 Chronicles 9 could have been procured from Ophir, and ivory and apes from Africa, 'the peacock is an Indian and not an African bird', its Hebrew name supposedly having Tamil roots.[63] The 'great oriental mart' on which the fleets of Hiram and Solomon descended triennially, Tennent concluded triumphantly, was Point de Galle in Ceylon.[64] His findings serve to underline a growing scholarly fascination with the Phoenicians as vectors for, and bridges between, Hebraic and Homeric mythologies.[65] Tarshish continued to attract attention, then, but not as a coded reference to or metaphor for Britain.

Yet seeing Tarshish for what it really was diminished its significance: it became an interesting if obscure fragment in a wider civilisational mosaic of which biblical history itself was increasingly only a part. When Matthew Arnold set forth *The Great Prophecy of Israel's Restoration arranged and edited for Young Learners* (1872) his intention was to make 'Hebrew literature in its perfection', namely Isaiah chapters 40–66 (as Deutero-Isaiah was then defined), accessible to young readers alongside the best of the Roman and Greek authors. Carefully sidestepping the question of whether or not they foretold the future, Arnold, like his father, held that the grandeur of the prophets lay in their unflinching moral courage and imagination.[66] His Isaiah still foresaw a time when the 'the isles shall wait for his law': but only because Arnold thought it sounded better than 'sea-coasts', which was the more accurate translation.[67] Deutero-Isaiah was read by Arnold as one among many beautiful and thus morally elevating ancient expressions of the universal 'human spirit'. There was no sense in which it foretold the future, or could be used to corroborate events in the present: it was simply a beautiful ancient poem.[68] Late Victorian schoolchildren looking for references to Tarshish, Tyre and Ophir would find them in Rider Haggard's 1885 adventure novel *King Solomon's Mines*, but they were designed to give a sense of the exotic rather than to bolster belief.

Conclusion

Like much current work on nineteenth-century religion, this chapter has sought to nuance received assumptions about the direction of cultural and intellectual travel. On the one hand it shares the scepticism of recent work towards the now tired paradigm of 'faith and doubt' that takes George Eliot, Arthur Hugh Clough and Thomas Hardy as reference points on a gradual but inevitable slide towards secularisation.[69] On the other it has used a particular set of texts to argue that, although prophecy and providential language retained rhetorical and homiletic purchase, by the end of the century even ardent believers did not believe that they could be applied in the ways that they had been a hundred years before. This has important implications for how we see the place of 'doubt' in nineteenth-century thought. Serious cases of doubt could indeed prove fatal to belief, but it is clear that in others shifting ideas about received aspects of Christianity did not lead to systemic collapse. As the previous section underlined, new discoveries in geography, natural science and biblical studies did not so much undermine faith as reshape its foundations. As threats to the Bible shifted, so too did the majority of interpreters in how they read significant passages.

This raises important issues for the study of prophecy. For here, too, unhelpful binary distinctions in the secondary literature between the mostly evangelical constituencies who 'believed' in the literal fulfilment of Scripture predictions and those who 'doubted' them has obscured the extent to which prophetic ideas and passages could infuse people's thinking in more subtle, more provisional ways. Such passages could soften into emblems or they could harden again into something more concrete: witness how General Allenby's entry into 'Jerusalem the Blessed' in December 1917, for example, prompted renewed adventist activity among British evangelicals in particular.[70] If this chapter leaves us with a disjuncture, it is between those who saw prophecy and its current or past fulfilment as apologetically useful, and those who did not. By that measure, both Chamberlain and the more up-to-date scholars who participated in Smith's *Bible Dictionary* were engaging in similarly apologetic endeavours, endeavours that higher criticism would expose as futile by showing prophetic texts to be subject to processes of composition, editing and redaction. Just as telling was the issue raised by Matthew Arnold and others: why would one need or want to confirm the archaeological veracity of a text whose content was moral or spiritual? Whether 'true' or not, biblical portrayals of Rome, Jerusalem and Babylon continued to provide poets and sermonisers with some of their most resonant metaphors of glory, power, luxury, commerce and corruption. Kipling was no orthodox believer, but his 'Recessional', printed in *The Times* as a would-be lay sermon against complacency commenting on Victoria's Silver Jubilee celebrations in 1897, was soaked in familiar scriptural-prophetic phraseology:

> Far-called, our navies melt away;
> On dune and headland sinks the fire:
> Lo, all our pomp of yesterday
> Is one with Nineveh and Tyre!
> Judge of the Nations, spare us yet,
> Lest we forget – lest we forget![71]

If the imagery was close to that of Chamberlain, the beliefs that animated it were worlds away. Ultimately, then, this chapter has identified a growing dichotomy in ideas about how prophecy was to be used. For those who imbibed modern scholarship, prophecy bore witness to the contexts in which it was written: it demonstrated the veracity of the Bible as a set of Near Eastern texts. For those like Kipling it provided ringing words. But as the twentieth century dawned there remained a significant subculture that saw prophetic passages as a prophylactic against doubt in a very different sense, as a code waiting to be unscrambled by faithful exegetes alert to the unfolding of events. Given that parts of the internet are populated with people still convinced that Britain (or the United States) really is Tarshish, that subculture continues to resonate with some even today.[72]

Notes

1 Walter Chamberlain, *Isaiah's Call to England: Being an Exposition of Isaiah the Eighteenth* (London: Wertheim, Macintosh and Hunt, 1860), pp. iv–v.
2 Chamberlain, *Isaiah's Call*, pp. 333, 341–4; 357–9.
3 Chamberlain, *Isaiah's Call*, pp. 423, 203–29.
4 Chamberlain, *Isaiah's Call*, p. 227.

5   Chamberlain, *Isaiah's Call*, pp. 422–4.
6   Boyd Hilton, *A Mad, Bad, and Dangerous People? England, 1783–1846* (Oxford: Oxford University Press, 2006), pp. 397–406.
7   [W. J. Conybeare], 'Church Parties', *Edinburgh Review*, 98 (1853), 297.
8   Chamberlain, *Isaiah's Call*, p. x.
9   J. and J. A. Venn, *Alumni Cantabrigienses, 2: From 1752 to 1900*, 6 vols (Cambridge: Cambridge University Press, 1940–54), II: p. 3.
10 Walter Chamberlain, *A Plain Reply to Bishop Colenso* (London: Wertheim, Macintosh and Hunt, 1863).
11 See, for example, Martin Spence, *Heaven on Earth: Reimagining Time and Eternity in Nineteenth-Century British Evangelicalism* (Eugene, OR: Pickwick Publications, 2015).
12 *Quarterly Journal of Prophecy*, 12 (1860), 395–7; see also *London Review and Weekly Journal of Politics, Literature, Art, and Society*, 4 October 1862, p. iv.
13 Elliott, like Chamberlain, was a learned man: a one-time fellow of Trinity College, Cambridge, he ended his days as incumbent of St Mark's, Kemptown, in well-heeled Brighton: see J. Bateman, *The Life of the Rev. Henry Venn Elliott* (London: Macmillan and Co., 1868).
14 Crawford Gribben and Timothy C. F. Stunt, eds, *Prisoners of Hope? Aspects of Evangelical Millennialism in Britain and Ireland, 1800–1880* (Carlisle: Paternoster, 2004), pp. 1–17; see also Ralph Brown, 'Victorian Anglican Evangelicalism: the Radical Legacy of Edward Irving', *Journal of Ecclesiastical History*, 58 (2007), 675–704.
15 W. H. Oliver, *Prophets and Millennialists: The Uses of Biblical Prophecy in England from the 1790s to the 1840s* (Auckland: Auckland University Press, 1978), pp. 239–40.
16 Arthur Penrhyn Stanley, *The Life and Correspondence of Thomas Arnold*, 2 vols (London: B. Fellowes, 1844), I: pp. 65, 177–80.
17 The erstwhile Brethren leader Benjamin Wills Newton was especially scornful of Elliott's argument: see Benjamin Wills Newton, *Aids to Prophetic Enquiry*, 3rd edn (London: James Nisbet and Co., 1881), p. 241n.
18 Samuel Minton, *The Merchants of Tarshish, or, England, America, and Russia in the Last War* (London: Seeley, Jackson, and Halliday, 1868), p. iv.
19 See Michael Ledger-Lomas, 'Conder and Sons: Dissent and the Oriental Bible in Nineteenth-Century Britain', in Ledger-Lomas and Scott Mandelbrote, eds, *Dissent & the Bible in Britain, c.1650–1950* (Oxford: Oxford University Press, 2013), pp. 205–22.
20 The recent literature on this is vast. Highlights include Alexandra Walsham, *Providence in Early Modern England* (Oxford: Oxford University Press, 1999), pp. 281–325; Pasi Ihalainen, *Protestant Nations Redefined: Changing Perceptions of National Identity in the Rhetoric of the English, Dutch and Swedish Churches, 1685–1772* (Leiden: Brill, 2005); John Coffey, *Exodus and Liberation: Deliverance Politics from John Calvin to Martin Luther King Jr.* (Oxford: Oxford University Press, 2014), pp. 25–78.
21 Coffey, *Exodus and Liberation*, pp. 36–7.
22 Daniel Defoe, *The Lay-Man's Sermon upon the Late Storm* (London: [s.n.], 1704), p. 6.
23 E.g. Samuel Stennett, *A Sermon in Commemoration of the Great Storm of Wind* (London: J. Buckland and R. Bishop, 1788).
24 J. H. Pratt, ed., *Eclectic Notes: or, Notes of Discussions on Religious Topics at the Meetings of the Eclectic Society, London, during the Years 1798–1814*, 2nd edn (London: J. Nisbet, 1865), p. 330.
25 Paul J. Korshin, *Typologies in England, 1650–1820* (Princeton, NJ: Princeton University Press, 1982).
26 Walsham, *Providence*, p. 299.
27 John Ruskin, *The Stones of Venice: The Foundations* (London: Smith, Elder and Co., 1851), p. 1.
28 Thomas Newton, *Dissertations on the Prophecies*, 3 vols, 3rd edn (London: J. and R. Tonson, 1766), I: pp. 314–51, extensively cited travellers' accounts by Richard

Pococke, Thomas Shaw and Henry Maundrell; Thomas Hartwell Horne's *Landcape Illustrations of the Bible*, 2 vols (London: John Murray, 1836; n.p.) supplemented these with accounts from modern travellers, including William Jowett and James Silk Buckingham.

29 Herman Melville, *Moby-Dick; or, The Whale* (New York: Harper and Brothers, 1851), p. 46 (ch. 9).
30 For Bochart, see Zur Shalev, *Sacred Words and Worlds: Geography, Religion, and Scholarship, 1550–1700* (Leiden: Brill, 2012), pp. 141–204.
31 And in variations elsewhere: see 2 Chronicles 9:21.
32 George Horne, *A Commentary on the Book of Psalms*, new edn (London: W. Tegg and Co., 1849), p. 283.
33 See Donald M. Lewis, *The Origins of Christian Zionism* (Cambridge: Cambridge University Press, 2009), pp. 25–48, for a useful summary of seventeenth-century puritan interest in the subject.
34 Mayir Vereté, 'The Restoration of the Jews in English Protestant Thought 1790–1840', *Middle Eastern Studies*, 8 (1972), 3–50; Nabil Matar, 'The Controversy over the Restoration of the Jews', *Durham University Journal*, 87 (1990), 29–44.
35 Stuart Semmel, *Napoleon and the British* (New Haven, CT: Yale University Press, 2004), pp. 72–106.
36 C. D. A. Leighton, 'Antichrist's Revolution: Some Anglican Apocalypticists in the Age of the French Wars', *Journal of Religious History*, 24 (2002), 125–42.
37 Henry Kett, *History the Interpreter of Prophecy*, 2 vols (4th edn; London: Bye and Law, 1801), II: pp. 291–2 n.
38 Ralph Wedgwood, *The Book of Remembrance: The Outline of an Almanack on the Ancient Cycles of Time* (London: [s.n.], 1814), p. 46; original emphasis.
39 James Hatley Frere, *A Combined View of the Prophecies of Daniel, Esdras and St John*, 2nd edn (London: W. Clowes, 1815), p. 114.
40 James Bicheno, *The Restoration of the Jews, the Crisis of all Nations*, 2nd edn (London: J. Barfield, 1807), pp. 227–35.
41 'Eben-Ezer' [Ebenezer Aldred], *The Little Book; or, a Close and Brief Elucidation of the 13, 14, 15, 16, 17, and 18th Chapters of Revelations* (London: C. Stower, 1811), p. 69.
42 'Sermons in Aid of the Waterloo Subscription', *Critical Review*, 5th ser., 2 (1815), 523–8; see also 'Art. VII', *Monthly Repository*, 11 (1816), 216–17.
43 Edward Bickersteth, *A Scripture Help* (12th edn; London: L. B. Seeley and Son, 1825), pp. 240–1; Adam Clarke, *The New Testament of Our Lord and Saviour Jesus Christ*, 2 vols (New York: Abingdon Press, 1831), II: p. 1048; Alexander Keith, *Signs of the Times, as Denoted by the Fulfilment of Prophetic Predictions ...*, 2 vols, 2nd edn (Edinburgh: William Whyte and Co., 1832), II: pp. 120–9; Edward Bishop Elliott, *Horae Apocalypticae*, 3 vols, 3rd edn (London: Seeley, Burnside, and Seeley, 1847), III: pp. 329–30.
44 W. T. Gidney, *The History of the London Society for Promoting Christianity amongst the Jews, from 1809 to 1908* (London: London Society for Promoting Christianity Amongst the Jews, 1908), pp. 51–200; Lewis, *Christian Zionism*, pp. 67–106.
45 Edwin Hodder, *The Life and Work of the Seventh Earl of Shaftesbury*, 2 vols (London: Cassell and Co. Ltd, 1886), I: p. 378. He was conflating Isaiah 43:6 and 60:9.
46 T. R. Birks, *Memoir of the Rev. Edward Bickersteth*, 2 vols, 2nd edn (London: Seeleys, 1852), II: pp. 182–3.
47 William Cuninghame, *The Political Destiny of the Earth, as revealed in the Bible*, 3rd edn (London: J. Nisbet and Co., L. B. Seeley and Co., and J. Cochran ..., 1842), p. xii.
48 Britain's acquisition of Cyprus ('Kittim') particularly excited E. J. Hytche, 'The Ships of Tarshish', *The Prophetic News and Israel's Watchman*, April 1881, 89–91. Americans who disapproved of the British Empire dwelt with gloomy relish on the vengeance promised to *all* nations, predicting divine leniency for their own land alone because of its favourable treatment of Jewish immigrants: George N. H.

Peters, *The Theocratic Kingdom*, 3 vols (New York: Funk and Wagnalls, 1884), II: pp. 778–80.

49 Alfred Ollivant, *The Duty of a Christian Nation to her Colonies and Foreign Dependencies* (Cambridge: Deighton, and Macmillan and Co., 1850), p. 27.
50 For accounts of the spectacle, see *Illustrated London News*, 17 June 1843; 5 June 1847.
51 Charles Richard Sumner, *The Duties of a Maritime Power* (London: J. Hatchard and Son; C and J. Rivington and Co., 1824), p. 21.
52 Richard Mant, *The Sovereignty of God in the Natural World, and the Agency of Man, Practically Considered* (London: F. C. and J. Rivington, 1818), William Whewell, *A Sermon Preached on Trinity Monday ... 1835* (London: Charles Whittingham, 1835), pp. 17–18.
53 Samuel Lee, *An Inquiry into the Nature, Progress, and End of Prophecy* (Cambridge: Cambridge University Press, 1849).
54 'Ships of Tarshish', *Naval Journal and Sailor's Magazine*, 10 (1837–38), 346–7.
55 E. B. Pusey, *The Minor Prophets* (Oxford: J. H. and J. Parker, 1860), p. 267.
56 Gidney, *London Society for Promoting Christianity amongst the Jews*, pp. 51–200; Lewis, *Christian Zionism*, pp. 67–106.
57 Edward S. Creasy, *History of England from the Earliest to the Present Time*, 5 vols (London: James Walton, 1869–70), I: p. 18.
58 See Michael Wheeler, *The Old Enemies: Catholic and Protestant in Nineteenth-Century English Culture* (Cambridge: Cambridge University Press, 2006), pp. 51–76.
59 F. Max Müller, 'Are there Jews in Cornwall?', in Müller, *Chips from a German Workshop*, 4 vols (London: Longmans, Green, 1867–75), IV: pp. 299–329; John Bannister, '"Jews in Cornwall"; and "Marazion"', *Journal of the Royal Cornish Institution*, 2 (1867), 324–42.
60 See John Wilson, *Our Israelitish Origin* (Cheltenham: Mimpriss, 1840), for one of the earliest developed statements of this position.
61 William Aldis Wright, 'Metals', in William Smith, ed., *Dictionary of the Bible*, 3 vols (London, 1860–3), II: pp. 341–3; John Saul Howson, 'Ship', *Dictionary*, II: pp. 1282–7; Edward Hayes Plumptre, 'Solomon', *Dictionary*, II: pp. 1342–54; Edward Twisleton, 'Tarshish', *Dictionary*, II: pp. 1438–41.
62 James Edward Tennent, 'Tarshish', in *Encyclopaedia Britannica*, 22 vols (Edinburgh, 1853–60), XXI: pp. 26–8; see also William Houghton, 'Peacocks', in Smith, ed., *Dictionary*, II: pp. 763–4.
63 Twisleton, 'Tarshish', p. 1441.
64 Tennent, 'Tarshish', p. 28.
65 See, for instance, Ernest Renan, *Mission de Phénicie* (Paris: Imprimerie Impériale, 1864); William Ewart Gladstone, *Juventus Mundi: The Gods and Men of the Heroic Age*, 2nd edn (London: Macmillan and Co., 1870), especially pp. 119–50; George Rawlinson, *History of Phoenicia* (London: Longmans, Green, 1889).
66 Matthew Arnold, *The Great Prophecy of Israel's Restoration*, 4th edn (London: Macmillan and Co., 1875), p. xxix.
67 Arnold, *Great Prophecy*, p. xvii.
68 Arnold, *Great Prophecy*, pp. xxxv–xxxvi.
69 For a good recent summary, see Kirstie Blair, *Form and Faith in Victorian Religion and Poetry* (Oxford: Oxford University Press, 2012), pp. 1–20.
70 D. W. Bebbington, 'The Advent Hope in British Evangelicalism since 1800', *Scottish Journal of Religious Studies*, 9 (1988), 103–14.
71 *The Times*, 17 July 1897, p. 13. It was later sung to the tune MELITA ('Eternal Father, Strong to Save'), which had strong maritime connections.
72 See, for example, 'Is America in Bible Prophecy?', accessed 8 August 2015, https://www.raptureready.com/featured/ice/AmericaInBibleProphecy.html.

CHAPTER FOUR

Jeremiah in Tara: British Israel and the Irish past
Brian H. Murray

In his ramble through the *Historical Memorials of Westminster Abbey* (1865), A. P. Stanley, Dean of Westminster, pauses portentously before the greatest relic of this 'British Valhalla': a 'primeval monument which binds together the whole Empire'. The ragged surface of the Stone of Scone, a rock set beneath the Coronation Chair, bears 'witness to its long migrations':

> It is thus embedded in the heart of the English monarchy – an element of poetic, patriarchal, heathen times, which, like Araunah's rocky threshing-floor in the midst of the Temple of Solomon, carries back our thoughts to races and customs now almost extinct; a link which unites the Throne of England to the traditions of Tara and Iona, and connects the charm of our complex civilisation with the forces of our mother earth.[1]

The Stone, brought to Westminster from Scotland as booty by Edward I, had long been associated with the rocky pillow of the visionary patriarch Jacob (Genesis 28:11). But the sequence of long migrations (via Ireland and Scotland) described by Stanley is the product of genealogies cooked up by medieval historians and elaborated by imaginative antiquarians ever since. From the fourteenth century onwards, chroniclers have claimed this relic as an embodiment of national sovereignty and divinely sanctioned rule. The tale has as many versions as tellers, but in the standard medieval account the stone is brought out of Egypt by Pharaoh's daughter Scota, the mother of the Scots (or, in Irish versions, the Gaels or Milesians). In some versions, the Stone spends several generations in Ireland before it is eventually transferred to Scotland by the conquering Kings of Dál Riada (progenitors of the modern Scottish and English thrones via Kenneth MacAlpin and the Stuarts). Occasionally, these historical foundation myths intersect with biblical narratives. An English poem of 1307 (*La Pierre d'Escoce*), for example, depicts Moses prophesying to the Scots before they depart Egypt, asserting that

'Whoso will possess this stone / Shall be the conqueror of a very far-off land.'[2] As Nick Aitchison points out, these myths were mobilised in opposition to Edward I's cynical appeal to British myths of origin (via Brutus of Troy) to justify his usurpation of the Scottish throne. In the Brutus myth the Scots are descended from Brutus's second son, while the English descend from his elder son and heir.[3] The passage of Genesis pertaining to Jacob's pillow concludes with the patriarch's famous dream, in which the Lord promises his descendants a vast legacy:

> [13]And, behold, the Lord stood above it, and said, I am the Lord God of Abraham thy father, and the God of Isaac: the land whereon thou liest, to thee will I give it, and to thy seed;
>
> [14]And thy seed shall be as the dust of the earth, and thou shalt spread abroad to the west, and to the east, and to the north, and to the south: and in thee and in thy seed shall all the families of the earth be blessed.

Dean Stanley was careful not to endorse the historicity of the Stone's reputed origins in druidic Ireland or Ancient Palestine. Nevertheless, his lyrical account makes a case for the emotional truth of these legends. Whether or not this revered British relic is an authentic fragment of Biblical antiquity, sincere pilgrims have believed it to be so.

The present chapter concerns a group of Stanley's contemporaries who insisted that the Coronation Stone represented far more than a mere concatenation of myth, legend and history. The British Israelites were a loose Protestant sect united by their belief that the Anglo-Saxon race was descended from the Lost Tribes of Israel and that biblical prophecies on the future of 'Israel' and 'Judah' actually referred to the British Empire. For British Israelites, the stone provided a vital archaeological thread connecting the British monarchy with the biblical Kingdom of David. Although reliant on established medieval genealogies, the British Israelites adapted the legend to emphasise both the unbroken lineage that supposedly connected Israel and Britain and the identification of the Stone of Scone with the Irish *Lia Fáil* (the coronation stone of the High Kings of Ireland). A pamphlet from 1937 gives a good summary of the British Israelite versions of events at this date. It picks up the story with Nebuchadnezzar's conquest of Jerusalem and the extinction of the Kingdom of Judah:

> What happened to Jacob's pillar-stone at the end of Zedekiah's reign, when the Davidic Dynasty was overthrown in Jerusalem and the Temple destroyed? Jeremiah the Prophet was divinely commissioned to transplant the Royal House of David to another land. Tradition states that soon afterwards he went to Spain and thence, in a Danaan ship to Ireland, where he arrived under the historic name Ollam Fodla (signifying 'wonderful prophet'). With Jeremiah on this journey were Baruch (or Bruch) and

King Zedekiah's two daughters, Tamar Tephi and Scotta ... Princess Tamar Tephi married the then head king of Ireland, Eochaidh Heremon, whose ancient genealogy shows him to be also of the Tribe of Judah. As queen of Ireland, she was dearly loved, as proved by the ancient Irish folklore. Through the line of the Irish and Scottish kings, the present King of Great Britain is a direct descendant of that queen.[4]

Medieval Irish chroniclers and early modern historians had always been keen to integrate biblical and Gaelic chronologies. Throughout the eighteenth and nineteenth centuries Irish antiquarians, poets and romantic nationalists often self-identified as 'Milesians' and argued for the Phoenician origin of Irish language and culture.[5] On one hand this gave the Irish a cosmopolitan origin myth that ran parallel to the biblical history of Israel and could stand in opposition to Anglo-Saxon narratives. The British Israelites also co-opted the Irish claim to Semitic inheritance, but to very different ends. The spurious identification of the obscure Irish King Ollamh Fodhla (or Ollam Fotla) with the biblical prophet Jeremiah provided British Israelites with the missing link that proved Anglo-Saxons were the true Chosen People. And yet, the same figures who placed so much weight on the ancient literature of Ireland as an accurate sequel to Scripture were quick to denigrate the present-day Irish. Despite their fascination with druidical mysteries and the relics of pre-Christian Ireland, most British Israelites were arch-imperialists, staunch anti-Catholics and vigorous opponents of Irish Home Rule. So why did the same myth-history prove so attractive to both Irish patriots and Anglo-Saxon imperialists? Why was a movement that assumed the innate superiority of Anglo-Saxon civilisation interested in the history and literature of the Celtic Irish? This chapter tells the story of how biblical narratives were combined with previously obscure Irish sources to construct a myth-historical bridge between the Bible lands of antiquity and the islands of the North Atlantic.

Anglo-Saxons and British Israel

Many commentators have argued that racial thinking is a distinct historical product of the Enlightenment and the movement towards explaining human difference in 'scientific' terms. On one hand, this led to a preoccupation with physiognomy and language as markers of identity and the obsessive classification of peoples into distinct races. Edward Beasley has suggested that there was no 'idea of race as we have come to know it' until the nineteenth century.[6] But even if the concept of race was given a scientific and philological makeover in the period, an understanding of the world's populations in terms of genealogical taxonomy is as old as the Bible itself. As David Livingstone has shown, by the seventh century BCE, cartographers considered the populations of Asia, Africa and Europe to be peopled respectively by the descendants of Shem, Ham and Japheth.[7] Likewise, Colin Kidd argues that scholars and commentators have treated the Bible as 'a source book of evidence for the dispersion of races and the beginnings of racial divisions and patterns' since the early modern period.[8] Even in the nineteenth century, secular accounts of the Anglo-Saxon race as an inevitably expansive and conquering 'nation' resorted to biblical tropes (such as providence and covenant) to explain British supremacy. The historian J. R. Seeley famously quipped that the English had 'conquered half the world in a fit of absence of mind', but for another commentator on the relentless expansion of 'Greater Britain', the Liberal MP Charles Dilke, this absent-minded imperialism also involved genocidal acts of biblical proportions. Observing the decline of indigenous populations in North America and Australasia, Dilke noted (with some pride) that the 'Anglo-Saxon is the only extirpating race on earth'.[9] As Gareth Atkins has shown in the previous chapter, apologists for empire frequently cited Scripture in vindication of Britain's 'providential' rule. British Israelites, however, pushed this rhetoric further by arguing that biblical prophecies could be read literally as prognostic accounts of the expansion of the British Empire and diffusion of the Anglo-Saxon race. As Kidd suggests, 'British Israelism came to function as the spiritual counterpart of Anglo-Saxon racialism' and its adherents 'elevated the white man's burden on to a theological plane'.[10]

As Atkins mentions, Rudyard Kipling's 1897 poem 'Recessional' exemplifies many aspects of *fin-de-siècle* imperial providentialism. In 1902, however, the influential British Israelite pastor J. H. Allen, an American Methodist, rebooted Kipling's 'Recessional' as a hymn to the God-given might of the Anglo-Saxon race. Allen's 'Concessional' purges Kipling's verse of all humility and freely indulges in exactly the kind of hubristic bluster the original poem had warned against.

> Still we call to our God of old;
>   God of the *'far off'* Isaac line;
> Our God, whose word doth make us bold
>   To claim *our* heritage divine.
> The Lord of hosts is with us yet,
> Doth He forget? Doth He forget?
>
> It cannot be that *Isaac* dies;
>   His people and his kings depart;
> Before his God the *Saxon* lies,
>   Glad and brave, but with contrite heart
> The Lord of hosts is with us yet,
> Doth He forget? Doth He forget?

> Called in Him we are today
>   No longer passing through the fire;
> Altho' we were but yesterday
>   As one of Nineveh and Tyre.
> The Lord of *nations* guide us yet.
> Doth He forget? Doth he forget?[11]

Unimpressed by British Israel's claim to hold the monopoly on truth, critical and historical accounts have tended to focus on the movement as an ideology or as a political network. J. Wilson identifies some of its key ideological traits as ardent monarchism, fundamentalist Protestantism and shrill imperialism.[12] The fact that Wilson could still observe these tenets first-hand in 1968 also indicates the staunchly conservative nature of the movement. It emerged from a specifically late Victorian confluence of khaki conservatism and evangelicalism. By the early twentieth century, Anglo-Israelism claimed to have 2 million followers in Britain and the United States. While this may have been an exaggeration, by 1929 a meeting of the British Israel World Federation could still fill the Royal Albert Hall. Although it was dominated by middle-class Anglicans, Kidd suggests that the movement had 'multi-denominational appeal', ranging from Anglicanism to American Pentecostalism, and that 'its attractiveness was not limited to any particular type of Protestantism'.[13] Michael Barkun likewise describes the organisation as an 'interdenominational fellowship'.[14] Unsurprisingly, however, this cult of empire, race and monarchy never attracted much interest from Roman Catholics, Jews or other non-Christians.

The focus on the *politics* of British Israel, however, downplays what British Israel tracts, periodicals and books actually spend most of their time doing. Unlike other forms of evangelical Protestantism, British Israelism did not radiate around the pulpit or the revival tent. Nor was it particularly interested in ritual (aside from royal pageantry). Above all else, British Israelism was a network of literary production. This emphasis on print was not uncharacteristic of nineteenth-century religious movements and revivals. But what is striking about British Israel is the generic homogeneity of its productions. We find few sermons on ethical or moral themes, and little or no interest in theological questions as an end in themselves. Almost all British Israel publications are either historical essays or scriptural commentary (usually a blend of both). The unity of British Israel lies in its epistemological assumptions: most importantly, the conviction that the Bible functions as a minutely accurate prophetic roadmap, revealing the historical fate of peoples, 'nations' and 'races'. The lack of interest in British Israel as a *scholarly* tradition is understandable. One of the few historians to explore their researches in detail, Tudor Parfitt, notes that the 'various proofs produced by the British Israelites ... are of a feeble composition even by the low standards of the genre'.[15] It is my contention, however, that the most interesting ideological tensions of this popular and resilient phenomenon only become evident once we interrogate the modes of argument and proof utilised by British Israelites.

In search of Lost Tribes

Since the Middle Ages, scholars, divines and eccentrics have suggested the possibility of genealogical or racial links between British Christians and the Jews of ancient Palestine.[16] Most scholars agree, however, that modern British Israelism begins with the prophetic career of the Newfoundland-born naval lieutenant Richard Brothers. In 1794 Brothers announced to London society that he was heir to King David, and that he would shortly assume the British throne and lead the Jews back to Israel. Amidst the turmoil and paranoia of war-torn Europe, Brothers's *Revealed Knowledge of the Prophecies and Times* (1784) attracted much attention (multiple editions appeared in Britain, Ireland, France and the United States). The publication led to his trial, arrest and eventual confinement.[17] Brothers made little effort to connect Britain and Israel through the kind of careful genealogical analysis that characterises later British-Israel tracts. His prophetic writings need to be read in the context of a larger craze for prophetic analysis sparked by the upheavals of the French Revolution and the Napoleonic Wars, as discussed by Gareth Atkins in Chapter 3.[18] But British-Israel thinking only really flourished during the mid-century *Pax Britannia*, when the key geopolitical context was no longer war in Europe but the growth of European empires overseas and, more specifically, the relentless expansion of the English-speaking settler colonies.

Late in his career, Brothers broadened his ethnographic speculation with his *Correct Account of the Invasion of England by the Saxons, Showing the English Nation to be Descendants of the Lost Ten Tribes* (1822).[19] However, it took John Wilson, a Scottish-born autodidact living in Ireland, to transform British Israelism from a 'loose strain of speculation into a more disciplined school of biblical interpretation'.[20] In *Our Israelitish Origin*, Wilson deploys the language of scientific racism and phrenology in his account of the progress of the 'children of Shem, generally called the Caucasian race'.[21] Importantly, Wilson explicitly excludes present-day Jews from his imagined Israel of prophetic inheritance. This exclusion is rooted in an important distinction that Wilson makes between the ten tribes of Israel and the two tribes of Judah. 'In speaking of the chosen people of God,' he argues, 'it is proper that we discriminate clearly between the two houses, generally distinguished by the names Ephraim, or Israel, or the house of Isaac, for the ten tribes; and Judah, or the Jews.'[22] Wilson's Israelites, reimagined as ancestors of the Gothic peoples, trek north-westward along the fringes of the great empires of Persia, Hellenistic Greece and Rome. Wilson's method is rooted in biblical exegesis, supported by a loose chain of archaeological evidence, folk etymology and the testimony of Classical authors. But in a move that becomes characteristic of British Israelite argument, he suggests that Britain's imperial standing in the present day is the best evidence for its 'chosen' status.

> Only look for a moment at the important position which this people now occupy, – whose name but lately was a name for barbarism. They possess the most improved portion of our globe, – the greater part of which was but a wilderness when they took possession of it. There is scarcely any place of much importance, in any part of the world, that they do not occupy, – except, indeed, their own land of Israel ... Israel have colonised, or are colonising all the new world.[23]

Although influential on latter British Israelite writing, Wilson's 'Israel' is still a relatively capacious category: it includes most vaguely Germanic peoples and the bulk of Western Europe. Nor does he claim any precise genealogical connection between the British monarchy and biblical rulers or prophets. Interestingly, although Wilson spent much of his life in Ireland, he shows little interest in distinguishing between the Celtic, Anglo-Saxon and Norman inhabitants of Britain and Ireland. As I will show, the denigration of the Catholic Irish is an important feature of British Israelite writing after Wilson. Paradoxically, this anti-Irish position would be built upon the philological and historical speculations of Irish antiquarians.

Irish Phoenicians

Recent work on Irish antiquarianism and Orientalism has shown that Ireland's imagined cultural isolation on the north-western edge of Europe paradoxically offered a means through which it could be associated with the East.[24] At the end of the eighteenth century, many Irish scholars and antiquarians reinvigorated Celtic origin myths preserved in medieval manuscripts. These stories narrated the epic migration of the Gaels or Milesians via the Greek and Phoenician colonies of the Mediterranean before settling in Galicia, where the sons of the eponymous warrior Míl Espáine (Milesius) launched an invasion of Ireland. As Joseph Lennon has suggested, this foundation myth perpetuated a narrative in which the 'Irish ancestors departed Egypt and wound up, eventually, in a land analogous to the Jewish "promised land"'.[25] In the eighteenth century, Irish antiquarians were influenced by the theories of the French Protestant philologist and biblical critic Samuel Bochart. Bochart had erroneously traced the Celtic languages back to the ancient Semitic Phoenician, a discovery which seemed to vindicate Milesian tales from the Irish Bardic tradition.[26] Charles O'Conor of Belanagare (1710–91), a remnant of the diminishing class of landed Catholic aristocracy, drew on the Milesian narratives in his *Dissertations on the Antient History of Ireland* (1753). In O'Conor's efforts to prove that early Irish culture was civilised and literate – and that modern Irish Catholics could be loyal and law-abiding subjects of the Crown – the Phoenicians of the Levantine coast (often regarded as inventors of the first alphabet) proved useful antecedents.[27]

One figure proved particularly amenable to O'Conor's project. Ollamh Fodhla was an honorary title bestowed on Eochaid, a semi-legendary High King of Ireland thought to have reigned around the first millennium BCE.[28] Eochaid is reputed to have inaugurated a triennial gathering of nobility at Tara, the *Feis Teamhrach*, and he is also credited with building the *Múr nOlloman* (or Scholar's Rampart) on the Hill of Tara. O'Conor describes Ollamh Fodhla as 'our first celebrated Legislator', and praises his 'excellent Institutes for the Regulation of Religion and Government'.[29] The subjects of this benevolent monarch were, we are told, 'a free and learned People' who enjoyed 'reasonable, equitable, and true Liberty' supported by a constitution that 'was founded originally upon democratic Principles' and a policy of religious toleration.[30] In his evocative sketch of pre-Christian Gaelic enlightenment, O'Conor lays particular stress on religion and ritual. The Celtic religion had originally been austere and purely monotheistic before eventually succumbing to 'polytheism', 'superstition' and 'Druid craft'.[31] This early monotheistic druidism was, according to O'Conor, remarkably similar to the faith of the 'old Patriarchs' of Israel.[32] At the centre of Ollamh Fodhla's court stood 'the oracular *Lia-Fail*, or famous *Stone of Destiny*, so sacredly preserved, through all Ages, by the Druids [as] ... the Palladium of their Empire'. And while O'Conor rejects the identification of the stone with Jacob's Pillow, his account of enlightened Phoenician druidism offered much to tempt later scholars in search of Lost Tribes.[33]

In his *General History of Ireland* (1775), the Irish Catholic surgeon Sylvester O'Halloran followed O'Conor's lead, suggesting that 'Greece, Italy, in short no other polite nation of antiquity can boast so perfect a legislator' as the benevolent Ollamh Fodhla.[34]

> The reign of this prince and the great reforms he made in the constitution, form a memorable epoch in Irish history. In the preceding reigns, the reader must have perceived the gradual advances to politeness and sound

> legislation. The completion of this grand system was reserved for the present time. Eochaidh was a prince of great erudition, and on this account he got the name Ollamh-Fodhla, or the Learned Doctor, or Legislator.[35]

If O'Conor and O'Halloran's reflections on the druidical past were rose-tinted, they at least had a sincere appreciation of the value of their rare manuscript sources. The same cannot be said for the rebel, fantasist and forger Roger O'Connor – a former United Irishman and father of the Chartist leader Feargus O'Connor. Previous scholars were prone to flights of fancy when expanding on the terse descriptions of early annals. But O'Connor offered something entirely new: a previously undiscovered manuscript with detailed accounts of the wandering Gaels and the subsequent reigns of the High Kings (including Eochaid). O'Connor's *Chronicles of Eri* (1822) were supposedly 'translated from the original manuscripts in the Phoenician dialect of the Scythian language'. The 'original manuscripts' were suspiciously destroyed in a house fire, but not before O'Connor had dutifully translated his venerable Phoenician manuscript into the comfortingly familiar English of the King James Bible. O'Connor's expanded account of the reign of Eochaid would prove instrumental in forging a later chain of spurious philological and historical connections. Most importantly, he insisted that King Eochaid and 'Olam of Ullad' (his version of Ollam-Fodhla) were in fact two distinct figures. The latter was judge, priest and prophet, and the author of an account of the reign of Eochaid and the travels of the Lia Fáil.[36] By the 1880s, most standard accounts of British Israel 'identity' would cite O'Connor's forgeries as evidence for the identification of Ollamh Fodhla – the guardian of the 'Stone of Destiny' – with the Hebrew prophet Jeremiah.

British Israelites in Ireland

The first British Israelite to argue that Jeremiah made a journey to Ireland was the retired soldier and clergyman Frederick Glover. In *England, the Remnant of Judah and the Israel of Ephraim* (1861), Glover builds upon Charles O'Conor's arguments for the Hebraic civility of pre-Christian Tara and Roger O'Connor's entirely invented account of Ollam Fodhla. Glover's innovation is to map figures from the Bible onto the Irish myth-history through a series of false etymologies and homophonic coincidences. An analysis of Ollam Fodhla's name and deeds reveal him to be no less than 'a Prophet and Hebrew'.[37] 'These Hebrew Words, Things, and Institutions, therefore clustered at Tara (cir. B.C. 580) constitute full evidence, that the whole Institution, as remodelled by the Hebrew Innovator, was, in a sort, a Transplanted Jerusalem.'[38] In the biblical account, the daughters of Zedekiah are only mentioned in passing and never named (Jeremiah 43:6–7). But through a little philological wrangling, Glover determines that the ancient Irish capital of Tara (*Teamhair* in Irish) must have been named after a Princess of Judah called Tamar.[39] Medieval traditions suggested that Scota, a Pharaoh's daughter, had brought the Stone of Destiny out of Egypt, but Glover suggests that this is a distorted account of the exile of Jeremiah and the daughters of Zedekiah at Tahpanhes in Egypt (Jeremiah 43:7). Glover concludes his account by marrying off the invented figure of Tamar to King Eochaid, thus setting up an uninterrupted genealogy from the Line of David to the House of Hanover (via the Irish kings of Dál Riada and the Stuarts). The presence of the Lia Fáil at each transition ensures that the torch of Israel passes seamlessly from Jerusalem to Westminster (via Tara and Scone).

Glover, a graduate of Cambridge and Sandhurst, had a career typical of the upper middle-class professionalism that characterised British Israelism in the period. Having served as an infantry officer in the First Anglo-Asante War (1826), he pursued holy orders on retirement and was later appointed chaplain of the British Consulate at Cologne. His son, John Hawley Glover, was a successful colonial administrator in West Africa and later Governor of Newfoundland.[40] Although Glover's method was routed in intense though misguided philological and historical analysis, he occasionally lets his antiquarian mask slip to reveal the petty jingoism and anti-semitism that underpins his theory. 'Where are we to find the Indestructible Throne of David?', he asks, 'Is it in 'Change Alley? – or in the Jew's Quarter in Frankfort? Is money, or money-dealing the foundation or manifestation of the Throne which was never to be without an occupant of the Stem of Jesse?' Surely the 'manifestation of fulfilled prophecy' must be sought rather in 'present circumstances of the British Empire'?[41]

The most important figure in popularising Glover's theories, and in promoting British Israel as an organised religion, with services, meetings, committees and periodicals, was the charismatic bank clerk turned lecturer Edward Hine. Hine's *The English Nation identified with Lost Israel* (1871) combined the prophetical exegesis of Brothers and Wilson with Glover's Irish theories. The result was 'twenty-seven identifications' which, in Hine's opinion, irrefutably proved England's direct inheritance from the Lost Tribes (the evidence expanded to forty-seven identifications in subsequent editions). Hine's tract sold a quarter of a million copies and was instrumental in popularising British Israelism in the United States where Hine travelled, lectured and published between 1884 and

1888.[42] Hine's brand of evangelical jingoism did not take much tweaking to become an endorsement of America's 'manifest destiny' to colonise the West and expand its hegemonic ambitions in the Pacific. His message was amplified and supported in America by Charles Totten, an artillery lieutenant who had briefly lectured in 'military science' at Yale.[43] Along with his supporter Edward Wheler Bird, a retired Anglo-Indian judge, Hine managed to unite various groups under the banner of the Anglo-Israel Association, and by the 1870s 'British Israelism achieved a measure of doctrinal coherence'.[44] Hine's success in establishing a kind of Anglo-Israelite orthodoxy also meant that Glover's story of Jeremiah and daughters of Zedekiah now became canonical. Indeed, a version of Jeremiah's residence at Tara appears in most British Israelite accounts of the wanderings of Israel and the Stone of Destiny to the present day.

But how, if at all, did the success of Anglo-Israelism impact on British attitudes towards Ireland in the period? Colin Kidd has suggested that British Israelites relaxed at least one of 'the principal racial classifications operating in nineteenth-century culture, by conflating the Anglo-Saxon and Celtic peoples of the British Isles as Israelites'.[45] But while it may be true that British Israelite myth muddied the waters of the Celt–Saxon distinction, this did not stop individual authors from making subtle distinctions between tribes and ethnic groups, often at the expense of contemporary Irish Catholics. Glover, for example, suggested that Eochaid, the Celtic King who welcomed Jeremiah and married the daughter of Zedekiah was – as a proud Ulsterman – a descendant of the tribe of Dan and the progenitor of northern Protestants. In British Israelite newspapers and periodicals, the Catholic Irish were frequently portrayed as irredeemably inclined towards superstition and idolatry. With the re-eruption of Fenian disturbances in 1881, the lead article in one British Israel newspaper called for habeas corpus to be suspended and lambasted Gladstone's leniency towards Fenians and Home Rulers. In support of their case, the editors attached an extract from an essay by Hine describing the bulk of the Irish population as a 'Canaanitish' race destined for extinction. The current population of the island, explained Hine, was made up of 'two distinct elements'. The first was 'the so-called Norman element, which is part of ourselves' and 'purely Israelitish':

> These, our kindred, have supplied us with some of the finest blood and talent our country has owned; some of our best statesmen and warriors have come to us from our own race in Ireland. But the second element, most certainly is not Israelitish, but Gentile ... this Gentile portion now in Ireland, and who swarm in certain parts of all our large cities, not only in the United Kingdom, but in America, and in all our Colonies,

are literally and positively no other than descendants of the Canaanites, the seven nations that were in Canaan prior to the possession of the land by our forefathers, in times of old.[46]

By viewing modern politics through the lens of biblical empires, the British colonisation of Ireland was literally rendered as a recapitulation of Israel's conquest of Canaan. And if these Celtic Canaanites were still giving Israel trouble it was because the Chosen People had, from antiquity to present, been far too humane in their treatment of their providently enshrined enemies: 'our forefathers were commissioned by God to *exterminate*, but they disobeyed God by failing to do so ... Our mission now is as clear as it was to our forefathers ... these Irish Canaanites are to us as aborigines, and have to come under the "dying out" process'.[47] Hine's position on Ireland was perfectly in line with his general policy of celebrating Britain and America's absent-minded genocide of non-white peoples:

> We have literally fulfilled Israel's mission by pushing the aborigines of our colonies to the ends of what was once their own country ... This we have done to the Caffres, the Maoris, the Bushmen of Australia, and notably by our kindred, who are pushing the American Indians to the backwoods ... All our aborigines are positively dying out, gradually but surely, before us.[48]

The transatlantic nature of the Fenian threat also sparked the interest of North American Anglo-Israelites, many of whom were already attracted by the movement's vocal opposition to popery. As J. H. Allen explained: 'it is a well-known fact that the settlers of *southern* Ireland are a vastly different people from those of *northern* Ireland, and that the difference is in their origin, for they sprang from a different race'. Did not the Fenians themselves 'boast of their Phoenician origin'? The Canaanites, it seems, were destined to be 'thorns in the side and pricks in the eyes' of Israel wherever she roamed (Numbers 33:55).[49] In British Israelite periodicals, such arcane and bookish justifications for racism and imperial conquest were frequently intermingled with more vulgar manifestations of prejudice. In December 1881, the *British Israel* newspaper featured an analysis of a political cartoon portraying Fenians with 'brutal gorilla-like faces':

> [It] is almost impossible for anyone to look upon the picture without acknowledging that it is a question of race; and we, who believe in our Identity with Israel, see, in the brutal and callous faces depicted, the types of our relentless and vindictive enemies, the Canaanites.[50]

As odd as it may seem, this popular antagonism to the Irish Catholic masses existed alongside a fascination with Celtic antiquities and a market for picturesque renderings of Jeremiah's 'transplanted Jerusalem' at Tara. The same issue of *British Israel* that called for the extermination of Fenian Canaanites also includes an advertisement for a set of chromolithographic 'mementos of Tara' ('of highest interest to all British Israelites as depicting the scenery of that district in which is centred so much of vast import to the Identity cause') (see Figure 4.1).[51] The literary endeavours of British Israelites were usually restricted to historical essays interspersed with the occasional didactic poem, but one interesting exception is Alfred Morris's historical novel, *Eochaid the Heremhon: Or, The Romance of the Lia Phail* (1900). The first chapter takes place in the Egyptian city of Tahpanhes, where we encounter 'two men attired in the then recognised garb of the Jews, with flowing gabardine and turbanned heads' (Jeremiah and Baruch). The prophet is described as 'a man about sixty-five years of age, of a stately presence ... and almost ascetic of figure, [possessing] one of those remarkable faces which impress the beholder with an irresistible conviction of character and power'.[52] Jeremiah and Baruch lament the backsliding of their fellow Israelites, who have been busy 'prostrating themselves before the accursed idol' of the Egyptians. 'The sober ceremonial of our ancient and true faith', laments Jeremiah, 'catcheth not the imagination like the gorgeous cult of this Egyptian priesthood.'[53] Morris thus sets up a familiar Protestant opposition between the sincere and sober religion of the book and the gorgeous ritual and fawning superstition of a false creed. The same theme extends to Ireland, where Jeremiah must next do battle with the Arch-Druids of Baal. At Tara, the prophet finds a people cowed by druidical priestcraft:

> The Druidical form of worship then ... can hardly be distinguished, as to its forms and ceremonies from the old Oriental worship of Baal; and, at the time of which we now write, no reforming influence had been felt even in Ireland, although, as we shall presently see, great changes ensued in that country shortly afterwards.[54]

The novel presents Jeremiah as both missionary and 'reformer', confronting the Druids with passionate recitations from his 'well-worn copy of the sacred writings of his race'.[55] When the Druids attempt to stage a human sacrifice, Jeremiah prays for divine intervention. The Druids are immediately struck down by a flash of lightening and the sacrificial fires of the wicker man are mercifully quenched by a sudden downpour. Shortly afterwards, Jeremiah manages to convert Eochaid by revealing the King's descent from 'the Israelitish tribe of Dan' and persuading him of the sovereign power of the Lia Fáil. In the key conversion scene, the prophet bombards the Irish King with a crash course in British Israel genealogy:

> 'O! Eochaid, king of Ulster and Pentarch of Ireland, art thou so sure that thou art not a prince of Israel, or that thy people are not of the tribe of Dan?'
>
> 'Great Baal! Tuatha de Dannan, the tribe of Dan; this is not the first time that I have heard this said, but if it be so, how makest thou me a prince of Israel; I am of the stock of Heber, the Milesian prince, who conquered this land five hundred years ago.'
>
> 'Be it so, Heber is an Israelitish name, and it is well recorded among us that the Milesians of Spain were originally an Israelitish colony from Dan and Simeon.'[56]

Eochaid eventually accepts 'the Lord God of Israel' and pledges to leave off 'the worship which revolted my heart with its cruelty, and confused my mind with its superstition'.[57] The reformation complete, Jeremiah turns matchmaker and persuades Princess Tamar to marry Eochaid, thus ensuring the survival of the House of David in a new land. As with most British Israel tracts – and many colonial adventure novels – Morris's 'romance' flirts with the attractions of an exotic and primitive past before ultimately endorsing a teleology of colonisation and conversion: Jeremiah's civilising mission to the savage Irish.

Morris died before the novel's completion, but it was edited, completed and published after his death by Denis Hanan, a Church of Ireland minister from Tipperary and the president of the British-Israel Association of Ireland (established 1897).[58] Hanan was also a member of the Royal Society of Antiquaries of Ireland, and a key promoter of a one of the most controversial British-Israel schemes: an archaeological expedition in search of the Ark of the Covenant at Tara. As Mairéad Carew has shown, the Irish branch of British Israel was already well integrated in antiquarian circles: eight council members of the British-Israel Association of Ireland were also members of the Royal Society of Antiquaries of Ireland.[59] Nonetheless, sporadic attempts to excavate the site between 1899 and 1902 were interrupted by the protests of Irish nationalists and conservationists. On Christmas Day 1900, the nationalist journalists and agitators Arthur Griffith and Maud Gonne trespassed deliberately on the site. On reaching the Hill of Tara, Gonne apparently fell to her knees and experienced a vision which she later recounted in an article for Griffith's *United Irishman* newspaper:

> The wind blew wildly with a sobbing sound among the fir trees, and I seemed to see shuddering, misty forms gazing curiously at us. A weird procession wound round the great raths where the palaces had stood.

Some tossed white arms as they moved in rhythmic circles, and was it the sound of the wind among the trees, or was it the echo from the harp, held high up in the air by the leader of the shadowy dance – Tara, Tara of the Kings, desolation.[60]

If Jeremiah had stripped the altars of Tara in the name of Jewish 'reformation', Gonne was keen to resuscitate the Druids as emblems of a revolutionary future.[61] In July 1902, under the guise of her radical *Inghinidhe na hÉireann* ('the Daughters of Ireland'), Gonne again marched on Tara for a 'Patriotic Children's Treat'. She led a procession of 300 children waving banners and singing national songs in Irish and English. Their arrival frustrated the plans of Tara's landowner, Gustavus Villiers Briscoe, who had prepared a bonfire in honour of the coronation of Edward VII. Gonne promptly set fire to the pile herself 'in honour of an Independent Ireland' and led the children in a chorus of 'A Nation Once Again'.[62] In the same year Gonne's most famous admirer, the poet William Butler Yeats, wrote to one tenant of Tara complaining of a 'monstrous' desecration 'being done by the fanatics, who are looking for the Ark of the Covenant'.[63] In June 1902, Yeats, together with the novelist George Moore and the poet Douglas Hyde (a future President of Ireland), wrote to the London *Times* demanding an immediate cessation to the excavations. 'Tara is', they claimed, 'probably the most consecrated spot in Ireland, and its destruction will leave many bitter memories behind it.'[64] So long as the British Israelites' historiographical exertions were restricted to their own networks and readerships, they ruffled few feathers. But their one notable venture into archaeology was met with fierce resistance from those who rejected their racial, political and theological assumptions. The excavations at Tara were meant to reveal material evidence of Jeremiah's reformation of Ireland and in so doing further enshrine Britain's imperial status. Ironically, the most immediate effect was to bring together a diverse group of cultural and political nationalists under a common banner that would soon be raised in open rebellion to British rule.

Conclusion

The legacies of British Israelism are complex and diverse, and the movement has spawned distinct offshoots in different regions of the English-speaking world. Following Hine's evangelising lecture tour of North America, and the development of his theories by Totten and Allen, British Israel ideas were picked up by several influential leaders of Pentecostal and revival movements. Allen, who started out as an

Figure 4.1 *British Israel, and Judah's Prophetic Messenger & Universal News* (2 September 1880). The front page includes a detachable chromolithograph image of Tara

orthodox Methodist, became one of the founders of a 'Holiness' Church in Missouri and later California. Charles Fox Parham, one of the principal founders of the modern Pentecostal movement, was also a committed opponent of racial integration and miscegenation. His theology was indebted to both 'Anglo-Israelism' and a form of 'pre-Adamite racialism' that denied the common humanity of 'lesser races'.[65] As Michael Barkun has shown, 'Parham and Allen infused British Israelism into the premillennial evangelical sects that were emerging out of Midwestern Methodism.'[66] In the United States, the racist underpinnings implicit in British Israelism fed into the related but distinct Christian Identity movement. As it developed in the aftermath of the Second World War, Christian Identity combined aspects of British Israelism with a fundamentalist version of 'pre-Adamite polygenesis' to further claims of white supremacy and advocate extreme forms of racial segregation.[67]

Some of the last strongholds of British Israel identity are among the extremist fringes of white Protestant communities in South Africa and Northern Ireland, groups with covenantal settler identities that have been forged against a background of racial and sectarian conflict.[68] At the close of the nineteenth century, large swathes of British-Israel publications took up Boer-bashing amid the rise of khaki populism and war in South Africa. Yet British-Israel ideas continued to have purchase within pro-apartheid Afrikaner communities and churches well into the late twentieth century: proof enough perhaps, that British-Israel ideas have most often been enlisted to give a theological veneer to underlying prejudices.[69]

A recent *British-Israel-World Federation Newsletter* demonstrates the movement's ongoing commitment to interpreting current events within an exegetical and millennial framework. The election of President Donald Trump 'confirms that the Spirit of the Lord is moving to revive the covenant nations of Joseph's sons and their prophetic descendants'. An essay by the current president of the British-Israel-World Federation defends Trump's Mexican border policy in response 'to various wall-bashing statements from the Pope'.[70] Given British Israelites' obsession with empire and Anglo-Saxon sovereignty, it is no surprise that they are also enthusiastic about the UK's decision to leave the European Union. The *Newsletter* for January 2017 begins with a 'Proclamation of Freedom from the EU' equating Brexit with 'the Exodus from Egypt by our forebears'.[71] An accompanying essay on 'The Positive Way Forward for the Island of Ireland' warns that around 'much of the Brexit, or "Brexodus," negotiations with the EU, we are hearing increasing sounds of "Pharaoh's chariots"'. Most troubling are 'the sounds of Irish Republicans in Belfast and Dublin using the Brexit process as an opportunity to push through a referendum on [Irish] reunification' and 'spurious fears of trade problems with the EU being put forth over the ... border with Northern Ireland and the Republic'.[72] The myth of Jeremiah's mission to Ireland continues to have a healthy afterlife in British-Israel publications and websites, but the Canaanites it seems are still 'pricks in the eyes, and thorns in the side' of 'Israel'.

Notes

1. A. P. Stanley, *Historical Memorials of Westminster Abbey*, 2nd edn (London: John Murray, 1868), pp. 66–7.
2. Nick Aitchison, *Scotland's Stone of Destiny: Myth, History and Nationhood* (Stroud: Tempus, 2000), p. 14. See also Richard Welander, David J. Breeze and Thomas Owen Clancy, eds, *The Stone of Destiny: Artefact and Icon* (Edinburgh: Society of Antiquaries of Scotland, 2003).
3. Aitchison, *Scotland's Stone of Destiny*, p. 35.
4. Adam Rutherford, *The Coronation Chair and the Stone of Destiny* (London: Covenant Publishing, [1937]), p. 6.
5. Joep Leerssen, *Remembrance and Imagination: Patterns in the Historical and Literary Representation of Ireland in the Nineteenth Century* (Cork: Cork University Press, 1997); Joseph Lennon, *Irish Orientalism: A Literary and Intellectual History* (Syracuse, NY: Syracuse University Press, 2002); Clare O'Halloran, *Golden Ages and Barbarous Nations: Antiquarian Debate and Cultural Politics in Ireland, c. 1750–1800* (Cork: Cork University Press, 2004); Colin Kidd, *British Identities before Nationalism: Ethnicity and Nationhood in the Atlantic World, 1600–1800* (Cambridge: Cambridge University Press, 1999), pp. 146–81.
6. Edward Beasley, *The Victorian Reinvention of Race* (New York: Routledge, 2010), p. 1. See also George Mosse, *Toward the Final Solution: A History of European Racism* (New York: Howard Fertig, 1978); Edward Said, *Orientalism* (New York: Pantheon Books, 1978); Robert J. C. Young, *Colonial Desire: Hybridity in Theory, Culture and Race* (New York: Routledge, 1995); Patrick Brantlinger, *Dark Vanishings: Discourse on the Extinction of Primitive Races, 1800–1930* (Ithaca, NY: Cornell University Press, 2003); Maurice Olender, *The Languages of Paradise: Race, Religion, and Philology in the Nineteenth Century* (Cambridge, MA: Harvard University Press, 1992); Tzvetan Todorov, *On Human Diversity: Nationalism, Racism, and Exoticism in French Thought*, trans. Catherine Porter (Cambridge, MA: Harvard University Press, 1993).
7. David N. Livingstone, *Adam's Ancestors: Race, Religion and the Politics of Human Origins* (Baltimore, MD: Johns Hopkins University Press, 2011), p. 6.
8. Colin Kidd, *The Forging of Races: Race and Scripture in the Protestant Atlantic World, 1600–2000* (Cambridge: Cambridge University Press, 2006), pp. 17, 168.
9. J. R. Seeley, *The Expansion of England* (London: Macmillan, 1883), p. 8; Charles W. Dilke, *Greater Britain: A Record of Travel in English-Speaking Countries*, 3rd edn (London: Macmillan, 1869), p. 224. See also Duncan Bell, *The Idea of Greater Britain: Empire and the Future of World Order, 1860–1900* (Princeton, NJ: Princeton University Press, 2007); Bernard Porter, *The Absent-Minded Imperialists: Empire, Society, and Culture in Britain* (Oxford: Oxford University Press, 2004).
10. Kidd, *Forging of Races*, pp. 212, 204.
11. J. H. Allen, *Judah's Sceptre and Joseph's Birthright* [1902], 7th edn (Boston: A. A. Beauchamp, 1930), pp. 331–2; original emphasis.
12. J. Wilson, 'British Israelism: A Revitalization Movement in Contemporary Culture', *Archives de Sociologie des Religions*, 13 (1968), 74–5.
13. Kidd, *Forging of Races*, pp. 209–10; A. M. Hyamson, 'Anglo-Israelism', in J. Hastings, ed., *Encyclopaedia of Religion and Ethics*, 13 vols (Edinburgh: T.&T. Clark, 1908–26), I: pp. 482–3.

14 Michael Barkun, *Religion and the Racist Right: The Origins of the Christian Identity Movement* (Durham, NC: University of North Carolina Press, 1994), p. 14.
15 Tudor Parfitt, *The Lost Tribes of Israel: The History of a Myth* (London: Phoenix, 2003), p. 61.
16 Parfitt, *Lost Tribes*, pp. 41–4.
17 Parfitt, *Lost Tribes*, pp. 44–7; Timothy C. F. Stunt, 'Brothers, Richard', *ODNB*/; Deborah Madden, *The Paddington Prophet: Richard Brothers's Journey to Jerusalem* (Manchester: Manchester University Press, 2010).
18 W. H. Oliver, *Prophets and Millennialists: The Uses of Biblical Prophecy in England from the 1790s to the 1840s* (Auckland: Auckland University Press, 1978); Clarke Garrett, *Respectable Folly: Millenarians and the French Revolution in France and England* (Baltimore, MD: Johns Hopkins University Press, 1975); Stuart Semmel, *Napoleon and the British* (New Haven, CT: Yale University Press, 2004), pp. 72–106.
19 Parfitt, *Lost Tribes*, p. 45; Kidd, *Forging of Races*, p. 206.
20 Kidd, *Forging of Races*, p. 206. J. Wilson, 'British Israelism: The Ideological Restraints on Sect Organisation', in B. R. Wilson, ed., *Patterns of Sectarianism: Organisation and Ideology in Social and Religious Movements* (London: Heinemann, 1967).
21 John Wilson, *Our Israelitish Origin; Or, British Christians a Remnant of the True Israelites* (London: Nisbet, 1844), p. 21.
22 Wilson, *Israelitish Origin*, pp. 52–3.
23 Wilson, *Israelitish Origin*, pp. 80–1.
24 Joep Leerssen, 'On the Edge of Europe: Ireland in Search of Oriental roots, 1650–1850,' *Comparative Criticism*, 8 (1986), 94–6; Brian H. Murray, 'The Last of the Milesians: In Search of Ireland's Biblical Past, 1760–1900', in Bradford Anderson and Jonathan Kearney, eds, *Ireland and the Reception of the Bible: Social and Cultural Perspectives* (London: Bloomsbury, 2018), pp. 137–53; Norman Vance, 'Carthaginians and Constitutions: Anglo-Irish Literary Relations, 1780–1820', *Irish Historical Studies*, 22 (1980), 226; Mairéad Carew, *Tara and the Ark of the Covenant: A Search for the Ark of the Covenant by British-Israelites on the Hill of Tara (1899–1902)* (Dublin: Royal Irish Academy, 2003), pp. 23–37.
25 Lennon, *Irish Orientalism*, p. 11.
26 Leerssen, *Remembrance and Imagination*, pp. 72–4.
27 O'Halloran, *Golden Ages*, pp. 23–9; Clare O'Halloran, 'Ownership of the Past: Antiquarian Debate and Ethnic Identity in Scotland and Ireland', in S. J. Connolly, R. A. Houston and R. J. Morris, eds, *Conflict, Identity and Economic Development: Ireland and Scotland, 1600–1939* (Preston: Carnegie, 1995), pp. 141–5.
28 Ollom Fotla means the 'the scholar of Fódla'. Fódla was a Celtic goddess and a poetic personification of Ireland. Ollom Fotla's reign is briefly described in the twelfth-century *Lebor Gábala* and his story is also incorporated into later Gaelic Annals, such as the *Annals of the Four Masters*, c.1632.
29 Charles O'Conor, *Dissertations on the Antient History of Ireland* (Dublin: James Hoey, 1753), pp. 56–7.
30 O'Conor, *Dissertations*, pp. 85–7.
31 O' Conor, *Dissertations*, pp. 99–102.
32 O' Conor, *Dissertations*, pp. 92–5.
33 O' Conor, *Dissertations*, pp. 103–4.
34 O' Halloran, *General History*, pp. 129, 133.
35 O' Halloran, *General History*, p. 128.
36 Roger O'Connor, *Chronicles of Eri; Being the History of the Gaal Sciot Iber: or, the Irish People*, 2 vols (London: Richard Phillips, 1822), II: p. 95.
37 F. R. A. Glover, *England, the Remnant of Judah and the Israel of Ephraim*, 2nd edn (London: Rivington, 1861), p. 21.
38 Glover, *England, the Remnant of Judah*, p. 133
39 Glover, *England, the Remnant of Judah*, pp. 88–9.
40 John Venn and J. A. Venn, eds, *Alumni Cantabrigienses*, 2 vols in 10 (Cambridge: Cambridge University Press, 1922–54), II: part 3, p. 66; Roger T. Stearn, 'Glover, Sir

John Hawley', *ODNB*; 'An English Church at Cologne', *The Colonial Church Chronicle and Missionary Journal* (Jan. 1859), 28–9.
41 Glover, *England, the Remnant of Judah*, pp. 118–19.
42 Parfitt, *Lost Tribes*, pp. 55–6. Barkun, *Religion and the Racist Right*, p. 19.
43 Barkun, *Religion and Racist Right*, p. 19. Totten elaborated on Hine and Glover's ideas in a multi-volume racial history of the world from creation to the present day. C. A. L. Totten, *Our Race: Its Origin and Destiny* (New Haven, CT: Our Race Publishing, 1893).
44 Kidd, *Forging of Races*, p. 209.
45 Kidd, *Forging of Races*, p. 211.
46 'Edward Hine on Ireland', *British Israel and Judah's Prophetic Messenger*, 6 January 1881, pp. 5–6, citing Edward Hine, *Forty-Seven Identifications of the British Nation with the Tribes of Israel* (London: S. W. Partridge, 1874), pp. 84–6.
47 'Hine on Ireland', pp. 5–6.
48 Edward Hine, *The English Nation Identified with the Lost Ten Tribes of Israel: A Lecture* (Warrington: George Powlson, 1872), p. 26.
49 Allen, *Judah's Sceptre*, pp. 287–8. On Allen see Barkun, *Religion and the Racist Right*, p. 21; Kidd, *Forging of Races*, p. 216.
50 'Israel in Ireland', *British Israel and Judah's Prophetic Messenger*, 15 December 1881, pp. 589–90. The cartoon appeared in *Moonshine*, an imitator of *Punch*. The latter had pioneered the racist convention of the simian Irishman. See L. P. Curtis, *Apes and Angels: the Irishman in Victorian Caricature* (Washington, DC: Smithsonian Books, 1971).
51 *British Israel and Judah's Prophetic Messenger*, 6 January 1881, p. 12.
52 Alfred Morris, *Eochaid the Heremhon: Or, The Romance of the Lia Phail*, ed. and compiled by Denis Hanan (London: Robert Banks and Son, 1900), p. 23.
53 Morris, *Eochaid*, p. 23–4.
54 Morris, *Eochaid*, p. 41.
55 Morris, *Eochaid*, p. 162
56 Morris, *Eochaid*, p. 169.
57 Morris, *Eochaid*, p. 184.
58 Carew, *Tara*, p. 2.
59 Carew, *Tara*, p. 28.
60 *The United Irishman*, 5 January 1901, quoted from Carew, *Tara*, p. 79. See also Bender, *Israelites in Erin*, pp. 28–9.
61 Gonne converted to Roman Catholicism in 1903, shortly before her marriage to the nationalist activist and soldier John McBride.
62 Carew, *Tara*, p. 97.
63 Carew, *Tara*, pp. 87–8.
64 W. B. Yeats, George Moore, and Douglas Hyde, 'The Hill of Tara', *The Times*, 27 June 1902, p. 11; Carew, *Tara*, p. 88.
65 Kidd, *Forging of Races*, p. 214.
66 Barkun, *Religion and the Racist Right*, p. 21.
67 Kidd, *Forging of Races*, pp. 216–18; Livingstone, *Adam's Ancestors*, pp. 214–18.
68 See Donald Akenson, *God's Peoples: Covenant and Land in South Africa, Israel, and Ulster* (Ithaca, NY: Cornell University Press, 1992). The current board of management of the British-Israel-World Federation includes the former Northern Ireland Assembly Member Nelson MacCausland, who is also a representative of the Democratic Unionist Party on Northern Ireland's controversial 'Commission on Flags, Identity, Culture and Tradition', accessed 24 June 2018, https://www.fictcommission.org/en/commission.
69 Chris Greyling, 'From Hyper-Imperialist to Super-Afrikaner: The Developments within a White Theology', *Journal of the Study of Religion*, 5 (1992), 47–63. The *Covenant Nations* magazine, published by the British Israel-World-Federation, often includes revisionist and apologetic accounts of apartheid South Africa and Rhodesia. The cover design for the magazine includes the pre-1994 flag of South Africa.

70 'The US Presidential Election Result', *British-Israel-World Federation Newsletter*, January 2017, p. 1; Clare Foges, 'Our turbulent world needs strong walls', *The British-Israel-World Federation*, accessed 28 June 2018, http://www.britishisrael.co.uk/showart.php?id=118.
71 'The Proclamation of Freedom from the EU', *British-Israel-World Federation Newsletter*, January 2017, p. 1
72 Michael A. Clark, 'The Positive Way Forward for the Island of Ireland', *British-Israel World Federation*, accessed 28 June 2018, www.britishisrael.co.uk/showart.php?id=116.

PART II

The Bible in transit and translation

CHAPTER FIVE

The British and Foreign Bible Society's Arabic Bible translations: a study in language politics

Heather J. Sharkey

In 1804, a group of British Protestant men founded the British and Foreign Bible Society, or BFBS, in London. Initially inspired by a girl named Mary Jones, who had allegedly crossed mountains to find a Welsh Bible, they insisted that individuals should be able to acquire Bibles and understand them. 'If for Wales,' they continued by asking, 'why not for the kingdom? Why not for the world?'[1] Eager to expand access to Bibles in Britain and beyond, the BFBS went on to sponsor translations of 'portions' – single books like Genesis – or entire Old and New Testaments. The society appointed translators of various nationalities, Protestant churches and missions, and published and sold the results at cheap prices.[2] The BFBS issued its first translation, a Mohawk edition of the Gospel of John, in 1805; continued with British languages, as in 1819, with an edition in Manx for the Isle of Man; and expanded throughout the British Empire, initially among sailors.[3] By the First World War, the society claimed involvement in all inhabited regions of the world.[4] By 1965, the society listed 872 Bible versions on its roster – though some, by this time, had become relics of dead or dying languages, with Manx, again, an example.[5]

The following pages consider the history of one set of these 872 Bible versions: the editions that the BFBS produced in nine forms of North African Arabic between 1908 and 1965.[6] Unlike the American Bible Society (ABS, founded in New York in 1816), with which it worked closely, the BFBS did not produce its own Bible in literary Arabic. That is, it did not develop its own edition in al-'arabiyya al-fusha, literally, 'the most eloquent Arabic' (sometimes called classical Arabic), for which the Qur'an historically offered the highest example. The BFBS instead published its Arabic editions in 'ammiyya – the 'common' language of the masses – meaning in forms of Arabic that were regionally and socially variable and that closely resembled what people spoke. (Note that English-speaking academics tend to translate ʿammiyya as 'colloquial', and refer to its forms as 'dialects'.)

The choice of the BFBS to translate and publish in colloquial Arabic had political implications. By undermining the primacy of literary Arabic during an age of incipient anti-colonial Arab nationalism, and by fostering a new and more popular culture of Arabic reading that included men and women from modest social classes, these BFBS editions had the potential to shift extant social hierarchies.[7] At the same time, their distribution had the potential to make and remake communities of readers within territories that bore some relation to colonial borders, which Britain (in what is now Egypt and Sudan) and France (in the Maghreb) were imposing during the late nineteenth and early twentieth centuries. The society's Bibles thereby had the potential to inform competing visions of Arab(ic) identity in ways that paralleled, for example, the work of Protestant translators in South India, where variant Bibles empowered different notions of Tamil language and Tamil community.[8]

Looking with dismay at the fragmented, post-Ottoman map of the Middle East and North Africa, certain mid- to late twentieth-century Arab nationalists argued that colloquial Arabic publications, like the BFBS Arabic translations, had been a Christian missionary and British imperial manoeuvre to divide Arabs from each other.[9] Colloquial Arabic print may indeed have made it harder for Arab nationalists to sustain the idea of linguistic unity across, and in spite of, borders. And yet, these colloquial Arabic editions were not simply products of a premeditated imperial scheme to inhibit pan-Arab nationalism, as the most strident postcolonial Arab critics maintained. Other factors also inspired the BFBS in its choices regarding Arabic, including British attitudes towards linguistic egalitarianism as well as rivalries – in the Middle East and other parts of the world – with the American Bible Society. In short, the society's collective experiences influenced what it did in North Africa. The BFBS North African Bibles thereby belonged and contributed to a convoluted history that tied together Britain and America; North Africa and western Asia (or 'the Middle East'); and other parts of the globe. They emerged from a broader British national and imperial history that crossed the New and Old Worlds while jumping across continents as the British Empire was approaching its zenith.

Historical features of the BFBS: setting the stage for the North African Bibles

The BFBS held what the literary scholar Isabel Hofmeyr called 'evangelical theories of language[,] by which texts [have the power] to seize and convert those they encounter'. (Hofmeyr based her analysis on central and southern African translations of John Bunyan's *The Pilgrim's Progress* into languages such as Kongo, Xhosa and Tumbuka.[10]) These ideas about the power of language endowed the BFBS with an egalitarian approach to translation, notwithstanding the British Empire's inclinations towards cultural imperiousness.[11] The society expressed this egalitarianism in 1829 when it published a 'Negro-English' Bible for slaves in Surinam. Although some British critics called this edition a 'degraded travesty of divine revelation', and objected that its language was unworthy of the Bible – in the process implying the racial and social inferiority of its designated readers – the society persisted in promoting it.[12] The society's commitment to the Negro-English Bible of Surinam anticipated its behaviour towards Arabic almost a century later. Indeed, during the early twentieth century, certain prominent British and American missionaries, who were working on the ground in North Africa and who were eager to appeal to Arab elites, expressed deep misgivings about the society's willingness to publish versions for the *hoi polloi*.

Leaders of the BFBS were keenly aware of earlier objections to English-language Bible publishing within England, and this awareness of English history also influenced their philosophy of translation in ways that anticipated the later treatment of Arabic. The society celebrated William Tyndale (c.1494–1536), the Protestant who had dared, between 1525 and 1535, to translate the Bible into English from Hebrew and Greek. For this heresy, emissaries of King Henry VIII captured Tyndale near Brussels and had him strangled and burnt at the stake. Writing in 1926, the society hailed Tyndale as one of the 'greatest of God's Englishmen', the forerunner of Shakespeare, who made it possible for 'every ploughboy [to] know the Scriptures'.[13] Heeding this history, BFBS executives rejected the notion that any language was too low for the Bible.

The society's extreme openness to biblical translatability contrasted sharply with the historic Muslim insistence on the *un*translatability of the Qur'an and its Arabic. During the early to mid-twentieth century, when the BFBS produced its colloquial Arabic translations, many Muslims cited one verse from the Qur'an – 'Indeed, we [meaning God] have sent it down as an *Arabic* Qur'an, so that you may understand' (2:12) – to support the idea that the Qur'an's Arabic and revelation were inseparable. Even Marmaduke ('Muhammad') Pickthall, the British convert to Islam who produced in 1930 the first English translation of the Qur'an by a Muslim, called his text *The Meaning of the Glorious Koran*, because, as he averred, 'The Koran cannot be translated.'[14] Likewise, the Muslim scholar Abdullah Yusuf Ali, a Cambridge University graduate from Lahore, called his influential 1938 English rendition *The Meaning of the Holy Qur'an*, and not simply 'The Holy Qur'an'.[15] Meanwhile, among Muslim and Christian Arabic literati alike, the prestige of the Qur'an as a paragon of Arabic beauty informed a general preference for *al-fusha* (again, highly eloquent or literary) Arabic for learned discourse, especially for religious affairs.[16]

Despite the fact that the BFBS enshrined Britishness in its name, the society was not parochially British in operations on the ground. Its executives were willing to sponsor a multinational array of Protestant missionary translators – Germans, Swedes, and above all, Americans, most of whom were also native English speakers. (Exceptions were Americans who spoke other European languages as their mother tongues, like the prominent missionary Samuel Zwemer (1867–1952) of Michigan, who was a native speaker of Dutch.) The society's pragmatism exercised itself in another way, too: it sometimes calibrated the rigour of its translations to the skills of translators available. Translations therefore varied in quality, as BFBS executives privately acknowledged in letters.

Significant to the BFBS, too, was the society's consciousness of Protestant pluralism – a feature that was written into its constitution and became central to its identity within the increasingly plural religious world of nineteenth-century Britain. To foster Protestant unity amid diversity in the United Kingdom and abroad, the BFBS insisted on printing Bibles 'without note or comment', aiming thereby to avoid doctrinal disputes and to include Anglicans, Methodists, Baptists and others as subscribers, translators and directors.[17] That principle also fitted it well for an empire whose expansion opened up new spaces for a variety of religious groups: notably, Scottish Presbyterians.[18] This non-sectarian principle led the society to reject Bibles – including some early twentieth-century colloquial Arabic Bible texts from Egypt – whose translators insisted on including explanatory notes.[19] In cases where a translator slipped in extra material – as the translator of the 1805 Mohawk edition did when he inserted 'a lively introduction to the gospel in the form of a spirited *Address to the Six Nations* [of the Iroquois]' – the BFBS retracted copies or forced changes before issuing a second edition.[20]

Finally, one other major historical input influenced the BFBS as it considered the Arabic-speaking lands. This was Britain's close yet tense relationship with the United States, its former colony, as well as the society's relationship with its 'sister' organisation and chief rival, the American Bible Society of New York.[21] This tense relationship manifested itself in the society's very first sponsored translation: the Mohawk Gospel of John, prepared by John Norton, also known as Tyonenhokarawen. Born in 1760, Norton had a Scottish mother and grew up in Scotland but claimed that his father was Cherokee from Tennessee. In the 1780s, Norton joined a British regiment in North America.

Through a murky process, he later became adopted as Iroquois, and rose to become an honorary Mohawk chief near Fort Niagara, in what is now southern Ontario.[22] In this capacity, Norton produced his Mohawk translation with a grant from the BFBS to publish two thousand copies. Its target audience consisted of Britain's Native American allies who had lost land in New York during the American War for Independence and who received compensation in 'Upper Canada', i.e. Ontario.[23] The society's Mohawk Gospel of John offered a textual affirmation of political borders newly drawn by war.

Norton exemplified what I would call 'political translation', suggesting the inextricable links between translation, power and posturing. He consciously appealed with his translation not to all Mohawks but rather to the ostensible royalists or loyalists among them. He also modelled the complex, friendly but fraught relationship that prevailed between Britain and the United States, and between the British and American Bible societies, during the nineteenth and early twentieth centuries. Indeed, officials of the ABS in New York praised John Norton's Mohawk Bible translation in their annual report of 1818. Writing six years after the War of 1812, ABS officials in New York agreed with the British society that *'the worship of God is ... as acceptable in Indian* [here meaning Native American] *as in English'* [sic]. Why, the ABS continued, adapting a biblical verse (Colossians 3:11), 'should we imagine that God, with whom "there is neither Jew nor Greek, Barbarian, Scythian, bond nor free", may not in his mercy open the hearts of the red men?'[24] In other words, notwithstanding the Norton translation's specific British Canadian rationale after an Anglo-American war, the ABS applauded his text's potential to evangelise Native Americans in this period when Protestant societies regarded missions to 'Indians' on North American turf as *foreign* missions akin to work among Indians in India and Levantines in greater Syria.[25] The ABS liked his translation so much, in fact, that they printed copies for circulation among Mohawk on the US side of the border.[26] With the Mohawk Bible, we can see glimmerings of the competition and co-operation, which, in the Middle East, later characterised the work of the American and British Bible societies with their nearly identical missions and evangelical attitudes.

The heyday of foreign missions and the challenge of the American Arabic Bible

The landscape of Anglo-American Bible translation changed considerably in the century after Norton's translation appeared, as the Protestant missionary enterprise expanded globally. This process accelerated in the Middle East in 1819, when two American Protestant missionaries or 'pioneers' left Massachusetts for Syria, where their activities and attitudes built upon the precedents of missions to Native Americans and to the people of the Sandwich Islands (now Hawaii).[27] They met and worked alongside Britons who were already active in eastern Mediterranean sites such as Malta, and many more missionaries followed in decades ahead, representing a range of churches and societies and including Americans, Britons, Germans, Swedes and others.[28] Soon, short-term travellers and pilgrims reached the region as well, and produced a stream of information and imagery in the form of letters, travel accounts, paintings and photographs, which stimulated popular fascination for the 'Bible lands' in the English-speaking world.[29] The opening of the Suez Canal in 1869 facilitated this travel and exchange. So did steamships and tourism, as companies like Thomas Cook and later American Express devised luxury trips in Palestine and Egypt.[30] European colonial expansion was decisive: by 1882, Britain had occupied Egypt while France was already controlling large parts of the Maghreb. In practice, both powers offered diplomatic protection to Christians, whether Protestant or Catholic, in areas where Islamic states had historically ruled.

Together, these circumstances favoured the expansion of British and American Protestant missions to the Middle East and North Africa from the 1880s onwards. Missions increased in both scope and ambition, and began to challenge centuries-old Islamic state restrictions on Christian evangelisation by appealing to local Christians as well as to Muslims and Jews. The fact that Islamic states had historically banned conversion from Islam to Christianity, but had not banned shifts between Christian sects, helps to explain why earlier Roman Catholic missions to the eastern Mediterranean region had focused efforts – including eighteenth-century publishing ventures – almost exclusively on 'Eastern' Christians, such as Maronite, Greek Orthodox and Coptic Orthodox Christians.[31] Evangelical Protestant missions in the nineteenth century – including the BFBS and ABS – aspired, by contrast, to universal evangelisation, although given their limited resources they undoubtedly saw the pragmatic benefits of 'awakening' Christian groups across the region. And again, the growing presence of British and French imperial power on the ground allowed Protestant missions to entertain the possibility of circulating Christian texts to Muslims and Jews.

Historians of Protestant missions later described the half-century from 1880 to 1930 as a 'golden age' of foreign missions.[32] This was definitely true in the Middle East, where missionaries were numerous, well-funded and (relative to prior and later conditions) freer in what they could do. This was a golden age for the BFBS, too. It was an era of high productivity in Bible translation, when the society published for languages all over the world, as in 1920, for example, when it issued one Gospel of Mark in 'Mataco' spoken by an 'Indian tribe' on the lower reaches of the Rio Bermejo (an area corresponding with south-eastern Bolivia, western Paraguay, and northern Argentina), and another Gospel of Mark in 'Mackenzie Island Eskimo', for Inuit or Inuvialuit people on the western Arctic coast.[33] Yet, despite these developments, prospects for the BFBS in Arabic were dimmer. By 1918, the society's executives admitted behind closed doors in London that they had no really good translation in literary Arabic to claim as their own. Confident, bold, even over-confident vis-à-vis many parts of the world, executives of the BFBS were less sure-footed in the Middle East, the historic lands of the Bible.

In fact, during the opening years of the twentieth century, the BFBS had what its agents regarded as a rather good literary Arabic Bible available for sale. The only problem was that this Arabic edition was an American, not British, production. This was the so-called Van Dyck Bible, published in 1865 after years of effort led by two American missionaries in Beirut, Eli Smith (1801–57) and Cornelius Van Dyck (1818–95), who worked from the Hebrew and Greek. Van Dyck was brilliant: a Dutch-American New Yorker, he was a professor of pathology at the Syrian Protestant College (renamed the American University of Beirut in 1920), where he wrote Arabic textbooks on medicine, chemistry and astronomy, and favourably considered Darwin's theories of evolution – much to the dismay of mission sponsors in New York.[34] Smith and later Van Dyck worked on their Bible translation with certain leading Christian and Muslim Arab thinkers of the nineteenth-century Arabic cultural renaissance, or *nahda*. One of these *de facto* Arab 'team members' was Butrus al-Bustani (1819–83) – a Maronite Catholic convert to Protestantism – who also produced the first Arabic encyclopedia and influential Arabic translations of works like Daniel Defoe's *Robinson Crusoe*.[35] Another was Nasif al-Yaziji, a Melkite (Greek) Catholic from Lebanon who tried to emulate early Islamic-era classical Arabic in his own writings. A third was Yusuf al-Asir (1815–90), a Muslim graduate of al-Azhar in Cairo who authored works on Arabic grammar and who brought his knowledge of the Qur'an to bear on this Bible's literary style. Yusuf al-Asir's contribution was especially welcome, because the Americans saw the Qur'an as a rival text – just as they saw Islam as a rival religion – and wanted their Bible to be similarly august and magnificent.

The Arabic of the Van Dyck Bible was sufficiently eloquent that when it appeared in 1865, the BFBS quickly abandoned the rough early eighteenth-century translation that it had been selling and began to circulate it.[36] And yet, elegance aside, its Arabic was not especially lucid. The historian David D. Grafton has recently argued that the

Figure 5.1 'Three Bible Women, Assiut Conference', Assiut, Egypt, 1916. The American Presbyterian mission, which sponsored these Bible women, distributed the Van Dyck Arabic Bible – not the colloquial Arabic versions. Anna B. Criswell Papers. Presbyterian Historical Society (Philadelphia)

Van Dyck translation was 'antiquated' from the start, and sometimes used archaic and obscure language to make it seem old instead of modern.[37]

From the 1860s onwards, the British society sold this 'American' Arabic edition but without ever fully agreeing over who had rights to print it. As the twentieth century opened, the BFBS was itching either to control publication of the Van Dyck edition or to own an equivalent. As early as 1918, BFBS executives in London privately discussed their desire to secure a lofty Arabic Bible that would be exclusively their own and not tied to New York. They wanted a *British* Arabic Bible, not an *American* Arabic Bible, and for a while they thought they had found the man to make one. This was the Anglican W. H. T. Gairdner (1873–1928), of the Church Missionary Society in Egypt, who admitted that he thought of the Van Dyck Bible as 'incomprehensible or inelegant' in parts.[38] Even today, historians of Protestantism recognise Gairdner as a chronicler of the World Missionary Conference in Edinburgh in 1910, which propelled the Protestant ecumenical movement and anticipated the World Council of Churches founded in Geneva in 1948.[39] Gairdner loved Arabic in all its forms, considered himself a missionary to Muslims, and relished the challenge of directing a major literary Arabic translation, which he hoped to model on the Qur'an.[40]

Meanwhile, in 1923, officials in the New York and London offices squabbled anew over printing rights within their transatlantic correspondence. Representatives of the BFBS wanted to print the Van Dyck Bible in London, using plates they had obtained many years before; ABS representatives now insisted that only the American missionaries in Beirut and the ABS itself had printing rights.[41] Nowadays we might hear the terms 'copyright infringement' or 'piracy' to describe the printing and selling of unauthorised copies, but the American society did not use these terms. '[I]f the B.F.B.S. did any further printing from its Arabic plates in London', the American society warned simply, then the American society 'would consider itself free to print any of the versions which are exclusively the property of the B.F.B.S.' In fact, the BFBS had not always been generous with its own printing permissions. As far back as 1860, the BFBS had denied the ABS the right to print its Bulgarian Bible (which a team of American missionaries and a leading Bulgarian intellectual had produced with BFBS funding). A report drafted in New York in 1964 shows that the memory of this denial persisted and informed the American society's reluctance to cede rights to the Van Dyck Arabic edition during the late nineteenth and early twentieth centuries.[42] This report showed the capacity of the American and British Bible societies to hold multi-generational grudges, and to connect, through institutional memories, widely disparate translations such as the BFBS Bulgarian edition and the ABS Arabic Van Dyck.

Alas, W. H. T. Gairdner, who had agreed to translate the Bible into a new and very classical Arabic, died suddenly in 1928, within ten years of starting the project, without making much progress. His death made it clear that the British society would be 'stuck' with the American Van Dyck edition.

The Society's vernacular ('ammiyya) North African Bibles

The Anglo-American rivalry of the London and New York executives did not extend to British and American missionaries on the ground. Missionaries who worked *in situ* shared common challenges of evangelising in Islamic societies, encountering Muslims who identified their presence with imperial aggression, and competing with Catholic missionaries with whom, in this pre-Vatican II period, they were often not on speaking terms. Beleaguered, English-speaking and Protestant together, Americans and Britons co-operated in the Middle East. Where they differed in their opinions about Arabic Bible translations, their differences cut across national lines and reflected the literacy thresholds of their target audiences.

By the 1920s, for Arabic speakers who had minimal literacy, the BFBS already had some Arabic Bible portions that no other society was selling or claiming. These were what they called 'vernacular' or what Arabic scholars would now call 'colloquial' translations, produced as single portions in regionally and socially variant forms of Arabic. The British society was willing to support colloquial Arabic editions because its executives approved, in principle, of making Scriptures comprehensible to the masses. Executives in London were also glad to produce editions that the ABS could not claim.

The BFBS sponsored colloquial versions for a third reason, too: its leaders listened to certain British and American missionaries (Anglicans, Methodists and others among them) who expressed grave doubts about what the ABS Van Dyck Arabic Bible was and what it could do. These sceptics felt that the Van Dyck translation was *too* literary, too centred on intellectual elites – perhaps too koranic in grandeur – to be useful where literacy rates were so low. In Egypt in 1898, for example, only an estimated 8 per cent of men, and one-fifth of 1 per cent of women, knew how to read and write.[43] In places like Morocco and Sudan the rates were much lower. Without Bibles in easy language that echoed what people spoke, missionaries feared that they could not convey biblical learning to the vast majority of Arabic-speaking men and women, and especially peasants and workers. BFBS executives found these arguments persuasive, and agreed, from 1908, to sponsor colloquial Bible portions which it printed and sold very cheaply. The fact that the British society was active in all of North Africa as far west as Morocco and deep into the Sahara, and that it was also active throughout Sudan as far south as its borders with Uganda and the Belgian Congo and to the south-east in Ethiopia, gave the BFBS an edge in appealing to North African readers. By contrast, in North Africa, the ABS limited itself mainly to Cairo, and sought niches elsewhere in the Middle East – notably in greater Syria, Turkey and Iran, where the US government, though still a minor regional power in this pre-Second World War period, was strengthening its foothold.

Regarding those who supported the colloquial North African Arabic Bibles of the BFBS, two trends stand out. First, missionaries (whether British or American) who worked among poor people generally welcomed colloquial versions, while those who worked among highly educated people undoubtedly favoured the Van Dyck edition. These Bible translations had a class dimension, with the Van Dyck imprints of the American society being far more elitist. Second, although Protestant missionaries to the Middle East mostly succeeded in attracting Middle Eastern Christians, the colloquial Arabic Scriptures of the BFBS targeted Muslims and Jews almost exclusively. To be sure, there were no indigenous Christian communities west of Egypt, anyway. But in Egypt, where Coptic Christians counted for perhaps a tenth of the population and had access to Protestant and Catholic mission schools, Christians had higher literacy rates than Muslims, according to early twentieth-century Egyptian government census data, and favoured the Van Dyck translation. For these reasons, again, Protestant missionaries and the BFBS geared colloquial versions to non-Christians, and that meant to Muslims and Jews.[44]

The British society's two earliest North African Arabic translations were Gospels of Luke printed in 1908. One was based on an initial translation by a Swedish missionary, which an American then revised with 'native assistance', for Muslims who lived around Constantine, in north-east Algeria. The other was produced by a British missionary from Belfast in Northern Ireland who worked among poor Muslim town-dwellers in the Egyptian Delta. The BFBS went on to publish many more portions in Egyptian and Algerian Arabic, and also printed translations in Moroccan, Tunisian and Sudanese Arabic. Their last colloquial editions were a full Moroccan Arabic Bible, and a 'union' Algerian and Tunisian Arabic New Testament, completed in the 1950s but only published in 1963 and 1965, respectively. Meanwhile, two editions published in Tunisia in 1910 and 1922 appeared in Hebrew characters, in what linguists call 'Judaeo-Arabic', and thus were intended for use by British missions to Jews, whose spoken Arabic included many word borrowings from Hebrew, Aramaic and Berber. Other colloquial versions – such as the ones produced in Khartoum, Sudan – were translated by two British women who had limited linguistic expertise and – judging from other CMS ventures in Sudan – were working on a shoestring budget.[45] Their Sudanese translations apparently reflected the Arabic of the poor Muslim females among whom they worked. Indeed, some educated Sudanese men reportedly mocked these texts for conveying a 'women's Arabic' of the kitchen![46] Clearly, Arabic translations could capture differences in spoken language according to region, class, religion and even gender – suggesting that possibilities for translation and for the identification of languages were theoretically bounded only by numbers of speakers.

While the BFBS's colloquial editions had some vocal missionary supporters, the most prominent and most highly educated missionaries regarded them as rather ridiculous. This was the case, for example, with Samuel Zwemer, of the Reformed Church of America, who considered himself a missionary to Muslims and who was still attracting ardent retrospective admirers (especially among American evangelical Christians) and bitter opponents (especially among Egyptian Islamists) as the twenty-first century opened.[47] Writing confidentially in 1917 to an executive from the BFBS, Zwemer expressed deep embarrassment with regard to these colloquial Bible editions. Zwemer described Muslim sheikhs who collapsed into laughter upon hearing the Christian Scriptures translated into low-class Arabic: one verse about Mary came out sounding scandalous. Zwemer warned that the colloquial Scriptures made Christianity look ridiculous to Muslims because their Arabic contained the 'vulgarisms of the slums'.[48]

Faced with such criticism, advocates of the colloquial Arabic versions insisted on their value. Consider the American Methodist missionary and translator in Algeria, Percy Smith, who published articles on the subject in a prominent missionary journal in 1914, 1917 and 1919. 'What is the living language of the people?', the Reverend Smith asked. 'Is it the Literary Arabic, practically the same as that of a thousand years ago, or is it the Common Speech used by everyone in daily intercourse?' Common speech, Smith concluded, was the living Arabic. While recognising that Muslims regarded the beautiful Arabic of the Qur'an as 'its permanent attesting miracle', Smith observed that it would be 'a bold step, but ... a necessary one, [to ... follow] the Christian tradition of publishing the Word of God in the simple language of the people'.[49] Again, for mixed reasons, BFBS executives in London agreed. Their print runs were very small, however – in some cases just a couple of thousand volumes – and unlike the Van Dyck Arabic Bible, they seldom sold from the Bible society's depots in major cities. To the extent that the colloquial editions circulated, it appears that the individual missionaries who supported them promoted them on the ground.

One last point about the BFBS editions is worth making. Surviving records of the BFBS say little to nothing about the local language experts who assisted with colloquial Arabic translations. Their absence recalls Jeffrey Cox's observation, in his history of British missions abroad, that 'The overwhelming majority of non-western participants in the missionary enterprise are nameless ... in the missionary narratives of white, male, clerical heroism.'[50] The historian can sense the presence of local language experts in the BFBS translations via passing references to 'native helpers' without being able to 'see' or 'hear' these individuals in the archives directly. Certainly the colloquial translations had no Arab contributors like the formidable encyclopedist, Butrus al-Bustani, who worked on the Van Dyck edition.

Conclusion: the BFBS and the making of Arab communities

The BFBS published colloquial Arabic Bible translations until the 1960s. But then many factors combined to end these efforts. For a start, decolonisation changed the political circumstances of Bible publishing and forced missions to consolidate and scale down. Increasing Arabic literacy rates made colloquial print less appealing to those who could read something more eloquent. Among Muslims, the rise of secular Arab nationalism, together with tensions surrounding the Arab–Israeli conflict, boosted pan-Arabism, making Modern Standard Arabic (a somewhat simplified but still very literary form) a *sine qua non* for cultural unity.[51] Among Jews from the Maghrib, meanwhile, the rise of French-language culture through schools, and then the near-total emigration of North African Jewish communities – also amid the tensions of the Arab–Israeli conflict – pushed the distinctly Jewish variants of spoken Arabic into extinction.[52] In the Bible Society's book vaults deep within Cambridge University Library, fragile copies of the Judaeo-Arabic translations from Tunisia now sit on the shelves as relics of a dead language. They serve as reminders of the fragility of language and of the capacity of print culture's architects to make, break, or reconfigure communities of readers.

Which communities did the BFBS either recognise or try to contrive by means of its Arabic editions? By publishing Arabic Bible portions which they called, for example, 'Sudanese' and 'Algerian' – even if these particular versions were actually based on speech from around Khartoum and Constantine, respectively – the BFBS proposed or tried to promote visions of language on the scale of the colony and the postcolonial nation state. This point was true even for its Judaeo-Arabic versions developed in Tunis, which conceived of the language of the local Jews as broadly 'Tunisian'. A notable exception occurred with its last colloquial Arabic edition – the 'union' Algerian and Tunisian New Testament of 1965 – which suggested the British society's tendency to imagine these two French post-colonies as a unit.

Mid- to late twentieth-century Arab nationalists denounced the Bible society's territorially focused colloquial Arabic printing as part of a larger British imperial scheme – pursued by Christian missionaries as well as by merchants, military strategists and others – to divide Arab peoples into smaller bounded lands in order to weaken, control or reconfigure them. The most influential denunciation appeared in 1953, in a book by two academics from Beirut and Damascus named Mustafa Khalidi and ʿUmar Farrukh. Their account of 'Evangelism and Imperialism in the Arab Countries' influenced a generation of Arab thinkers who came from both secular leftist and conservative Islamist backgrounds.[53] Recalling Benedict Anderson's notion that print cultures stimulate nationalism in the form of 'imagined communities', the BFBS's insistence on a plurality of Arabics may indeed have made Arabic speakers more aware of regional barriers to communication and therefore communion across the region, while fortifying conceptions of communities built within narrower state borders, among Egyptians, Algerians and the like.[54]

And yet, as we have seen above, this divisive impact may not have been consciously intended, suggesting that colloquial print was not the imperial ploy that Arab nationalists imagined it to be. Recalling ideas that the historian Bernard Porter advanced in his 2004 book, *The Absent-Minded Imperialists*, about Britain and its domestic experience of empire, I suggest that if the society's Arabic Bibles had some imperialistic dimensions, then their imperialism was more absentminded or inadvertent, and less intentional or controlled, than Arab nationalist critics believed.[55] That is because, in North Africa as elsewhere, the society's translators had different agendas; variable levels of language expertise; constraints of funding, time and opportunity; and different target audiences. The colloquial Arabic Bibles were the outcome of these constraints, set against the context of an evangelical philosophy that valued vernacular Scriptures and regarded translations as valid and indeed essential.

In sum, the colloquial North African Arabic Bibles of BFBS came out of a distinctly British and Anglo-American context, and reflected global encounters and historical experiences with a variety of peoples and languages. The society aimed to promote broadly comprehensible 'vernacular' or 'colloquial' Bibles in Arabic-speaking societies where longstanding assumptions about Islamic history, associated with the Qur'an, had shaped very different attitudes towards Arabic and its culture. At the same time, the choices that the British society made vis-à-vis Arabic reflected its ongoing rivalry with its American counterpart. What we have here, therefore, is a tale of translation that swept across Britain, North America, and parts of Asia, Africa, and the wider world; linked regions, colonies, nations and empires; and included Christian, Muslim, Jewish and other people – perhaps believers as well as doubters and cynics among them – within a single historical frame. Thus viewed, the history of places like Ontario and Tunisia; of Bulgaria, Beirut and the western Arctic; and of South America's Rio Bermejo valley and Egypt, begin to look like pieces of a common puzzle.

Notes

1 William Canton, *The Story of the Bible Society* (London: John Murray, 1904), p. 5.
2 Leslie Howsam, *Cheap Bibles: Nineteenth-Century Publishing and the British and Foreign Bible Society* (Cambridge: Cambridge University Press, 1991); Stephen Batalden, Kathleen Cann and John Dean, eds, *Sowing the Word: The Cultural Impact of the British and Foreign Bible Society, 1804–2004* (Sheffield: Sheffield Phoenix Press, 2004). On the society in the early twenty-first century, see Matthew Engelke,

THE BFBS'S ARABIC BIBLE TRANSLATIONS

God's Agents: Biblical Publicity in Contemporary England (Berkeley, CA: University of California Press, 2013).

3 Roald Kverndal, 'Sowing by Sea: Empowering Seafarers with the Gospel', in Batalden, Cann and Dean, eds, *Sowing the Word*, pp. 327–43.

4 James Moulton Roe, *A History of the British and Foreign Bible Society, 1905–1954* (London: British and Foreign Bible Society, 1965), p. 29.

5 *The Gospel in Many Tongues: Specimens of 872 Languages in Which the British and Foreign Bible Society Has Circulated Some Portion of the Bible* (London: British and Foreign Bible Society, 1965).

6 There was also a tenth North African version, published by the BFBS, which was distinct not in its language (which was classical Arabic), but in its typography. This was the society's 1903 Gospel of Luke, intended for Tunisia but also circulated in Nigeria, which was 'hand-copied and photographically reproduced in the Maghribi style of Arabic calligraphy, without verse breaks or punctuation, for Muslim readers who had trouble deciphering Arabic print'. Heather J. Sharkey, 'The Gospel in Arabic Tongues: British Bible Distribution, Evangelical Mission, and Language Politics in North Africa', in Sharkey, ed., *Cultural Conversions: Unexpected Consequences of Christian Missionary Encounters in the Middle East, Africa, and South Asia* (Syracuse, NY: Syracuse University Press, 2013), pp. 203–21, especially p. 204.

7 In *Ordinary Egyptians: Creating the Modern Nation through Popular Culture* (Stanford, CA: Stanford University Press, 2011), the author Ziad Fahmy aimed 'to document the influence of a developing colloquial Egyptian mass culture as a vehicle and forum through which ... critiques of colonial and elite authority took place' (pp. 1–2). Yet, he did not mention the Christian missionaries' promotion of colloquial Arabic – which may hint at how enduringly unpopular Christian missionaries are in certain academic circles. On the spread of literary Arabic print culture, see Ami Ayalon, *The Arabic Print Revolution: Culture Production and Mass Readership* (Cambridge: Cambridge University Press, 2016).

8 Hephzibah Israel, *Religious Transactions in Colonial South India: Language, Translation, and the Making of a Protestant Identity* (New York: Palgrave Macmillan, 2011).

9 Heather J. Sharkey, 'Christian Missionaries and Colloquial Arabic Printing', *Journal of Semitic Studies*, Supplement 15: Philip Sadgrove, ed., *History of Printing and Publishing in the Languages and Countries of the Middle East* (Oxford: Oxford University Press, 2004), pp. 131–49; Heather J. Sharkey, 'Arabic Antimissionary Treatises: Muslim Responses to Christian Evangelism in the Modern Middle East', *International Bulletin of Missionary Research*, 28 (2004), 112–18. Besides works profiled in the latter essay, there was one important book about the Arabic language, written by an (Egyptian) Arab nationalist intellectual, which was not an anti-missionary tract but which hotly criticised the missionaries' colloquial ventures: Nafusa Zakariyya Sa'id, *Tarikh al-da'wa ila al-'ammiyya wa-atharuha fi Misr* ['The History of the Mission for Colloquial Arabic and Its Influences in Egypt'] (Cairo: Dar al-Ma'arif, 1980). See also John Eisele, 'Representations of Arabic in Egypt, 1940–1990', *Arab Studies Journal*, 6 (Fall 2000/Spring 2001), 47–60, esp. 53–5.

10 Isabel Hofmeyr, *The Portable Bunyan: A Transnational History of the Pilgrim's Progress* (Princeton, NJ: Princeton University Press, 2004), pp. 13–14.

11 Heather J. Sharkey, 'The Case of Henry Athanassian, an Armenian in the Suez Canal Zone: Questioning Assumptions about Missions and Missionaries', in Judith Becker, ed., *European Missions in Contact Zones: Transformation through Interaction in a (Post-)Colonial World* (Göttingen: Vandenhoeck and Ruprecht, 2015), pp. 267–85.

12 Canton, *Story of the Bible Society*, p. 202.

13 *The Hundred and Twenty-First Report of the British and Foreign Bible Society for the Year Ending March MCMXXV* (London: The Bible House, 1925), p. 1; David Daniell, *William Tyndale: A Biography* (New Haven, CT: Yale University Press, 1994).

14 Ziad Almarsafy, *The Enlightenment Qur'an: The Politics of Translation and the Construction of Islam* (Oxford: Oneworld, 2009), p. 184.

15. Khaleel Mohammed, 'Assessing English Translations of the Qur'an', *Middle East Quarterly*, 12 (2005), 58–71. The same applies to the translation of Muhammad Asad (the Austrian convert from Judaism formerly known as Leopold Weiss), who published his version as *The Message of the Qur'an* in 1980.
16. Cambridge University Library, Bible Society Archives (henceforth BSA), BSA/E3/3/18: Arabic Translation Papers, 1949–57.
17. Roger Steer, 'Without Note or Comment: Yesterday, Today, and Tomorrow', in Batalden, Cann and Dean, eds, *Sowing the Word*, pp. 63–80.
18. T. M. Devine, *To the Ends of the Earth: Scotland's Global Diaspora, 1750–2010* (Washington, DC: Smithsonian Books, 2011), especially 'The Missionary Dynamic', pp. 188–208; and Hilary M. Carey, ed., *Empires of Religion* (London: Palgrave Macmillan, 2008).
19. The society rejected the colloquial Arabic translations of Sir William Willcocks, a hydraulics engineer in Egypt and architect of the first Aswan Dam, who printed editions at his own expense. These translations included, for example, a joint Gospels of Matthew and Mark, published in Cairo in 1924, in which Willcocks added a preface claiming that 'The Egyptian language is basically the same language that Christ spoke.' *al-Arba' Bashayir bil-lugha a-misriyya, al-qism al-awlani: Bashayir Matta wa-Murqus*, trans. Sir William Willcocks (Cairo: Nile Mission Press, 1924), p. 6.
20. Steer, 'Without Note or Comment', p. 68.
21. John Fea, *The Bible Cause: A History of the American Bible Society* (Oxford: Oxford University Press, 2016).
22. Carl Benn, 'Missed Opportunities and the Problem of Mohawk Chief John Norton's Cherokee Ancestry', *Ethnohistory*, 59 (2012), 261–91, esp. 263–4.
23. Joyce Banks, 'The BFBS and Native Language Literature in Nineteenth-Century Canada', in Batalden, Cann and Dean, eds, *Sowing the Word*, pp. 316–26, esp. p. 317.
24. American Bible Society, Second Annual Report, cited in *Evangelical Recorder*, 4 July 1818, p. 257.
25. William R. Hutchison, *Errand to the World: American Protestant Thought and Foreign Missions* (Chicago, IL: University of Chicago Press, 1987), p. 46.
26. John Norton, trans., *Tsinihorighhoten Ne Saint John/The Gospel According to Saint John (in the Mohawk Language)* (New York: D. Fanshaw for the American Bible Society, 1818).
27. An early work that used the pioneer was David H. Finnie, *Pioneers East: The Early American Experience in the Middle East* (Cambridge, MA: Harvard University Press, 1967). On the relevance of Native American and Hawaiian precedents for the Middle East, see Ussama Makdisi, *Artillery of Heaven: American Missionaries and the Failed Conversion of the Middle East* (Ithaca, NY: Cornell University Press, 2008).
28. Gareth Atkins, 'William Jowett's *Christian Researches*: British Protestants and Religious Plurality in the Mediterranean, Syria and the Holy Land, 1815–30', in Charlotte Methuen, Andrew Spicer and John Wolffe, eds, *Christians and Religious Plurality, Studies in Church History*, 51 (2015), 216–31.
29. E.g. Yeshayahu Nir, *The Bible and the Image: The History of Photography in the Holy Land, 1839–1899* (Philadelphia: University of Pennsylvania Press, 1985).
30. F. Robert Hunter, 'Tourism and Empire: The Thomas Cook & Son Enterprise on the Nile, 1868–1914', *Middle Eastern Studies*, 40 (2004), 28–54; *Egypt and the Holy Land: Independent and Conducted Tours, Season 1923–4* (London: American Express Travel Department, 1923).
31. Bernard Heyberger, 'Livres et pratique de la lecture chez les chrétiens (Syrie, Liban), XVIIe – XVIIIe siècles', *Revue des Mondes Musulmans et de la Méditerranée*, 87–8 (1999), 209–23; Chantal Verdeil, ed., *Missions chrétiennes en terre d'islam (XVIIe–XXe siècles)* (Turnhout, Belgium: Brepols, 2013).
32. Hutchison, *Errand to the World*.
33. *The Hundred and Sixteenth Report of the British and Foreign Bible Society for the Year Ending March MCMXX* (London: The Bible House, 1920), p. 2.

34 Betty S. Anderson, *The American University of Beirut: Arab Nationalism and Liberal Education* (Austin, TX: University of Texas Press, 2011); Marwa Elshakry, *Reading Darwin in Arabic, 1860–1950* (Chicago: University of Chicago Press, 2013).
35 Rana Issa, 'Al-Bustānī, Buṭrus bin Sulaymān Hassan 'Ifrām', *Oxford Islamic Studies Online*, accessed 9 May 2019, http://www.oxfordislamicstudies.com/article/opr/t343/e0275.
36 John Alexander Thompson, *The Major Arabic Bibles* (New York: American Bible Society, 1956); Lamin Sanneh, 'Bible Translation, Culture, and Religion', in Lamin Sanneh and Michael J. McClymond, eds, *The Wiley-Blackwell Companion to World Christianity* (Chichester: Wiley Blackwell, 2016), pp. 265–81.
37 David D. Grafton, *The Contested Origins of the 1865 Arabic Bible: Contributions to the Nineteenth-Century Nahda* (Leiden: Brill, 2015).
38 BSA/E3/3/16/1: Translation Dept, Correspondence, Arabic (All Varieties March 1909–December 1919): Edit. Supt [Kilgour] to C. T. Hooper, 29 October 1918; C. T. Hooper to Revd R. Kilgour, Port Said, 22 April 1918.
39 Brian Stanley, ed., *The World Missionary Conference, Edinburgh 1910* (Grand Rapids, MI: Eerdmans, 2009).
40 Although he loved high literary Arabic (*al-fusha*), Gairdner was an expert on colloquial Arabic, too, and wrote the first English textbook on the subject: W. H. T. Gairdner, *Egyptian Colloquial Arabic: A Conversation Grammar*, 2nd edn (London: Oxford University Press, 1926). His works about Islam included *The Reproach of Islam* (Edinburgh: Foreign Missionary Committee of the Church of Scotland, 1911).
41 Rana Issa, of the American University of Beirut, told me that she saw papers in the Bible Society Archives at Cambridge suggesting that Cornelius Van Dyck himself had given printing plates to the BFBS.
42 American Bible Society (New York), Margaret T. Hills, A.B.S. Historical Essay #16, Part III-F, 'Text and Translation: F – Languages of the Near East, 1831–1860', typescript, 1964. On this Bulgarian Bible, which inspired important strands of Bulgarian nationalism, see Barbara Reeves-Ellington, 'Petko Slaveykov, the Protestant Press, and the Gendered Language of Moral Reform in Bulgarian Nationalism', in Mehmet Ali Doğan and Heather J. Sharkey, eds, *American Missionaries and the Middle East: Foundational Encounters* (Salt Lake City, UT: University of Utah Press, 2011), pp. 211–36.
43 Beth Baron, *Egypt as a Woman: Nationalism, Gender, and Politics* (Berkeley: University of California Press, 2005), p. 6.
44 Heather J. Sharkey, *American Evangelicals in Egypt: Missionary Encounters in an Age of Empire* (Princeton, NJ: Princeton University Press, 2008); Sharkey, 'American Missionaries, the Arabic Bible, and Coptic Reform in Late Nineteenth-Century Egypt', in Doğan and Sharkey, eds, *American Missionaries in the Modern Middle East*, pp. 237–59; and Sharkey, 'The Gospel in Arabic Tongues'.
45 Heather J. Sharkey, 'Christians among Muslims: The Church Missionary Society in the Northern Sudan', *Journal of African History*, 43 (2002), 51–75.
46 Sharkey, 'The Gospel in Arabic Tongues'; and 'Sudanese Arabic Bibles and the Politics of Translation', *The Bible Translator*, Technical Papers, 62 (2011), 37–45.
47 Alan Neely, 'Samuel Marinus Zwemer', in Gerald H. Anderson, ed., *Biographical Dictionary of Christian Missions* (New York: Macmillan Reference USA, 1998), p. 763; and Sharkey, 'Arabic Antimissionary Treatises'. Among Zwemer's books, for example, is the polemic called *The Disintegration of Islam* (New York: Fleming H. Revell Co., 1916).
48 Zwemer to Hooper, Cairo, 11 December 1917, in BSA/E3/3/16/1: Translation Dept, Correspondence, Arabic (All Varieties).
49 Percy Smith made these claims in three articles: 'A Plea for the Use of Versions of Scripture and of Other Literature in the Vulgar Arabic', *Moslem World*, 4 (1914), 52–63; 'A Plea for Literature in Vernacular Arabic', *Moslem World*, 7 (1917), 333–42; and 'Another Plea for Literature in Vernacular Arabic', *Moslem World*, 9 (1919), 351–62.
50 Jeffrey Cox, *The British Missionary Enterprise since 1700* (New York: Routledge, 2008), p. 16.

51 Yasir Suleiman, *The Arabic Language and National Identity: A Study in Ideology* (Washington, DC: Georgetown University Press, 2003). This was also an argument of Sa'id, *Tarikh al-da'wa ila al-'ammiyya wa-atharuha fi Misr*.
52 Moshe Bar-Asher, *La composante hebraïque du judéo-arabe algérien (communautés de Tlemcen et Aïn-Témouchent)* (Jerusalem: Hebrew University, 1992): see e.g. pp. 13–14; and Keith Walters, 'Education for Jewish Girls in Late Nineteenth- and Early Twentieth-Century Tunis and the Spread of French in Tunisia', in Emily Benichou Gottreich and Daniel J. Schroeter, eds, *Jewish Culture and Society in North Africa* (Bloomington: Indiana University Press, 2011), pp. 257–81.
53 Mustafa Khalidi and 'Umar Farrukh, *al-Tabshir wa'l-isti'mar fi al-bilad al-'arabiyya*, 2nd edn (Beirut, n.p., 1957).
54 Benedict Anderson, *Imagined Communities: Reflections on the Origin and Spread of Nationalism*, rev. 2nd edn (London: Verso, 1991).
55 Bernard Porter, *The Absent-Minded Imperialists: Empire, Society, and Culture in Britain* (Oxford: Oxford University Press, 2004).

CHAPTER SIX

Empire and nation in the politics of the Russian Bible

Stephen K. Batalden

The linkage of biblical translation with the development of the nation and the standardisation of spoken languages is not a new theme in scholarly studies of modern nationalism.[1] By extension, the issue of modern biblical translation also became drawn into the politics of empire. Whether explicitly stated or not, modern biblical translation often posed a challenge to imperial institutions, testing the limits of a national agenda, and illuminating the relationship between empire and nation. I argue that biblical translation was particularly politicised in the case of the Russian Empire because of the nature of the empire, which, as Robert Crews describes it, was a 'confessional state' wherein issues of religion, empire and political authority became tightly intertwined.[2] Indeed, the issue of the modern Russian Bible rose to the highest level of imperial and court politics repeatedly in the nineteenth century.[3] As this chapter documents, conflicts over the Russian Bible have continued in varied form, illuminating the politics of 'empire and nation' in modern Eurasia to the present.

In exploring this cultural and political divide over biblical translation, I explore four touchstone moments when the politics of empire and nation came to be sharply represented in conflicts over biblical translation – (1) the conflict in the early nineteenth century over the imperially sanctioned Russian Bible Society; (2) the internal debate of the 1850s in the Holy Synod over the reopening of modern Russian biblical translation; (3) the conflicts linking the Jewish question with biblical translation in the last half of the nineteenth century; and, very briefly, (4) the contemporary issue of biblical translation in the context of the current international conflict over Ukraine. In each instance, it seems to me, the politics of modern biblical translation help to frame the evolving relationship between 'empire and nation' in modern Eurasia.

In this discussion of empire and nation, the work of Robert Crews takes on special significance because he has helped to sharpen for us the peculiar nature of 'empire' in its Russian context. The Russian Empire was not just any multinational empire addressing problems of diversity, but rather it was an empire functioning as a confessional state in which both the dominant Orthodox state religion and non-Christian religions, including Islam, came to view the tsarist administration as an ally in advancing their own religious authority. Thus, Muslims, like their Christian and Jewish counterparts, turned to state authority as an arbiter of religio-political authority. The state, in turn, sought to use religion to govern the Empire, drawing to itself religious and confessional clients who not infrequently turned to state authority, including tsarist police and the courts, to further their own religious aims. Crews even suggests that this 'confessionalisation' of the Empire's peoples effectively permitted the Empire to rule with less violence and greater consensus than previously recognised. Such a harmonisation of the imperial confessional state with diverse religious and confessional elites effectively challenges popularised views of timeless conflict between Christianity and Islam, Europe and the East, in a 'clash of civilisations'.[4]

In this confessional state, the idea of the secular nation in the nineteenth century was not only narrowly confined to a small intelligentsia, but it also carried a potential threat to both imperial institutions and religious/confessional elites alike. For religious and confessional elites were also the beneficiaries of imperial patronage. Although they were not monolithic, such elite arbiters of Russian religious culture, including the Holy Synod and prominent members of the episcopate, remained largely wedded to the confessional state. The church's operative *diglossia* created a sharp and growing divide between a stylised and occasionally obscure Slavonic language of religious and liturgical texts, on the one hand, and a spoken and literary Russian more commonly understood by Russian laypeople, on the other.

The Russian Bible Society and the politics of the Russian Bible

It is in the context of that divide that the idea of a Russian Bible was introduced into the Russian Empire in the second decade of the nineteenth century at a time of international crisis following the 1812 Napoleonic invasion of Russia. The timing was critical not only because it corresponded to a wartime period when the enigmatic Emperor Alexander I was drawn to religious mysticism and new forms of religious piety, including Bible reading, but also because it followed the launch in 1804 of the British and Foreign Bible Society (BFBS), whose agents entered the Russian Empire in 1812 in connection with their wider travels in Scandinavia and Russian Finland. The founding of the Russian Bible Society (Rossiiskoe bibleiskoe obshchestvo, RBS) by imperial edict in December 1812 was a landmark event in modern Russian religious culture.

Having garnered the patronage of the Emperor and having limited their publications to the Slavonic Bible and to translations into non-Russian languages of the Empire, the RBS initially posed no threat to the established confessional state. By 1816, however, spurred on by the support of its interconfessional board of directors, the RBS secured authorisation from Emperor Alexander I to launch the translation and publication of the Bible in modern Russian. In the eight years that followed, the Russian Bible Society translated and published numerous editions of the Russian New Testament, in whole or in part. It also issued the first complete Russian translation of the Psalter, and prepared in unbound printed sheets a full translation of the first eight books of the Old Testament from the Hebrew Masoretic text. So efficient was its commercial RBS Press, which had imported the latest stereotype printing technology from England, that by 1824 the RBS had issued close to one million copies of Scripture in more than two dozen languages.

Despite more than 250 affiliated branch RBS chapters aiding distribution in cities across the Empire, the ambitious publishing enterprise of the RBS even outstripped the demand of a reading public. In the early 1820s the enterprising BFBS representatives, not wanting to curtail the massive printing effort, launched their own educational and prison-reform efforts along the lines pioneered by the Quaker Joseph Lancaster to generate a potentially expanded audience for its booming Scripture business. If demand was flagging, then the answer of the RBS founders was not to slow production, but stoke demand.

Despite the successes of its stereotype printing business, mounting opposition to the Russian Bible Society from the Holy Synod (the administrative arm of the Russian Orthodox Church), from leading conservative publicists and from senior government officials led to the effective closure of the RBS by the end of 1824. In 1826, the newly crowned Emperor Nicholas I formally declared the closure of the RBS, forbidding publication of Scripture in the Russian language. The closure left all the issues attending modern biblical translation in Russia unresolved: Who had the authority to translate and publish Scripture? Which base texts – Greek, Hebrew or Slavonic – were to be considered authoritative? What was the appropriate Russian language for the translation of sacred texts? At the end of the first quarter of the nineteenth century, the only answer to those questions was the official imperial rescript that concluded that the experiment of the Russian Bible Society was not to serve as a precedent for the future.

What was it that made modern Russian translation of Scripture so dangerous, and why was this first major experiment in Russian biblical translation aborted? Many reasons have been given for the RBS closure – scandals involving Catholic and other sectarian, non-Orthodox supporters of the Society, rising opposition to mystical and pietist movements entering Russia from the West that were perceived to be aligned with the Bible Society movement, and the official government crackdown known as the 'Arakcheevshchina' (after Russia's War Minister Aleksei Arakcheev), which closed freemasonic societies and sought to limit other incipient civil-society initiatives following the Napoleonic War and the Congress of Vienna.

Yet, at its core, there was a logic behind the closure of the Russian Bible Society that has too often been overlooked in the search for immediate villains. Quite simply, the egalitarian, interconfessional and entrepreneurial Bible Society movement and its modern language texts were at odds with the Russian Empire as a confessional state. In the confessional state, the emperor, his appointed senators and ministerial officials, and of course, the Holy Synod oversaw and arbitrated issues involving Russian religious culture. The state was both the protector and ultimate arbiter of religious and confessional practice – not the marketplace or the 'public' square, as enterprising Bible Society advocates may have sought. In the politics of empire and nation, the advocates of the Russian Bible were ultimately overwhelmed by their own success, not realising the danger that market-oriented Russian Bible production posed to the harmonious and hegemonial operation of the confessional state. The imperial state of Alexander I and Nicholas I was, in the end, incompatible with an empire of nations empowered by their own autonomous languages and cultures.

The politics of the Russian Synodal Translation

While there were several very interesting clandestine efforts to continue the translation work piloted by the Russian Bible Society in the thirty years following the Society's closure, it was not until the latter half of the 1850s and the reign of the 'Tsar Reformer' Alexander II that the issues of empire and nation earlier opened in the Bible Society era resurfaced more or less openly. It was at the time of the coronation of Alexander II that Russia's most notable prelate of the nineteenth century, Moscow Metropolitan (i.e. presiding archbishop) Filaret (born Vasily Mikhaylovich Drozdov, 1782–1867) – a former member of the Russian Bible Society board of directors and active biblical translator – approached

Alexander II about reopening Russian biblical translation. In 1856, the Moscow metropolitan persuaded his colleagues on the Holy Synod to petition the tsar to resume modern Russian biblical translation. In seeking to minimise opposition to Russian translation and rather appeal to traditional confessional loyalties, Filaret Drozdov of Moscow proposed to the Synod that the translation effort not be for liturgical use, but rather as a supplemental aid to believers who no longer could understand the more obscure passages of the Slavonic text.

Filaret Drozdov of Moscow was soon confronted with a major challenge to this proposal by his powerful conservative Synodal counterpart, Kiev Metropolitan Filaret (born Fyodor Georgievich Amfiteatrov, 1779–1857). Filaret Amfiteatrov of Kiev was sensitive to the controversies aroused by earlier Russian biblical translation. He had supported Holy Synod Ober-prokuror Protasov's effort to declare the Greek Septuagint and Slavonic biblical texts inviolate in the 1840s. Positioning himself as the defender of holy tradition, Filaret Amfiteatrov of Kiev believed that renewed translation would threaten the spiritual inheritance of Russia, especially the authority of the Slavonic Bible. In the conflict that ensued between the two Filarets, a politically contested setting was firmly established for Russian biblical translation in the last half of the nineteenth century.

In his response to the Synod's 1856 proposal to resume modern Russian biblical translation, Filaret Amfiteatrov of Kiev took a fundamentalist or essentialist position, arguing for the infallibility of the Slavonic text and the rejection of modern Russian translation. In his 'Zapiska' of 1857, penned shortly before his death, the Kievan prelate posed several forceful arguments against modern Russian translation. The first and most basic line of attack was the charge that translation and dissemination of the Bible in modern Russian would undermine the authority of the Slavonic text.[5] He decried modern language translation because of the threat that it posed to the sacred language of the Slavonic text. What was needed in his view was not renewed Russian translation, but more diligent training in the sacred Slavonic tongue. All that was needed for those who might be struggling with the Slavonic text was a Russian biblical commentary. The Kievan metropolitan argued that the Old Believer schism of the seventeenth century and the controversy spawned by biblical translation in the early nineteenth century developed out of a basic disregard for the holy and infallible Slavonic text.

In defending the Slavonic text, the Kievan prelate argued for retaining a liturgical, biblical language that was identifiably spiritual (*dukhovnyi*) in form and content. As an elite client of the confessional state, he was concerned for the maintenance of Church Slavonic as the sacred language for worship, much like the concern among Muslims for retaining the special authority of Arabic in the Qur'an or among Jews for the authority of Hebrew in the Bible. He claimed that the modern Russian language, especially the clerical Russian of the nineteenth-century Synod chancellery, was incapable of conveying the inspired Word of God in liturgical worship, and sought to defend the preservation of an appropriately 'spiritual' language for liturgical worship.

The issue of an appropriate medium or sacred language for modern Russian religious culture, enjoined in the battle over Russian biblical translation, has continued to be a focus of interest up to the present day, as in the deliberations of the All-Russian Church Council of 1917–18 and in debates carried on in the emigration and in the post-Soviet Russian Church. By the end of the nineteenth century, modern translations existed for most liturgical texts, despite continued strict adherence to the use of Slavonic texts in Russian church worship.[6] In the twentieth-century emigration, this concern for an appropriate sacred language for Russian Orthodox worship also came to divide prominent theologians, notably Father Georges Florovsky and Georgii Fedotov, the latter a church historian formerly of the Leningrad religious underground. The two twentieth-century émigré churchmen essentially re-engaged the issue hidden in the debate between the two Filarets in the 1850s. Fedotov argued that Holy Scripture offered divinely inspired narratives of simple fishermen, carpenters, lepers and nomads. Such narratives did not need to employ obscure or lofty language. As Fedotov concluded:

> Today in the Russian Church there are two deep streams of Russian spirituality vying: the Russian kenotic [sacrificial/suffering] tradition and Byzantine theurgy. They struggle not for destruction, of course, but for predominance and leadership. Who will win? St. Sergei of Radonezh or Areopagus? Upon the outcome of this spiritual duel depends also the fate of Slavonic or Russian liturgics![7]

While the positions of Fedotov and Florovsky were more nuanced than those of their nineteenth-century predecessors, the debate over renewed Russian biblical translation in the 1850s had opened a wider discursive issue over appropriate spiritual language that continues to the present.

A second line of argument posed by Kiev Metropolitan Filaret in the 1850s, however, reflected a much more defensive concern for empire. In the wake of incipient national movements the Kievan prelate feared that modern translation would undermine the established confessional order. His Moscow counterpart was concerned that the public needed recourse to sacred texts in Russian because of the obscurity and unintelligibility of Slavonic passages. Goading the venerable Moscow metropolitan, Filaret of Kiev wrote, 'If one is to translate Holy Scripture into Russian, then why not translate also into Ukrainian, Belarusian, and other languages?'[8] Filaret Drozdov's response, while it sought to counter the conservative Kievan prelate's position, nevertheless reflected the status of both prelates as guardians of official religious culture and dutiful clients of the confessional state. Filaret Drozdov's response to why translation should be undertaken into Russian, but not into Belarusian or Ukrainian, was quite simple:

> Because the Ukrainian and Belarusian languages are of a small minority and are little developed; because many (but not all) Ukrainians and Belarusians understand Russian and are able to read Holy Scripture in it; and, finally, because for church and civil unity it is more useful that a single Russian language rule in Ukraine.[9]

There could not be clearer testimony to the reality of the confessional state than the Moscow prelate's appeal to 'church and civil unity'. Filaret Anfiteatrov of Kiev countered that, if the revered Moscow metropolitan really wanted to promote unity, he ought to support the Slavonic text for both liturgical and home use. 'If one is to be concerned about church unity,' wrote the Kievan metropolitan, 'then it would be more useful for there to be one Slavonic language used by these Slavs and by us in both church worship and home reading.'[10] What this exchange between the two metropolitans revealed was not only the degree to which the Russian Bible had become politicised, but also the degree to which both prelates saw themselves functioning as clients of the confessional state, protecting the unity of empire. Indeed, the exchange confirmed that high-placed Russian prelates continued to view the Slavonic text as serving 'imperial' ends. In a sense, the importance of the Slavonic Bible rested in its capacity to serve as the architecture for an imperial civil religion. Today, in the context of the ongoing crisis in Ukraine, the common opposition of the two mid-nineteenth-century prelates to modern biblical translation in the 'little developed' Ukrainian and Belarusian languages sounds remarkably paternalistic. Yet, in the context of a confessional state in which they were among the elite arbiters of the religious culture, both prelates, despite their differences on the issue of renewed Russian biblical translation, were the co-opted defenders of empire. Interestingly, the Russian Orthodox Church canonised both metropolitans – Saints Filaret and Filaret – in the late twentieth century, just prior to the collapse of the Soviet Union.

Promulgated by Emperor Alexander II in 1858, the tsarist decree authorising the resumption of modern Russian biblical translation launched a process that yielded by 1875 a complete translation of the

Russian Bible – the authorised Holy Synod edition of the Russian Bible, the so-called *sinodal'nyi perevod*, or Synodal translation. The Russian Synodal translation has remained the most widely circulated Russian text of the Bible to this day, even though the text remains largely, though not entirely, absent from liturgical worship in the contemporary Russian Orthodox Church.

Biblical translation and the Jewish Question

In both the Russian Bible Society initiative of the early nineteenth century and the debate over renewed Russian biblical translation in mid-century, the Russian Bible tested the efficacy and limits of the confessional state and of religious elites in the arbitration of modern Russian religious culture. But what about the capacity of the confessional state to harmonise imperial interest with the concerns of minority religious communities of the Empire? Robert Crews addresses this question for Islam in his volume, *For Prophet and Tsar*. But, even more interesting for our purposes is the case of the Jewish community in the latter half of the nineteenth century. For, as in the case of modern Russian religious culture, so also for the Jews of Russia, biblical translation – in this case, translation of the Hebrew Bible into Russian – served as a challenge, testing the capacity of the confessional state to harmonise the conflicting interests of empire and nation. In the Jewish case, however, the role of the confessional state as an impartial protector and arbiter of religious communities came to be significantly compromised.

The Jewish Question intersected with modern biblical translation in the first instance because leading figures in the Jewish Enlightenment – the *maskilim* or Russian Jewish leaders of the Haskalah – undertook their own translations into Russian of portions of the Hebrew Bible, including editions of the Torah or Pentateuch. These Russian translations were intended for a Jewish audience and reflected a Russifying accommodation of the Jewish Enlightenment to Russian imperial rule – a carefully nuanced accommodation of the Russian-speaking Jewish *maskilim* to the confessional state. The accommodation of the Jewish enlighteners to Russian imperial rule, symbolised by the Jewish philanthropic organisation, the Society for the Promotion of Enlightenment among the Jews, even included rare instances of intermarriage and conversion to Russian Orthodox Christianity.[11]

The major translations of the Torah into Russian in the late tsarist era were tied to centres of Jewish Enlightenment in the north-west of the Empire, specifically Vil'na/Vilnius and St Petersburg. These Russian translations originated in the very heartland of the Russian Jewish *maskilim*. In an effort to sort out the variety of Jewish Enlightenment responses to Russian rule in the last half of the nineteenth century, John Klier has identified four varying intellectual streams. These range from what he calls the 'old *maskilim*', those who came out of the tradition of Moses Mendelssohn in eighteenth-century Germany, to a 'new *maskilim*', who were much more intent on developing Russian language training and enriching the curriculum of traditional Jewish state schools, to an even more secular Russian Jewish intelligentsia that was prepared to integrate Jewish schooling within mainstream Russian schools. At the extreme end of this spectrum were those whom Klier labelled the 'total assimilationists'. Somewhere towards the assimilationist end of that spectrum was the remarkable Orientalist and translator of the Hebrew Bible, Daniil Avraamovich Khvol'son, a convert to Christianity and yet loyal Jewish figure within the *maskilim* who became a central figure in modern Russian biblical translation.[12]

As Klier noted, one and the same person often moved across the spectrum of these varying positions. Whether it be the Gintsburg family and other wealthy notables who led the first generation of the Society for the Promotion of Enlightenment among the Jews of Russia (Obshchestvo dlia rasprostraneniia prosveshcheniia mezhdu evreiami v Rossii, OPE), founded in St Petersburg in 1863), or the official school inspectors and aides to local governors-general (the so-called Jewish experts, or *uchenye evrei*) in provincial postings, most Jewish enlighteners believed that emancipation, with its increased rights and privileges, would require a transformation of Jews themselves. The transformation necessitated rejection of 'Jewish fanaticism', a charge commonly brought by Russian officials seeking to equate Jewish identity with traditional Talmudic training. Central to such transformation sought by Jewish enlighteners was the embrace of the Russian language, recognised by even the older *maskilim* as an instrument for advancement that needed to be cultivated alongside traditional study of Hebrew.

It is these nineteenth-century enlighteners – the *maskilim* and the evolving Jewish intelligentsia – who initiated distinctive Russian translations of the Hebrew Bible in the last half of the nineteenth century. In assessing the historic place of these *maskilim*, Michael Stanislawski has cautioned that they not be viewed merely as a momentary phenomenon, a temporary way station towards some more fully formed nationalist or socialist Jewish intelligentsia:

> We have an image of the ideological development of East European Jewry as a neat case of doctrinal succession: traditional Judaism yielding to the Haskalah, whose naïve, optimistic view of the world crashes on the shores of anti-Semitism and radicalism and is transmuted into the more realistic and long-lived ideologies of modern Jewish nationalism and socialism.[13]

For Stanislawski, the problem with such a paradigm is that 'the vast majority of Jews in Russia ... never became Zionists or Bundists or Autonomists or any other "ists"'.[14] Like Klier's reference to Jewish enlighteners who moved along a spectrum of accommodation to Russian rule, Stanislawski sees most Jewish writers in Russia prior to 1917 as having one foot in their own traditional world and the other outside this world as they sought to respond to the challenges of modernity. It is from such a world of the *maskilim* and emergent Russian Jewish intelligentsia that there arose the Jewish translators of the Hebrew Bible into Russian.

The earliest of the translators was Leon Mandel'shtam, the first Jewish graduate of the University of St Petersburg. Born in the province of Vil'na in 1819, Mandel'shtam had initially enrolled at the University of Moscow in 1840 – he was the first Jew to enrol there. Transferring to St Petersburg, he graduated from its Faculty of Law in 1844 and was shortly thereafter hired by Sergei Uvarov, the Russian Minister of Public Instruction, as a 'Jewish expert' (*uchenyi evrei*) for the Ministry. Mandel'shtam embodied that characteristic ambivalence of the new *maskilim* who were rooted in traditional Talmudic training, but at the same time sought to advance their fellow Russian Jewish compatriots by encouraging secular study for the professions. He later wrote:

> I love my country and the language of my land [i.e. Russian] but, at the same time, I am unfortunate because of the misfortune of all my fellow Jews. Their rigidity has enraged me, because I can see it is destroying their gifts. But I am bound to their affliction by the closest of ties of kinship and feeling. My purpose in life is to defend them before the world and to help them to be worthy of that defense.[15]

Mandel'shtam briefly held the position of supervisor of Jewish schools in Russia before abandoning the Russian Empire in 1865 for a period of residency in Germany. Prior to his departure for Germany, he completed his Russian translation of the Torah, as well as his Hebrew–Russian, Russian–Hebrew dictionary. Unable to publish his translation of the Pentateuch in Russia, ostensibly because of Synod concern that the church had yet to issue its own authorised Russian edition of the Pentateuch, Mandel'shtam published his 1862 Hebrew–Russian diglot of the Pentateuch in Berlin.[16] Not insignificantly, the Mandel'shtam translation also apparently met with stiff resistance from Orthodox rabbis who considered translation of the Torah blasphemous.[17]

The 1862 Russian Pentateuch was prefaced by a lengthy note in Russian, 'To Jewish Instructors'. The note indicated he wished to dedicate the work to teachers of Jewish schoolchildren, enjoining the teachers to help 'turn Jews into real Russian citizens'. The *maskilim* spirit behind the translation was also clear from the analogy Mandel'shtam sought to draw between his own translation into Russian and earlier translations of Saadia Gaon (d. 942, early writer in both Hebrew and Arabic) and Moses Mendelssohn (1729–86, Jewish Haskalah translator of the Hebrew Bible into German). As Mandel'shtam put it, 'If Saadia Gaon found the need to translate Holy Scripture into Arabic, and if Moses Mendelssohn did so into German, and by means of such translations Jews were brought together and became close to their neighboring people, ... is it possible for there to be any doubt of the need for Jews of a Russian translation of the Bible?'[18]

Mandel'shtam's translation was a literal translation from the Hebrew, and its issuance as a diglot was clearly intended to serve the dual functions of religious training and language acquisition, much as the Mendelssohn translation had inspired study of German among the Jews of Germany from the eighteenth century onwards. The OPE subsequently subsidised an 1872 reprinting of the Mandel'shtam translation, buying up several thousand copies. Despite the interest among the *maskilim* in this early Russian biblical translation for the Jewish community, sales of the volume apparently lagged, with the OPE ending up some 4,000 roubles in the red on its purchase.[19] Some years later, Mandel'shtam returned to St Petersburg, dying there in relative poverty in 1889. Only after his death was his substantial personal library sold to the New York Public Library, where it became the foundation for its rich Judaica collection.

In the preface to his Hebrew–Russian diglot of the Pentateuch, Leon Mandel'shtam also noted that the diglot was to serve as a 'preliminary work', until a future translation of the Bible could be undertaken 'in a more elegant Russian language'.[20] The problem confronting translation and publication of a Russian text of the Bible for Jews did not, however, turn on the elegance of its Russian language. What transpired instead was that the OPE purchase of part of the 1872 edition of the Mandel'shtam diglot followed a quite dramatic internal conflict within the Russian Jewish community – one that set the stage for all subsequent Russian Jewish biblical translation and publication in the late tsarist era. Following the initial 1862 publication of the Mandel'shtam Torah diglot in Berlin, there had been several efforts by the OPE to secure Orthodox Church permission to circulate the text in Russia. In the face of the routine denial of these requests, Daniil Khvol'son proposed 'a compromise' solution to overcome the impasse. At his recommendation, the OPE would suggest to the Holy Synod that the Synod permit OPE to adopt as its own a modified Synodal Russian edition, reordering the books to make them conform to the Hebrew canon and introducing modest revisions of the translation so as to conform with Jewish practice.

Little did the OPE leadership know that Khvol'son had made essentially the same proposal to the British and Foreign Bible Society, which took up Khvol'son's offer at the end of the 1860s to revise the BFBS Old Testament translation exclusively from the Hebrew original. In May 1869, the OPE adopted Khvol'son's compromise suggestion, petitioning the Holy Synod for permission to revise the Synod's own edition, then still under preparation (by Khvol'son, among others), for distribution among the Jews of Russia. In September 1869, the Synod granted the OPE permission to prepare such a Jewish version of the Synodal text.[21]

Had the proposal become reality, the enterprising St Petersburg Orientalist Daniil Khvol'son would, in effect, have been working simultaneously on three separate, though very closely related, Russian translations of the Hebrew canon – one for the Holy Synod's Russian Old Testament, one for the BFBS Russian Old Testament, and one for an OPE Russian edition of the Hebrew Bible. No sooner had the Synod granted permission to the OPE for a Jewish revision of the Synodal text than open conflict broke out within the Jewish community over the very idea. The hostilities ultimately became so widespread that the idea was abandoned. The Odessa newspaper *Den'* attacked the proposal, claiming that the Jews of Russia deserved their own translation, not a Jewish version of a Russian Orthodox text. In his own defence, Khvol'son indicated he doubted whether the Synod would ever permit publication of such a rival Jewish translation, arguing that his own motives were pragmatically those of advancing the command of Russian among the Jews of Russia.[22]

By the spring of 1870, the conflict had taken an *ad hominem* and conspiratorial turn, with one OPE member, D. Slonimskii, claiming that Khvol'son was secretly trying to convert Jews to Christianity.[23] Because of the widespread concern expressed about the Khvol'son proposal, the OPE ultimately abandoned the idea. Khvol'son's accommodationist proposal had taken the OPE, and even its more secular *maskilim*, one step too far. After the dust cleared, OPE did gain Synod authorisation to purchase and sell several thousand copies of the 1872 Berlin reprinting of the Mandel'shtam Pentateuch diglot. But, the weak sale of those copies left the OPE budget in the red.

These secular, enlightened *maskilim* translators of the Hebrew Bible – a group that ultimately included not just Leon Mandel'shtam, but Iona Gordon, Lev Levanda, Yehoshua Shteinberg and Daniil Khvol'son – all had one foot in a confessional state, embracing Russian, and assimilating Russian institutions and western learning, while retaining much of their Jewish tradition. The OPE, for its part, needed and sought Holy Synod approval to undertake its own biblical translation. Even though it subsequently abandoned that effort and feared the repercussions of working with a figure of such prominence as Khvol'son, its embrace of Russian and its assimilationist profile fit the well-established pattern of other religious and confessional clients co-opted within the confessional state of the Russian Empire.

Bible translation, blood libel: the Saratov Affair

A second intersection of Jewish enlighteners with Russian biblical translation yielded even more dramatic results. This was the involvement of Russian translators of the Hebrew Bible, including notably Khvol'son himself, in a notorious anti-semitic case of blood libel, the Saratov Affair. In the Saratov Affair, key translators of the Russian Old Testament formulated an historic refutation of the blood libel charge, in the process challenging prevailing anti-semitism in post-serf emancipation (i.e. post-1861) Russia. The blood libel charges not only helped to stir the passions of early Jewish nationalism in Russia, but in mounting the refutation to the blood libel charge, modern secular translators of the Hebrew Bible revealed the increasing limitations and contradictions of a confessional state that often failed to be an impartial protector of interreligious harmony. In the Saratov affair, enlightened nineteenth-century Russian Hebraists launched one of the most significant challenges to the scourge of blood libel in modern European history, linking forever the history of Russian biblical translation with the Jewish Question in modern Russian history.

The development of Hebraic studies in nineteenth-century St Petersburg was closely identified with the work of three prominent translators of the Russian Old Testament – Gerasim Pavskii, Vasilii Levison and Daniil Khvol'son – all of whom taught Hebrew at one time or another at the St Petersburg Theological Academy. Pavskii and Khvol'son also taught at the University of St Petersburg. What brought the careers of these linguists momentarily together in the nineteenth century, however, was not their translation efforts, but their common involvement in the fate of modern Jewry in the Russian Empire. In a unique and largely forgotten instance of collaboration, these three Russian Hebraists shared joint membership on a special commission convened in 1855 to investigate the allegation in Saratov that there had been Jewish use of Christian blood for ritual religious purposes. In this Saratov Affair, Pavskii, Levison and Khvol'son came to the defence of Russian Jewry, challenging the prejudicial charges levied against the local Jews of Saratov.[24]

In December 1852, a 10-year-old Saratov boy, Feofan Sherstobitov, failed to return home from school; seven weeks later an 11-year-old, Mikhail Maslov, vanished in the same city. Saratov, a major port city on the south-central stretch of the River Volga, was far removed from the more restricted zone of Russian Jewish residence – the Pale of Settlement – but it was a city of mixed ethnic population, owing to its importance also as a centre of Volga German population in the Russian Empire. In March 1853, the bodies of the two boys were found. Local examination led to the allegation that the boys had been crudely circumcised, and then beaten to death. Further inflamed by the anti-Jewish sermon of a local cleric and by conflicts over destruction of a Jewish cemetery in the region, public outrage – based on rumour – led the authorities to launch an interrogation of all the Jews of Saratov, a relatively small population that included military personnel. The first individual to be arrested was an army private by the name of Shlifferman, identified as the sole person who conducted circumcision among local Jews. There was no evidence, however, linking Shlifferman with the time and place of the two disappearances.

When news of the disquieting events reached St Petersburg, the Ministry of Internal Affairs (MVD) sent one of its *chinovniki* (bureaucrats), N. S. Durnovo, to investigate the matter. With his mind already made up by earlier MVD reports about the ritual use of Christian blood by Jews, Durnovo presupposed the guilt of local Jews in the killing of the two boys and proceeded to direct a broad police surveillance of all Jews of the surrounding district, including baptised Christians of Jewish parentage.

Durnovo's attitude towards the question of ritual Jewish use of Christian blood was clearly influenced by the 1844 report of Vladimir Ivanovich Dal', *Rozyskanie ob ubienii evreiami khristianskikh mladentsev i upotreblenii krovi ikh* (An Inquiry concerning the Murdering by Jews of Christian Boys and the Use of Their Blood).[25] A Lutheran convert to Orthodoxy in his later years, Vladimir Dal' is mainly known in Russian history and philology because of his monumental four-volume dictionary of the Russian language, published in the 1860s. Under the patronage of the MVD, where he worked from 1843 to 1849, Dal' landed in St Petersburg, where he penned his anti-semitic treatise. The anti-semitism of Dal', visible in entries in his dictionary, was deeply embedded in the 1844 *Rozyskanie*, which claimed to be an objective history of what were, in fact, unsubstantiated cases of ritual use of Christian blood by Jews from the time of Constantine the Great to the celebrated Velishkoe Affair of 1823. The attention accorded Dal's anti-semitic *Rozyskanie* profoundly affected subsequent MVD proceedings, including the investigation at Saratov headed by the decidedly junior N. S. Durnovo.[26]

In this investigation, a succession of witnesses pointed the finger of blame at local Jewish military personnel and others of the small Jewish community. The expanding Durnovo investigation extracted ever more incredible testimony, slandering local Jewish citizens of Saratov. In the atmosphere established by Durnovo, the probe inevitably became broader with predictable 'findings' of wholesale kidnapping of young boys. In the end, the Saratov prisons and police-department jails were unable to hold all those arrested in the affair, with the result that private premises were rented for the incarceration of local citizens. Failing to contain the affair, Durnovo was finally told to close his investigation, and the ministry declared the preliminary investigation closed in November 1853.

In order to judge the guilt or innocence of those arrested, a committee of ministers, with the approval of Tsar Nicholas I, established in July 1854 a judicial commission (*sudebnaia komissiia*) under the presidency of Aleksandr Karlovich Giers, a section head for special affairs in the MVD and future minister of finance. The professional leadership that A. K. Giers brought to the judicial commission contrasted sharply with that provided earlier in Durnovo's Saratov investigation. The Giers judicial commission, which met from September 1854 to June 1856, was charged with determining the facts, including the allegation of official involvement in the murders, and specifically whether there were any secret dogmas of Jews that might explain their use of Christian blood.[27]

It was with respect to the charge bearing on Jewish dogmas that Giers decided to convene in late 1855 an internal 'special commission' (*osobaia komissiia*). This special commission was attached to the MVD's Department of Spiritual Affairs for Foreign Confessions (*departament dukhovnykh del inostrannykh ispovedanii*). Its composition included Giers (who presided), Daniil Khvol'son, Vasilii Levison, Gerasim Pavskii and one of Pavskii's students, Fedor Sidonskii, a graduate of St Petersburg Theological Academy. Thus, in 1855, the major St Petersburg Hebraists responsible for modern Russian Old Testament translation were drawn together 'to examine carefully whether in books or manuscripts anything could be found relating to the Jewish use of Christian blood for religious purposes'.[28]

Following a period of research into Hebrew sources, as well as into local lore, Pavskii, Levison and Khvol'son each submitted findings to Giers's special commission. On the basis of these findings, the special commission reported to the wider Saratov judicial commission that there was no documentary or other evidence whatsoever in the Hebrew tradition for the use of Christian blood in Jewish ritual observances. Indeed, it concluded that such a practice was in complete violation of Mosaic laws, which specifically forbade killing. In the most exhaustive effort undertaken by any commission member, Daniil Khvol'son prepared a lengthy report entitled *O nekotorykh srednevekovykh obvineniiakh protiv Evreev: Istoricheskoe issledovanie po istochnikamI* (Concerning

Some Medieval Accusations against Jews: Historical Source-based Research). First published in 1861, the Khvol'son work was issued in three subsequent editions, as well as in German translation. Frequently cited in German as well as in Russian literature on the blood libel question, the Khvol'son work is the most authoritative examination of sources ever consulted on the question, including use of works from the pre-Christian era down to the nineteenth century.[29] None of the members of the Giers special commission found any credible evidence for the Saratov allegations, nor for the longstanding mythical notion of Jewish use of Christian blood. In addition to his longer scholarly study, Khvol'son later prepared a separate brochure for a more popular audience, reviewing the findings of the Saratov special commission.[30] Khvol'son indicated that the special commission had also reviewed all the testimony offered before the Saratov judicial commission, and had found no support for the charges levied against local Jews.

The Saratov events did not end, however, with the findings of Pavskii, Levison and Khvol'son. In June 1856, Giers's wider judicial commission referred the entire affair to the sixth department of the State Senate in Moscow. Although the judicial commission recommended that the accused Saratov Jews be held in jail pending final judgement on the matter, its report included the finding that the judicial commission had discovered no evidence of guilt on their part. The Senate Department in Moscow confirmed the Giers judicial commission findings and called for the immediate liberation of all Jews confined in Saratov.[31]

The matter then passed to the State Council in St Petersburg, which had been created in 1810. Within this Council – the highest advisory body to the tsar – a committee of three ministers reviewed the prior findings. Despite the call from Minister of Justice Zamiatin for the unconditional acquittal of those wrongly accused, the full State Council reversed the Moscow Senate department's recommendation, voting by a margin of 22 to 2 to keep the falsely charged Jews under arrest. Tsar Alexander II added his name to the majority, thereby officially closing the matter in 1860.[32] The State Council's reversal of the Giers commission and the Moscow Senate findings sadly confirmed the precedent of an earlier ritual murder case, the notorious Velishskoe affair, in which Tsar Nicholas I had determined that, even if Jewish ritual use of Christian blood could not be proven, there may have been some deviant Jewish sect that retained responsibility.

What particularly troubled Professor Khvol'son in this matter was the news he received from his close acquaintance, Council member and Minister of Education Avraam Sergeevich Norov. Norov informed Khvol'son that the report of the Pavskii–Levison–Khvol'son 'special commission' regarding the spurious charge of ritual use of Christian blood by Jews was conspicuously missing from the file reviewed by the State Council on the Saratov affair. Emboldened by the discovery of this omission, Khvol'son committed himself to the full publication of his own findings on the matter. Shortly thereafter Kvol'son's work appeared as 'O nekotorykh srednevekovykh obvineniiakh protiv Evreev' (Regarding Some Medieval Accusations against the Jews), in the journal *Biblioteka dlia chteniia*.[33]

Later, following the deaths of Pavskii and Levison and in the aftermath of yet another set of blood libel allegations – the Kutaissi Affair (*Kutaisskoe delo*) – Khvol'son republished his work against blood libel and issued his more popular brochure challenging the repeated, unfounded charges in the slanderous works of his contemporaries, Ippolit Liutostanskii and N. I. Kostomarov.[34] Responding in *Novoe vremia* to Kostomarov, Khvol'son was particularly offended by two charges, the first an *ad hominem* attack, and the other directed more broadly at the Russian intelligentsia. On the *ad hominem* charge raised by Kostomarov that Khvol'son was merely driven by support for his fellow Jews, Khvol'son responded by saying:

> Mr. Kostomarov alludes to my 'patriotism' and speaks about my 'partiality toward Jews'. Yes, I admit that I nourish empathy for Jews, for I know not only their dark, but also their bright side. And I think that it is far more honest to defend those of my fellow race and my former religion from erroneous accusations than to slander them with various fabrications and with false representation of the most innocent facts. To be sure, a defender of Jews cannot count upon the approbation of the majority who invariably throw in their lot with the slanderers of Judaism. But why does an honest man need such approbation? I hold true to my conscience in struggling for justice and for truth.[35]

To this Kostomarev countered that, in the end, truth always wins out, and the very stridency of Khvol'son's defence of Russian Jewry cast doubt upon his case. Khvol'son's rejoinder constituted an appeal to the duty of the Russian intelligentsia:

> Mr. Kostomarov says that 'the light of truth by itself scatters the darkness of delusion'. Unfortunately, I am not such an historical optimist as Kostomarov ... Truth is not a material force, operating according to general physical laws. It is a spiritual power that does not act by itself, but requires assistance. If the intelligentsia quietly lays down its hands and awaits the 'power of truth', surely this power will never be made manifest 'by itself'. For as the Saviour said, 'If indeed the salt has lost its taste, how shall its saltiness be restored?' (Matt. 5:13).[36]

Daniil Khvol'son and his fellow Old Testament translators effectively challenged prevailing nineteenth-century superstitions directed against

Russian Jewry, and Khvol'son's published refutation has remained a landmark critique of the charge of blood libel, defending Jews against the claim of ritual murder.

In the end, it may not have been coincidental that the architects of Hebraic studies in Orthodox Russia – Gerasim Pavskii, Daniil Khvol'son and their students –should have become such outspoken defenders of Jews against the blood libel myth. For, as Ronald Hsia has noted in the case of Germany, so also in the case of Russia, the systematic scholarly refutation of the ritual murder charge invariably accompanied the advance of serious Hebraic studies in the academy.[37] The tradition of outstanding Hebrew scholarship in St Petersburg continued well into the twentieth century. The last major student of Khvol'son, Pavel Konstantinovich Kokovtsev (1861–1942), taught Hebrew at Leningrad State University and served well into the Soviet period as a distinguished research scholar in the Leningrad Division of the Institute of Oriental Studies of the Soviet Academy of Sciences.

But, for our purposes, what is noteworthy about the Saratov Affair is how it helps to sharpen our understanding of the confessional state. For when the State Council and Tsar Alexander II overruled the investigative commission and allowed the unfounded charges against Jews imprisoned in Saratov to stand, it revealed the limits of the confessional state in an age of popular demagoguery and anti-semitism. Unable to serve as an impartial arbiter of religious affairs, the Russian Empire as a 'confessional state' was dying. The decline of the myth of the saintly ruler was part of the dismantling of the confessional state. In that dismantling, the role of the secular intelligentsia – in this case, the role of the pioneers of modern nineteenth-century Russian biblical translation – has been under-appreciated.

Conclusion

There is a curious contemporary afterlife to these issues of empire and nation in the politics of the Russian Bible. In the contemporary Ukrainian crisis, the politics of the Bible has been playing out in a remarkably diverse confessional setting in which the majority of the participants – Russians and Ukrainians alike – claim loyalty to one or another Eastern Christian confessional body. Of the four major Eastern rite confessions, all but the Ukrainian Orthodox Church of the Moscow Patriarchate now operate with use of the Ukrainian language for liturgical worship. The translation of the Bible into Ukrainian was an important development of the late nineteenth century, its architects key figures in the Ukrainian national movement.[38] But, as elsewhere, traditional Church Slavonic liturgical practice continued into the post-Soviet period within most Ukrainian Orthodox parishes, and the appeal to conservative tradition may ironically have contributed to the maintenance of its large following throughout the Soviet period.

Rather dramatically, however, the Ukrainian–Russian conflict that reopened in 2013 effectively polarised the Ukrainian question, with many Ukrainian Eastern rite believers now migrating to the Ukrainian Orthodox Church, Kiev Patriarchate, which prominently employs the Ukrainian Bible in its liturgical worship. The Kiev Patriarchate's early support of the Maidan Square protest and its opposition to the ousted Ukrainian President Viktor Yanukovych was matched by its appeal to the use of the Ukrainian language. As Ger Duijzings noted in the quite different case of Kosovo, so also in Ukraine, international conflict has sharpened and 'ethnicised' otherwise more fluid lines of inter-ethnic confessional identity, forcing ethnic subjects into rival camps, and reinforcing for Ukrainians the political importance of Ukrainian in liturgical worship and the priority of the Ukrainian Bible over that of the Slavonic text.[39] Vladimir Putin and his loyal Moscow Patriarch may look with nostalgia at the confessional state of the nineteenth-century Russian Empire, as the current Ukrainian conflict curiously has confirmed the expectation of the conservative nineteenth-century Kievan Metropolitan Filaret Amfiteatrov, who fought against the Russian Bible, fearing the nationalising of religious practice and, with that, the demise of a confessional empire.

In contemporary Ukraine, as in nineteenth-century Russia, modern biblical translation, with its appeal to national languages, became embroiled in the conflict between empire and nation. In that conflict the modern Bible not only helped to fashion the nation, but subtly challenged the imperial claims and the authority of the confessional state.

Notes

1 See for example Adrian Hastings, *Construction of Nationhood* (Cambridge: Cambridge University Press, 1997); Lamin Sanneh, *Translating the Message: The Missionary Impact on Culture* (Maryknoll, NY: Orbis Books, 2009); Anthony D. Smith, *Chosen Peoples: Sacred Sources of National Identity* (Oxford: Oxford University Press, 2003); Hastings, 'Nationalism in Early Modern Europe', *History and Theory*, 44 (2005), 404–15.
2 Robert D. Crews, *For Prophet and Tsar: Islam and Empire in Russia and Central Asia* (Cambridge, MA: Harvard University Press, 2006). Crews's focus is on Islam, but his insights into the Russian Empire as a confessional state are of obvious relevance for the dominant Eastern Orthodox state religion as well.
3 See Stephen Batalden, *Russian Bible Wars: Modern Scriptural Translation and Cultural Authority* (Cambridge: Cambridge University Press, 2013).
4 Crews takes issue specifically with Samuel P. Huntington's *The Clash of Civilizations and the Remaking of World Order* (London: Simon and Schuster, 1997). Crews's

challenge to such notions of timeless conflict and religious fault lines within or between empires is anticipated by others, including Ger Duijzings, *Religion and the Politics of Identity in Kosovo* (New York: Columbia University Press, 2000), who argues similarly that the Ottoman frontier was a zone of relative peace and harmony broken only by international conflicts that only then sharpened lines of national conflict in what otherwise were zones of peaceful coexistence and harmonisation of fluid religious identities on the frontiers of empire.

5   'Otvetnaia zapiska', ROGPB, *fond* S.-Peterburgskaia dukhovnaia akademiia, *delo* A.I.80, *ll.* 95–104. See also Chistovich, *Istoriia perevoda Biblii*, 269–83, which summarises the arguments posed by Filaret Amfiteatrov.
6   On the modern Russian translation of liturgical texts, see B. I. Sobe, 'Problema ispravleniia bogosluzhebnykh knig v rossii v XIX–XX vekakh', *Bogoslovskie trudy*, 5 (1970), 25–68.
7   G. P. Fedotov, 'Slavianskii ili russkii iazyk v bogosluzhenii?', *Put'*, 57 (August–October 1938), 28.
8   ROGPB, *fond* S.-Peterburgskaia dukhovnaia akademiia, *delo* A.I.80, *ll.* 109ob. For the Chistovich account, which curiously omits this exchange between the two Filarets, see *Istoriia perevoda Biblii*, 275.
9   'Konfidentsial'naia zametka', *l.* 110; Chistovich, *Istoriia perevoda Biblii*, 290.
10 'Konfidentsial'naia zametka', *l.* 110.
11 On the Society and its work with biblical translation, see Brian J. Horowitz, *Jewish Philanthropy and Enlightenment in Late-Tsarist Russia* (Seattle, WA: University of Washington Press, 2009).
12 On Khvol'son, see Andrew C. Reed, 'For One's Brothers: Daniil Avraamovich Khvol'son and the Jewish Question in Russia, 1819–1911' (Ph.D. dissertation, Arizona State University, 2014).
13 Michael Stanislawski, *For Whom Do I Toil? Judah Leib Gordon and the Crisis of Russian Jewry* (New York: Oxford University Press, 1988), p. 5.
14 Stanislawski, *For Whom Do I Toil?*, p. 5.
15 Quoted in Zvi Gitelman, *A Century of Ambivalence: The Jews of Russia and the Soviet Union, 1881 to the Present* (New York: Viking Press, 1988), p. 6.
16 See 'Appendix', no. 54. On Synodal objection to its printing in Russia, see Horowitz, *Jewish Philanthropy*, p. 45
17 Horowitz, *Jewish Philanthropy*, p. 252 n. 21. Horowitz cites Il'ia Trotskii's account of the opposition to the Mandel'shtam translation from Orthodox rabbis. '"Samodeiatel'nost' i samopomoshch"', in *Kniga o russkom evreistve ot 1860-kh godov do revoliutsii 1917 g.: Sbornik statei* (New York: Soiuz russkikh evreev, 1960), p. 473.
18 'Evreiskim nastavnikam', in *Thora, t.e. Zakon, ili Piatiknishie moiseevo* (Berlin: K. Schultz, 1862), p. v.
19 Horowitz, *Jewish Philanthropy*, p. 45.
20 'Evreiskim nastavnikam', p. iii.
21 This account of the OPE appeal to the Holy Synod is drawn from John Klier, *Imperial Russia's Jewish Question, 1855–1881* (Cambridge: Cambridge University Press, 2005), pp. 251–4, which in turn is based on I. M. Cherikover, *Istoriia Obshchestva dlia rasprostraneniia prosveshcheniia mezhdu evreiami v Rossii, 1863–1913 gg.* (St Petersburg, 1913).
22 Klier, *Imperial Russia's Jewish Question*, pp. 252–3.
23 Klier, *Imperial Russia's Jewish Question*, pp. 252–3.
24 On the 'Saratovskoe delo', the most reliable secondary account, because of its appeal to the manuscript record of the investigations, is that of Iu[lii] Gessen, 'Saratovskoe delo', in *Evreiskaia entsiklopediia*, vol. 14 (St Petersburg, 1914), pp. 2–8. See also Gessen's work, *Istoriia evreev v Rossii* (St Petersburg, 1914); and P. Ia. Levenson, 'Esche o saratovskom dele', *Voskhod*, 4 (1881), 163–78.
25 V. I. Dal', *Rozyskanie ob ubienii evreiami khristianskikh mladentsev i upotreblenii krovi ikh* (St Petersburg: Suvorin Press – 'Novoe Vremia', 1913). For Dal's' 4-volume Russian dictionary, see *Tolkovyi slovar' zhivago velikorusskogo iazyka* (Moscow,

1863–66). On Dal', including his involvement in the blood libel issue, see A. Cherkas, '"Vladimir Ivanovich Dal'", Russkii biograficheskii slovar', 6 (St Petersburg, 1905), 42–8.

26 For an account of how Durnovo's Saratov investigation was affected by Dal's' own prejudicial work, see Aleksandr Alekseev, *Upotrebliaiut-li evrei khristianskuiu krov' religioznoiu tseluiu?* (Novgorod: 1886), pp. 10–12. Alekseev, an Orthodox Christian of Jewish parentage, was present in Saratov during much of the investigation. One can also trace the genealogy of the Dal' report in subsequent MVD writing on blood libel. Utilising the report nearly word for word, Valerii V. Skripitsyn, director of the MVD Department of Spiritual Affairs for Foreign Confessions, prepared an *otnoshenie* for Nicholas I on the Saratov affair, 'Svedeniia ob ubiistve evreiami khristian dlia dobyvaniia krovi [Information on the Murder by Jews of Christians for Obtaining Blood]'. Skripitsyn's slanderous and unfounded charges were later published in the 1878 volume of *Grazhdanin*, 23–8. The Skripitsyn–Dal' polemic set the tone for much subsequent anti-semitic propaganda. Dal's' *Rozyskanie* was republished posthumously in the wake of the celebrated Beilis Affair. Another work relating to the allegation of Jewish ritual use of Christian blood is the disturbing volume compiled by Ivan O. Kuz'min that perpetuates the old myths, *Materialy k voprosu ob obvineniiakh evreev v ritual'nykh prestupleniiakh* (St Petersburg, 1913).

27 See Gessen, 'Saratovskoe delo', 5. The contrasting styles of MVD bureaucratic response reflected in the widely differing leadership exercised in the Saratov affair by Giers and Durnovo were not uncommon in the MVD. See, in this regard, the analysis of Daniel T. Orlovsky, *The Limits of Reform: The Ministry of Internal Affairs in Imperial Russia, 1802–1881* (Cambridge, MA: Harvard University Press, 1981), pp. 204–5. Orlovsky notes 'the ideological conflict within the bureaucracy itself'.

28 The charge to the internal *osobaia komissiia* may also be found in Gessen, 'Saratovskoe delo', 7–8. For a more complete account of this charge to the special commission, see also the preface to the 1880 edition of Daniil Khvol'son, *O nekotorykh srednevekovykh obvineniiakh protiv Evreev: Istoricheskoe issledovanie po istochnikam.*

29 Khvol'son's work was first issued in the journal *Biblioteka dlia chteniia*, 164 (March 1861), 1–56 and (April 1861), 1–48; and 165 (May 1861), 1–60. The 1861 bound edition was expanded to 386 pages in the 1880 edition (St Petersburg: Tip. Tsederbauma i Gol'denbliuma), including the preface concerning the Saratov events. The German edition, *Die Blutanklage und sonstige mittelalterliche Beschuldigungen der Juden: Eine historische Untersuchung nach den Quellen*, was published in Frankfurt (J. Kauffmann Press, 1901), although it was printed in Vienna (L. Beck and Son). Gerasim Pavskii issued his own response, similar in tone to that of Khvol'son, but much shorter. For the Pavskii response, see N. I. Barsov, 'Mnenie protoierei G. P. Pavskago po voprosu ob upotreblenii evreiami khristianskoe krovi dlia religioznykh tselei,' *Tserkovnyi vestnik*, 20 (1879).

30 D. A. Khvol'son, *Upotrebliaiut-li evrei khristianskuiu krov'?* (St Petersburg, 1879), pp. 1–69. An expanded edition, printed in Kiev in 1912 shortly after Khvol'son's death, incorrectly identifies the author as A. D. Khvol'son.

31 Gessen, 'Saratovskoe delo', pp. 5–6.

32 Gessen, 'Saratovskoe delo', p. 6. On the *memoriia* of the State Council, Alexander II simply wrote alongside the position of the 22, 'i ia' [and I].

33 See note 28 above. Khvol'son's acquaintance with Norov dates from the time of Khvol'son's conversion to Russian Orthodoxy.

34 Ippolit Liutostanskii, basing his study on the work of Skripitsyn and Dal' (see note 3), first issued his anti-semitic polemic in 1876 under the title *Vopros ob upotreblenii evreiami-sektantorami khristianskoi krovi dlia religioznykh tselei v sviazi s voprosom ob otnosheniiakh evreistva k khristianstvu voobshche* (Moscow: 1876). This broadside prompted Khvol'son to republish *O nekotorykh srednevekovykh obvineniiakh protiv Evreev* (St Petersburg: Tip. Tsederbauma i Gol'denbliuma, 1880). Khvol'son also issued for a more popular audience his *Upotrebliaiut-li evrei khristianskuiu krov'?* [Do Jews Use Christian Blood?]. In turn, in 1880 Liutostanskii issued an expanded

two-volume edition of his 1876 work under the slightly revised title *Ob upotreblenii evreiami (talmudistskimi sektantorami) khristianskoi krovi dlia religioznykh tselei, v sviazi s voprosom ob otnosheniiakh evreistva k khristianstvu voobshche* (Moscow: 1880). This edition devoted a new preface, i–xviii, to a personal attack on Khvol'son. In his more popular 1879 work, Khvol'son also responded to the historian Kostomarov, who had repeated in the pages of *Novoe vremia* the charge of Jewish ritual use of Christian blood. See, within Khvol'son's *Upotrebliaiut-li evrei khristianskuiu krov'?*, the third appendix, 'Otvet na zamechanie N. I. Kostomarova, "po povodu broshiury, isdannoi g. Khvol'sonom: upotrebliaiut-li evrei khristianskuiu krov"?' Khvol'son's response addressed the criticism that Kostomarov first directed at him in the newspaper *Novoe vremia*, 1172, 5 June 1879.

35 D. A. Khvol'son, 'Prilozhenie 3: Otvet na zamechanie N. I. Kostomarova' (Kiev: 1912), 77.
36 Khvol'son, 'Otvet na zamechanie N. I. Kostomarova', 74–5.
37 On the linkage of the refutation of ritual murder accusations with the development of Hebraic studies, see Ronald Po-chia Hsia, *The Myth of Ritual Murder: Jews and Magic in Reformation Germany* (New Haven, CT: Yale University Press, 1988).
38 On the Ukrainian Bible and its place in the 'nationalising' of religious practice, see Ricarda Vulpius, *Nationalisierung der Religion: Russifisierungspolitik und ukrainische Nationsbildung, 1860–1920*. Band 64, 'Forschungen zur osteuropäischen Geschichte' (Wiesbaden: Harrassowitz Verlag, 2005), pp. 117–72.
39 The Duijzings reference is to *Religion and the Politics of Identity in Kosovo* (New York: Columbia University Press, 2001).

CHAPTER SEVEN

Contested identity: the Veda as an alternative to the Bible

Dorothy Figueira

The Western quest for origins received an initial formulation in the recognition of a philological relationship between Sanskrit, Latin, Greek and other languages of Europe in the sixteenth century. Already in the Enlightenment, there was much speculation regarding India, its culture, language and peoples. Many of the uninformed assessments of this time would resurface in subsequent Orientalist scholarship, Romantic mythography, nineteenth-century linguistic science and race theory. Excited by the linguistic affinity between Sanskrit and other languages, Orientalist scholars fostered the comparative science of religion and mythology that developed a vision of an Aryan race as the originator of Indian and European culture.[1] The belief in Indo-European origins further spurred European interest in Vedic Aryan sources. Certain Enlightenment thinkers idealised the Vedic past in an attempt to find a utopia outside Europe and as an alternative tradition to that of the Bible. Romantic mythographers not only accepted Aryan genius, but prioritised it. Speculation regarding the Aryan provided a means whereby Indian history could be used to create a fresh historical tradition that expressed specifically European political and ideological interests. What Europeans sought in India was not Indo-European religion, but a reassessment of Judaeo-Christianity.

India, What Can It Teach Us?

This question, adopted by Max Müller as the title of a collection of essays, addresses the fundamental concern of this chapter, namely, that a fictive India and fictional Aryan ancestors were constructed in the West to provide answers for questions regarding European identity. India enabled Europe to discover its supposedly 'true' past. Nowhere was this process more apparent than in the attempt of Voltaire

(1694–1778) to rewrite the history of religions and compare world mythologies.

In particular, it was in his understanding of the Fall of Man that Voltaire's true need to construct an Indian alibi (Latin: 'elsewhere') surfaced. Voltaire compared what he perceived as the Indian version of the Fall to the classical myth relating the revolt of the Titans and the apocryphal account of Lucifer's rebellion found in the Book of Enoch.[2] The common use of this myth in three traditions suggested to Voltaire that the Greeks and the Jews had knowledge of some common tradition consisting of brahmin mysteries. The Aryans, it seems, and not the Jews, provided the foundation for the entire Christian religion,[3] since they originated the concepts of Original Sin and the Devil who, as the agent of sin, animated all Judaeo-Christian theology.[4] If this genealogy was authentic, why, Voltaire asked, did Christianity bother to use a source as tenuous as a Jewish apocryphal book to explain the existence of evil?[5] Why did Christianity seek to base itself solely on a myth that did not even appear in the Old Testament?[6]

Voltaire posed these questions with a clear response in mind. By inserting this fundamental myth into an apocryphal book, he concluded that the Jews contrived to claim authorship for and displace the true founders of 'our' faith. He then concluded that it was the Aryans, the Vedic brahmins, who had, in fact, first developed these truths. The Jews subsequently repeated this mythology, after stealing it from its ancient Indian source.[7] Just as the Jews stole the source of religions, so too did they steal the idea of Adam as the progenitor.

> Did they get this from the Jews? Did the Jews copy the Indians, were both original? The Jews are not allowed to think that their writers took [ont puisé] anything from the brahmins, of whom they have never heard. It is not permitted to think about Adam in another way than do the Jews. I will be quiet and I will not think.[8]

Such is Voltaire's polemic: The Jews stole what was of worth in their religion from the Aryans, people whom they called Gog and Magog.[9] They then conspired to keep their fraud a secret. 'We, as Christians, have not dared to reveal this fraud, as our own beliefs are implicated.'[10] 'We have to believe the Jews, although we detest them, because they are regarded as our precursors and masters.'[11]

In order to prove that the Jews had appropriated the wisdom of the Aryans, Voltaire sought to reconstruct Aryan religion by discovering their sacred book and interpreting it.[12] Towards this end, he introduced the *Ezour Veidam*. With this text, a forgery most probably composed by Jesuits in India to aid them in their proselytising efforts,[13] Voltaire sought to attack the originality of the Hebrews and their religion. The *Ezour Veidam* allowed Voltaire to claim the anteriority of the Indians and, in doing so, effectively challenge the authority of the Bible. In Voltaire's estimation, India provided another basis for religion that was unencumbered by the Judaic tradition. This supposed Indian holy book also allowed Voltaire to make the argument that the Jews were the great plagiarists of history:

> Some very intelligent thinkers say that the brahmin sect is incontestably older than that of the Jews ... [They] say that the Indians were always inventors and the Jews always imitators, the Indians always clever and the Jews always coarse.[14]

In sections appended in 1769 to the *Essai sur les moeurs*, Voltaire specifically accuses the Jews of stealing from the Indians. The Jews did not set the stage for Christianity, rather it was the Aryans who bequeathed to us a religion based on universal reason that the Jews subsequently distorted. In a 1775 letter to Frederick the Great, Voltaire reiterated that Christianity was founded solely on what he called the ancient religion of Brama.

Voltaire's reading of the fraudulent Veda is, indeed, as ironic as it is inventive. He was able to imbue a clever piece of propaganda or a clumsy attempt at ecumenism with characteristics that suited his polemical needs. Vedic India became a privileged site of Deist rationalism. It could be enlisted to attack the pretensions of the Catholic Church (always a project for Voltaire), as well as being invoked in order to displace the Jews from their privileged position in history.

Voltaire had placed the origin of mankind in the East on the banks of the River Ganges, as opposed to the account found in Genesis. Johann Gottfried Herder (1744–1803) followed Voltaire in that he too discovered the cradle of humanity in India.[15] Since all men were descended from the same race,[16] Herder attributed the development of different cultures and languages to environmental forces.[17] Language, the purest expression of the spiritual character of a national group,[18] like man himself, descended from a unique source.[19] By positioning the childhood of humanity in India, Herder referred not only to the ancestors of Europeans, but also progenitors of all humankind. Already in Voltaire, we saw the Aryans inhabiting a Golden Age and their religion offering a tradition older than the Bible. Aryan India saw primitive revelation degenerate under the influence of a corrupt priesthood and monotheism reduced to polytheism.[20] Upon this script, Herder and the Romantics would project their own aesthetic need: the desire to discover a true national poetry.[21] It was to be found in whatever text they could identify as the 'Bible of India'. Once the *Ezour Veidam* was discovered to be a clever forgery, Romantic mythographers simply came up with other purported 'Vedas' to fit the bill as an Aryan revealed text.

The Heidelberg philologist Friedrich Creuzer (1771–1858) identified just such a text in Anquetil Duperron's Latin translation from a Persian rendition of the Upanishads, the *Oupnek'hat* or *Upnekhata*.[22] Creuzer remarked in his autobiography that one of the reasons he delved into the history of religion was Anquetil Duperron's seeming proof of the thesis that polytheism developed from primitive monotheism.[23] In his magisterial opus, *Symbolik und Mythologie der alten Völker, besonders der Griechen* (1822), Creuzer sought arguments to prove that Anquetil's 'translation' of the 'Veda' taught the most ancient religious system of the world, being an instance of authentic monotheism.[24]

The real innovation that Creuzer effected upon previous Western emplotments of India consisted in the role he ascribed to Aryan religion. While Herder and the Romantics touted the sublimity, purity and antiquity of Indian speculative thought relative to the Judaeo–Christian perspective, Creuzer specifically assigned it an equal position to that of the Hebrews. Creuzer claimed that the primitive worship of Brahma formed the basis of the Hebrews' religion. He also held that the purest cult of Jehovah, as practised by Abraham, represented an isolated branch of this old 'Brahmaism'.[25] With such assertions, Creuzer went further than other polemicists in de-emphasising the role of Judaism in the history of religions. The Jews were not the only recipients of the true doctrine.[26] For Creuzer, Israel now became an equal partner with Aryan India.[27]

A decade earlier, Joseph Görres (1776–1848) had also sought primitive religion beyond Judea. For Görres, Christianity constituted the penultimate stage in religious evolution. The fifth and final stage would consist in a return to primitive monism. From his comparative analysis, Görres concluded that in primitive times there existed one God, religion, cult, law and Bible.[28] He believed that this cradle of humanity was to be found in India.[29] Subsequent objects of worship among other peoples ranked only as imitations of this Aryan *Urreligion*.[30] He also noted that the closer the diverse religions were to India geographically, the more they retained a rich, pure and living form.[31] Görres, like Creuzer, reduced the religion of Judea to something he called primitive 'Brahmaism', a religion purportedly imparted by Brahma–Abraham.[32] The Jews thus owed their entire religion to the Vedic Indians and Christians worshipped the Aryan Brahma as Christ.

As others of his generation, Görres identified the Veda with the *Oupnek'hat*, which he took to be the oldest document known to humanity.[33] He identified ancient India's religion as the oldest religion in the world.[34] Dating at 2240 BCE, Görres also claimed that the 'Veda' was the source from which all other myths derived.[35] Here too, the centre of gravity had shifted from Judea to India; Görres claimed that the Hebrews were a subgroup of the true chosen people, who originated in India.[36]

While Herder tried to incorporate India within his exegesis of the Old Testament, Creuzer posited the equivalence of India and Judea, and Görres elevated Indian religion above Judaism. He associated other prophets (Toth, Zoroaster, Fohi, Theut and Othin) with Brahma (Abraham), only to the degree that their doctrines reflected those of the *Oupnek'hat*, viewed as the first, oldest, and most faithful repository of primitive revelation. Creuzer and Görres (as well as other Romantic mythographers, such as Majer and Kanne) attributed the universality of myth to divine revelation. They all situated this revelation in India. But the idea of the existence of a purely Indo–European religious community did not enter their formulations. It was the geographer Karl Ritter (1779–1859) who developed the first features of Indo-European primitive religion.

Ritter characterised India as the vestibule (*Vorhalle*) of Western history and charted the direct lineage from the Aryans to the Teutons[37] by establishing the bridge between Sanskrit and Old German.[38] In other words, Ritter revealed a civilisation, religion and language irreducible to that of the Hebrews. Judaeo–Christianity now became the intruder in his as well as other Romantic mytholographers' schemas. Indeed, it appeared to have derailed Europe from its historic path and subverted its true mission.

The historical school emphasised the national aspect of myth as popular phenomena. This conception of myth developed throughout the nineteenth century. When the Veda appeared in print in the West and finally permitted mythographers to compare Indo-European national mythologies, the Romantic thesis, especially that of Ritter, gained renewed prominence. Indian Scripture could now prove the existence of primitive monotheism and any illusions regarding the primacy of the Jews could be laid to rest. Speculations regarding the imagined Indo-European community that these Romantics developed would resurface with the eventual appearance of the *Rig Veda* in print and, in fact, would find their substantiation in the scientific research of its editor. Friedrich Max Müller (1823–1900) would popularise the important Romantic thesis that by the mid–nineteenth century was far from moribund – the idea of an Indo-European religious community inferred from the concept of an Indo-European linguistic community. With his edition of the *Rig Veda*, the West, it seemed, had finally discovered the true chronicle of its past.

We have seen how earlier European scholarship on India consisted of an internal conversation. Nowhere was this dialogue more forceful than in the Vedic scholarship of Max Müller. For Müller, as for others examined in these pages, the quest for the Aryan exhibited a very important cultural attempt to restore one's own tradition:

> I wished that the Veda and its religion and philosophy should not only seem to you curious or strange, but that you should feel that there was in them something that concerns ourselves something of our own intellectual growth, some recollections, as it were, of our own childhood, or at least of the childhood of our own race.[39]

More importantly, it offered 'solutions to some of the greatest problems of life, and the needed corrective for the inner life of Europe'.[40] Müller's task, as he envisioned it, was to discover the first germs of the language, religion and mythology of 'our' Aryan forefathers.[41] He asserted that the Veda was the most important document of 'Aryan humanity'[42] and the first book of the 'Aryan nations'.[43] It presented the 'sharp edges of primitive thought, the delicate features of a young language, the fresh hue of unconscious poetry'.[44] Until Müller's edition, 'our own' history was only gleaned through guesswork and endless, baseless speculations. Now, answers could be found in Müller's *editio princeps* of the *Rig Veda* (1849–74) and his numerous public lectures and books on India directed towards a general audience.

As we have noted, the traits of the representative groups who comprised 'Aryan humanity' had long captivated the European imagination. Max Müller merely continued this tradition. He identified the Aryans as 'our nearest intellectual relatives'.[45] They were the 'ancestors of the whole Aryan race, the first framers of our words, the first poets of our thoughts, the first givers of our laws, the first prophets of our gods and of Him who is God above all gods'.[46]

According to Müller, the Aryans[47] originated in the northern regions, living together within the same precincts as the ancestors of the Greeks, Italians, Slavonians, Germans, Persians, Hindus and Celts.[48] The actual site of the Aryan paradise, the 'cradle of our race', was not known.[49] However, Müller was sure that it was in the East, since the earliest centres of civilised life, he argued, were found in Asia.[50]

The Aryans were men of strong individuality and great independence. Early on, they separated into two branches.[51] The northern branch roamed north-westward and civilised the whole of Europe, completing the 'one act allotted to them on the stage of history'.[52] As the 'prominent actors in the great drama of history, they carried to their fullest growth all the elements of active life with which our nature is endowed'.[53] These Aryans 'perfected society and morals and taught us the elements of science, the laws of art, and the principles of philosophy'; they embodied man's historic character.[54] In this respect, they fundamentally differed from the southern branch of the Aryan race who represented the flipside of the human character, the passive and meditative who were 'absorbed in struggles of thought'.[55] This persona reached near completeness in India.[56]

> If I were to look over the whole world to find out the country most richly endowed with all the wealth, power, and beauty that nature can bestow – in some parts a very paradise on earth – I should point to India. If I were asked under what sky the human mind has most fully developed some of its choicest gifts, has most deeply pondered on the greatest problems of life, and has found solutions to some of them which well deserve the attention even of those who have studied Plato and Kant – I should point to India. And if I were to ask myself from what literature we, here in Europe, who have been nurtured almost exclusively on the thoughts of Greeks and Romans, and one Semitic race, the Jewish, may draw that corrective which is most wanted in order to make our inner life more perfect, more comprehensive, more universal, in fact, more truly human, a life not for this life only, but a transfigured and eternal life – again I should point to India ... I am thinking chiefly of India, such as it was a thousand, two thousand, it may be three thousand years ago – not of towns today but village communities.[57]

Within the fold of the Aryan race, Müller included the Hindus, the Persians, the Greeks and Romans, the Slavs, the Celts and 'last, not least, the Teutons'.[58] Certain groups, however, did not belong to his schema. For example, Müller excluded from the Aryan family the 'really barbarian races' such as Africans and American Indians[59] as well as the Turanian and Semitic races, all over whom the Aryans historically ruled.[60] Even before the initial dispersion, the Aryans lived separately from the Semites and Turanians.[61] Therefore, Europeans need claim no filiation with these races, either culturally or linguistically.

> We are by nature Aryan, Indo-European, not Semitic: our spiritual kith and kin are to be found in India, Persia, Greece, Italy, Germany; not in Mesopotamia, Egypt, or Palestine.[62]

Until the deciphering of the Veda, there had been

> but one oasis in that vast desert of ancient Asiatic history, the history of the Jews. The Veda now offers another such oasis (Müller 1895:1.5–6) as well as another instance of revelation (Müller 1895:1.17), the wisdom of Him who is not the God of the Jews alone.[63]

> Our knowledge of universal history is imperfect if we narrow our horizon to history of Greek and Romans, Saxons and Celts, with a dim background of Palestine, Egypt and Babylon, and leave out of sight our nearest intellectual relatives, the Aryas of India, the framers of the most wonderful language, Sanskrit, the fellow-workers in the construction of our

fundamental concepts, the fathers of the most transparent of mythologies, the inventors of the most subtle philosophy, and the givers of the most elaborate laws.[64]

In the contest between Sanskrit and Hebrew, it was necessary for Sanskrit to prevail. To do so, Müller first demoted Hebrew from its position as the *Ursprache*.[65] Next, he sought to isolate Sanskrit from any filiation with Hebrew. The linguistic similarities between Sanskrit and the Semitic language, he noted, were coincidences, as were any parallelisms between the Aryan and Semitic religions.[66] They were just too dissimilar; he noted that it was simply impossible to imagine that a Semitic language could ever have sprung from an Aryan or an Aryan language from a Semitic tongue.[67]

Similarly, in the contest between the *Rig Veda* and the Old Testament, it was clear which text Müller preferred. Since he could not fix the date of individual books of the Hebrew Bible, Müller simply dismissed them as unreliable guides to ancient history and religion.[68] The Old Testament merely revealed the extent to which decay was prevalent in the religion of the Jews. Although Old Testament writers had tried to hide the traces of degeneration, by placing the religion of the Jews before us as ready-made from the beginning, perfect, revealed and incapable of improvement, Müller claimed that they only succeeded in highlighting its pervasive decay.[69]

When Müller compared the Semites to the Aryans, he judged them to be deficient in scientific and philosophical originality. Their poetry was chiefly subjective. Müller thus sought to dismantle any Jewish pretensions to superiority. As we have seen elsewhere, the displacement of the Jews served as a prerequisite to the valorisation of the Aryan.

> We look in vain among their poets for excellence in epic and dramatic composition. Painting and plastic arts never more than at the decorative stage. Politics patriarchal and despotic, and their inability to organise on a large scale has deprived them of the means of military success. Perhaps the most general feature of their character is a negative one, – their inability to perceive the general and abstract whether in thought, language, poetry or politics; and, on the other hand, a strong attraction towards the individual and personal, which makes them monotheistic in religion, lyrical in poetry, monarchical in politics, abrupt in style and useless for speculation.[70]

Race was truly a metaphor for Müller. He spoke of the Aryan as a means of describing the ideal Self. To create a Self necessitated distinguishing an Other, lacking those qualities one attributed to the Self. The Jew, of course, became that Other. In this manner, the mythologisation of

THE VEDA AS AN ALTERNATIVE TO THE BIBLE

the Aryan completed the process of mythologising the Jew. But we are still in the realm of the imagination. Müller might say anything he wanted about Jews and Aryans, but he recoiled at the appropriation of his categorisations in the realm of the real.

On several occasions, he sought to distance himself from the misuse of his formulations by contemporary racial theorists[71] by distinguishing between linguistic and racial classification.

> I have declared again and again that if I say Aryas, I mean neither blood nor bones, nor hair nor skull; I mean simply those who speak an Aryan language. The same applies to Hindus, Greeks, Romans, Germans, Celts and Slaves. When I speak of them I commit myself to no anatomical characteristics. The blue-eyed and fair-haired Scandinavians may have been conquerors or conquered, they may have adopted the language of their darker lords or their subjects, or vice versa. I assert nothing beyond their language when I call them Hindus, Greeks, Romans, Germans, Celts and Slaves; and in that sense and in that sense only, do I say that even the blackest Hindus represent an earlier stage of Aryan speech and thought than the fairest Scandinavians. This may seem strong language, but in matters of such importance, we cannot be too decided in our language. To me an ethnologist who speaks of Aryan race, Aryan blood, Aryan eyes and hair, is as great a sinner as a linguist who speaks of a dolichocephalic dictionary or a brachycephalic grammar.[72]

Blood had nothing to do with language.[73] He maintained that Aryanness was an expression of culture. In other words, he firmly stated that one cannot base ethnological classification on linguistic and anthropological terms.[74] The science of language and the science of ethnology should not be mixed up. Races can change languages. Different languages can be spoken by our race and the same language by different races.[75] Of course, Müller spoke too little and too late. The great scholar of mythology did not, perhaps, realise that myths take on lives of their own, when they support the political interests of those in power or those seeking power.

> There is no Aryan race in blood, but whoever, through the imposition of hands, whether of his parents or his foreign masters, has received the Aryan blessing, belongs to that unbroken spiritual succession which began with the first apostles of that noble speech, and continues to the present day in every part of the globe. Aryan, in scientific language, is utterly inapplicable to race. It means language and nothing but language; and if we speak of Aryan race at all, we should know that it means no more than X + Aryan speech.[76]

In a long letter to the ethnographer and colonial administrator Sir Herbert Hope Risley commenting on his *Ethnological Survey of India*, Müller tried to exonerate himself from the mischief produced by employing the terminology of comparative philology in an ethnological sense.[77]

> My warnings have been of little effect; and such is the influence of evil communications, that I myself cannot help pleading guilty of having occasionally used linguistic terms in an ethnological sense. Still it is an evil that ought to be resisted with all our might. Ethnologists persist in writing of Aryas, Shemites and Turanians, Ugrians, Dravidians, Kolarians, Bantu races and c., forgetting that these terms have nothing to do with blood, or bones, or hair, or facial angles, but simply and solely with language. Aryas are those who speak Aryan languages, whatever their colour, whatever their blood. In calling them Aryas we predicate nothing of them except that the grammar of their language is Aryan. The classification of Aryas and Shemites is based on linguistic grounds and on nothing else; and it is only because languages must be spoken by somebody that we may allow ourselves to speak of language as synonymous with peoples.[78]

Müller's most public statement of position appeared in his *Antrittsrede* at the University of Strasbourg in 1872, when he reiterated that there existed only Aryan and Semitic linguistic families, but no Aryan race, blood or skulls. In later instances, Müller was clearly defensive. Eventually he did not speak of races and *Völkern*, rather 'the Aryan family', 'Aryan humanity' and 'the civilisation of the Aryan race, that race to which we and all the greatest nations of the world ... belong'.[79]

However, Müller's myth of the Aryan throughout the thirty-odd years of editing the *Rig Veda* entailed the very type of categorical mixing that he condemned in the Strasbourg lecture. How do we explain this paradox? I believe that it was far less an issue of Müller's blindness towards his methodology (though that too was at issue) than his adherence to a Romantic emplotment of India. His need to construct the Vedic Aryan from a text and identify with this Aryan stemmed from religious and aesthetic concerns far more akin to the aims of Romanticism than nineteenth-century race theory.

Müller would be shocked at an assessment of his work in light of Romanticism. He maintained that his Aryans were merely an earlier stage of our own race,[80] not a 'race of savages, of mere nomads and hunters', as he felt they had been presented by his academic rivals.[81] It was, he disclaimed, scholars like Pischel and Geldner[82] who were under the influence of Rousseau regarding the simplicity and innocence of primitive man versus the 'modern' Aryans who had reached the summit of civilisation. Müller did not recognise his penchant for lyricism, even when he spoke of Aryan 'home-grown poetry'[83] as 'natural growth'[84] that has been 'carried down the stream of time, and washed up on the shores of so many nations'[85] or their 'home-grown religion' that history has preserved for us 'in order to teach us what the human mind can achieve if left to itself, surrounded by a scenery and by conditions of life that might have made man's life on earth a paradise if man did not possess the strange art of turning even a paradise into a place of misery'.[86] But a Romantic he was and not just in a rhetorical sense.

One can see a pattern in Müller's classifications of language, gods and mythology. His analyses move from the material to the immaterial, the concrete to the abstract, the simple to the complex and the single to the general. Just as language began as monosyllabic and developed agglutination and inflection, so then did Müller conclude that monotheism preceded polytheism.[87] He placed mythology and polytheism at the door of language. Müller's reading of the Veda verified the Romantic claim that India was the original seat of true poetry, primitive revelation and the site of its degeneration. Max Müller was a worthy heir to his father, the German Romantic poet Wilhelm Müller.

This Indologist, a final avatar of Romanticism in service of linguistics, popularised an ideal vision of the Aryan that would have serious repercussions. Although he himself tried to resist 'patriotic' impulses, Müller had to admit that he would be as proud as anyone to look upon 'Germany as the cradle of all Aryan life'[88] and 'Teutonic speech as the fountain of all Aryan thought'.[89] So, indeed, did the non-specialists who expanded upon his theories.[90]

Conclusion

Let us remember the dates of Müller's Veda (1849–74). Rather than have it begin our examination of the reception of the Veda in the West, we have allowed it to mark the end of our inquiry. The Veda as a 'real' text was either unknown or little known to Western authors before Müller. Nevertheless, it played a significant role in Enlightenment, pre-Romantic and Romantic literary and philosophical speculation. As an absent text, it wielded great authority. Although neither discovered nor fully translated, the Veda served as an important tool in formulating European discourse concerning poetry, race and religion. The possibility of the existence of the Veda affected a renewed interest in the Romantic theses of a revealed and primitive monotheism and the degeneration of Greek culture.

It is to be remembered that the Romantics held that the simplicity of religious dogmas defined the original state of man and its corollaries that monotheism was anterior to polytheism and primitive revelation had progressively degenerated. Once a people has unfolded its spirit to its fullest expression – from the Romantic point of view – it has fulfilled its role in history and only 'repetition' (revivals), stagnation and decay could follow. Müller's conclusions concerning the Veda recapitulated this central Romantic thesis.

Moreover, Romantic concepts regarding the degeneration of primitive monotheism into polytheism and the view of history as an unfolding expression of the spirit of a people followed by decay and stagnation continued to influence the European intellectual climate late into the nineteenth century. Stagnation would become a keyword in characterising Indian civilisation and would eventually find its way into the general writings of philosophers like Hegel, Marx and Spengler.

History was in a state of motion, a living organism. Universal history was structured organically and could be reduced to certain recurring elementary phenomena with the birth, development and death of the individual or group organism as eternal. Decadent cultures distinguished themselves from cultured populations. Decadent peoples consisted of those cut off from the soil, hovering between peace and war, the national and international. The cultured were those bound by a common destiny. Culture was Faustian, constantly in progress. The *Rig Veda*'s 'appearance' in Max Müller's abundant commentary merely confirmed these Romantic hypotheses.

The discovery that there existed in India a tradition older or, at least, as old as the biblical tradition was regarded as an event of the first magnitude, only to be compared in its consequences to the rediscovery of classical antiquity in the Renaissance. Through the study of India's past, it was hoped that scholars could reconstruct the history of mankind's past and origin, the development of religions and philosophies. By giving Vedic Aryans a place in universal history, a not-too-subtle displacement of the Jews was effected. Much of the discourse concerning the Veda effectively resulted in assigning the Jews a subaltern role in history. In Voltaire's case, we saw how the valorisation of the Aryans, who had been ignored by the Bible and universal histories, necessarily entailed a devaluation of the Judaeo-Christian tradition. Voltaire was always motivated by his need to challenge the primacy of the Church. For others, the motivations for this displacement were less clear.

One can distinguish, therefore, two motives for the beginnings of Vedic scholarship in the West. First, there entailed the search for the oldest forms of religion and language. Secondly, it set the stage for the inquiry into the origin and past of the Anglo-Saxon people through information drawn from ancient Sanskrit sources. With the twentieth-century legacy of Aryanism fresh in our memory, it is difficult not to overstate the argument. We can acknowledge, however, that the European discourse on the Veda (even when an absent text) created a portrait of pure and cultivated Aryan ancestors which wielded such authority that the subsequent discovery of the text could not alter the welter of assumptions and fantasies that formed its initial interpretation. This ideology of the Aryan participated in the formation of a new mythology of the past. This mythology was fuelled by irrational impulses growing out of anxiety regarding questions of national identity and mission. Specific themes resonating in the works of the authors examined here found their way into the new mythology: the displacement of the Jews from a central position on the stage of history; theories regarding the degeneration of peoples and religions from unity and purity to multiplicity and polytheism; and the idealisation of imaginary ancestors and their fictitious descendants. Thus, the myth of the Aryan was employed not only to construct the origins of society, but also to foster nationalism. In its latter configuration, it could be used to disarticulate existing society and rearticulate an alternative noteworthy for its identification of a mythic scapegoat.

Notes

1 There has been a spate of books in the 2000s on the intellectual history of race and Orientalist/Indological scholarship such as Urs App, *The Birth of Orientalism* (Philadelphia, PA: University of Pennsylvania Press, 2010); David Chidester, *Empire of Religion: Imperialism and Comparative Religion* (Chicago, IL: University of Chicago Press, 2014); Suzanne Marchand, *German Orientalism in the Age of Empire: Religion, Race and Scholarship* (New York: Cambridge University Press, 2005) and Colin Kidd, *The Forging of Races: Race and Scripture in the Protestant Atlantic World, 1600–2000* (Cambridge: Cambridge University Press, 2006). For a much fuller exposition of the Aryan hypothesis from a literary perspective and thus different in focus and pre-dating the spate of books in the first decades of the 2000s see Dorothy Figueira, *Aryans, Jews, Brahmins: Theorizing Authority through Myths of Identity* (Albany, NY: State University of New York Press, 2002).
2 Voltaire, *Oeuvres Complètes*, ed. L. E. D. Moland and G. Bengesco, 52 vols (Paris: Garnier Frères, 1877–85), XVIII: p. 34.
3 Voltaire, *Oeuvres Complètes*, XI: p. 184.
4 Voltaire, *Oeuvres Complètes*, XXIX: p. 482.
5 Voltaire, *Oeuvres Complètes*, XI: p. 551.
6 Voltaire, *Oeuvres Complètes*, XXVIII: p. 139.
7 Voltaire wrote:
'Ce ne fut que dans le premier siècle de notre ère qu'un faussaire très maladroit, soit juif, soit demi-juif et demi chrétien, ayant appris quelque chose de la religion des brachmanes, fabriqua un écrit qu'il osa attribuer à Enoch. C'est dans le livre d'Enoch qu'il est parlé de la rébellion de quelques puissances célestes que le faussaire appelle anges' (Voltaire, *Oeuvres Complètes*, XXVIII: p. 138).
8 Voltaire, *Oeuvres Complètes*, XXIX: p. 59.
9 Voltaire, *Oeuvres Complètes*, XXIX: p. 471.
10 Voltaire, *Oeuvres Complètes*, XXIX: p. 481.
11 Voltaire, *Oeuvres Complètes*, XI: p. 47.
12 Voltaire, *Oeuvres Complètes*, XXIX: p. 184.
13 For an exhaustive analysis of this text, see Ludo Rocher, ed., *Ezourvedam: A French Veda of the Eighteenth Century* (Amsterdam and Philadelphia, PA: John Benjamins, 1984).
14 Cited in Daniel S. Hawley, 'L'Inde de Voltaire', *Studies on Voltaire and the Eighteenth Century*, 120 (1974), 151.

15 J. G. Herder, *Sämtliche Werke*, ed. B. Suphan, 33 vols (Berlin: Weidmannsche Buchhandlung, 1877–1913), XIII:, pp. 38, 399, 403, 406. For India as the site of the Garden of Eden, see Voltaire, *Oeuvres Complètes*, XIII: p. 423.
16 Herder, *Sämtliche Werke*, V: p. 447; XIII: pp. 252, 405.
17 Herder, *Sämtliche Werke*, V: p. 539.
18 Herder, *Sämtliche Werke*, XVII: pp. 58–9.
19 Herder, *Sämtliche Werke*, XXX: p. 8.
20 As Brian Pennington has noted, missionary attacks on Hindu polytheism usually recycled anti-Catholic tropes. See Brian Pennington, *Was Hinduism Invented? Britons, Indians and Colonial Construction of Religion* (Oxford: Oxford University Press, 2005), pp. 67–9, 71–2.
21 See Jonathan Sheehan, *The Enlightenment Bible: Translation, Scholarship, Culture* (Princeton, NJ: Princeton University Press, 2005).
22 Georg Friedrich Creuzer, *Symbolik und Mythologie des alten Völker, besonders der Griechen*, 6 vols (Leipzig and Darmstadt: Heyer und Leske 1819–23), I: pp. 551, 554.
23 Georg Friedrich Creuzer, *Aus dem Leben eines alten Professors* (Heidelberg, Leipzig and Darmstadt: Heyer and Leske, 1840), p. 65.
24 Creuzer, *Symbolik und Mythologie*, I: pp. 546–7.
25 Creuzer, *Symbolik und Mythologie*, I: p. 570.
26 Creuzer, *Symbolik und Mythologie*, II: pp. 375–6.
27 Creuzer, *Symbolik und Mythologie*, I: p. 575.
28 Joseph Görres, *Mythengeschichte der asiatischen Welt*, 2 vols (Heidelberg: Mohr and Zimmer, 1810), I: pp. 13–14; II: p. 649.
29 Görres, *Mythengeschichte der asiatischen Welt*, I: pp. 37–40.
30 Görres, *Mythengeschichte der asiatischen Welt*, II: p. 611.
31 Görres, *Mythengeschichte der asiatischen Welt*, I: p. 54.
32 Görres, *Mythengeschichte der asiatischen Welt*, II: pp. 329, 435–6, 556.
33 Görres, *Mythengeschichte der asiatischen Welt*, I: pp. 117–19.
34 Görres, *Mythengeschichte der asiatischen Welt*, I: p. 569.
35 Görres, *Mythengeschichte der asiatischen Welt*, I: p. 571.
36 Görres, *Mythengeschichte der asiatischen Welt*, I: pp. xxxi–xxxvi.
37 Karl Ritter, *Die Vorhalle der Europäischen Völkergeschichte vor Herodots, un den Kaukasus und an den Gestaden des Pontus* (Berlin: G. Reimer, 1820), pp. 33–4.
38 Ritter, *Die Vorhalle der Europäischen Völkergeschichte vor Herodots*, pp. 23–4, 26.
39 Friedrich Max Müller, *India, What Can It Teach Us?* (London: Longmans, Green and Co., 1892), p. 254.
40 Müller, *India, What Can It Teach Us?*, p. 6.
41 Friedrich Max Müller, *History of Ancient Sanskrit Literature so far as It Illustrates the Primitive Religion of the Brahmins* (New York: AMS Press, 1978), p. 3.
42 Friedrich Max Müller, *Physical Religion* (London: Longmans, Green and Co., 1891), pp. 148–9.
43 Friedrich Max Müller, *Chips from a German Workshop*, 5 vols (New York: Charles Scribner's Sons, 1895), p. 167.
44 Friedrich Max Müller, *Rig-Veda-Samhita: The Sacred Hymns of the Brahmins*, 6 vols (London: William H. Allen, 1849–74), III: p. xliii.
45 Müller, *India, What Can It Teach Us?*, p. 15; see also *Chips from a German Workshop*, I: p. 63.
46 Müller, *India, What Can It Teach Us?*, p. 117.
47 His terms were *Arier* and *Indo-Germanen*. See Müller, *Chips from a German Workshop*, I: p. 65.
48 Müller, *History of Ancient Sanskrit Literature*, p. 14; see also *Chips from a German Workshop*, I: pp. 63–4, 66; II: p. 20.
49 Friedrich Max Müller, *Biographies of Words and the Home of the Aryans* (London: Longmans, Green and Co., 1888), pp. 91, 127.
50 Müller, *Biographies of Words*, p. 117.
51 Müller, *History of Ancient Sanskrit Literature*, p. 12.

THE VEDA AS AN ALTERNATIVE TO THE BIBLE

52 They travelled along two possible paths, through Russia to the shores of the Black Sea and Thrace, and from Armenia across the Caucasus or across the Black Sea to northern Greece and along the Danube. See Friedrich Max Müller, *The Science of Language* (London: Longmans, Green and Co., 1899), p. 298. See also Müller, *Chips from a German Workshop*, I: p. 61; *History of Ancient Sanskrit Literature*, p. 14.
53 Müller, *History of Ancient Sanskrit Literature*, p. 14.
54 Müller, *Chips from a German Workshop*, I: pp. 63–4.
55 Müller, *Chips from a German Workshop*, I: pp. 65–6.
56 Müller, *India, What Can It Teach Us?*, p. 95.
57 Müller, *India, What Can It Teach Us?*, pp. 6–7.
58 Müller, *India, What Can It Teach Us?*, p. 116; see also Müller, *Physical Religion*, p. 21.
59 Müller, *History of Ancient Sanskrit Literature*, p. 558.
60 Müller, *History of Ancient Sanskrit Literature*, p. 15.
61 Müller, *History of Ancient Sanskrit Literature* p. 14; see also Müller, *Chips from a German Workshop*, I: pp. 63–6.
62 Müller, *Chips from a German Workshop*, I: p. 4.
63 Müller, *History of Ancient Sanskrit Literature*, p. 3. See also Müller, *India, What Can It Teach Us?*, p. 112: 'I maintain that to everybody who cares for himself, for his ancestors, for his history, or for his intellectual development, a study of Vedic literature is indispensable; and that, as an element of liberal education, it is far more important and far more improving than the reigns of Babylonian and Persian kings, yea even, than the dates and deeds of many of the kings of Judah and Israel.'
64 Müller, *India, What Can It Teach Us?*, p. 15.
65 The fact that we cannot explain how so many dialects could be traced back to Hebrew (although many have tried) suggested to Müller that the problem had been misformulated. See Müller, *The Science of Language*, p. 147. Also see Friedrich Max Müller, *Lectures on the Origin and Growth of Religion as Illustrated by the Religions of India* (London: Longmans, Green and Co., 1879), pp. 246–7.
66 Müller, *Physical Religion*, p. 274.
67 Müller, *Science of Language*, p. 324.
68 Müller, *Physical Religion*, p. 214.
69 Müller, *Lectures on the Origin and Growth of Religion*, p. 125.
70 Müller, *Chips from a German Workshop*, I: p. 339.
71 Friedrich Max Müller, *Essays*, 4 vols (Leipzig: W. Engelmann, 1869–76), IV: pp. 103–27.
72 Müller, *Biographies of Words*, p. 120.
73 Müller, *Biographies of Words*, p. 108.
74 Friedrich Max Müller, *Über dies Resultate des Sprachwissenschaft. Vorlesungen gehalten der Kaiserlichen Universität zu Strassburg am xxiii anni MDCCCLXXII* (Strasbourg: K. J. Trübner, 1872), p. 17.
75 Müller, *Science of Language*, p. 450.
76 Müller, *Biographies of Words*, pp. 89–90.
77 After qualifying his position as a longstanding one, Müller offers Risley his advice: 'If you were to issue an interdict against any of your collaborateurs using linguistic terms in an ethnological sense, I believe that your Ethnological Survey of India would inaugurate a new and most important era both in the science of language and in the science of man.' See Müller, *Biographies of Words*, p. 247.
78 Müller, *Biographies of Words*, pp. 244–5.
79 Müller, *India, What Can It Teach Us?*, p. 116.
80 Müller, *Physical Religion*, pp. 385–6.
81 Müller, *Chips from a German Workshop*, II: p. 40.
82 Richard Pischel, a German Indologist and professor of comparative linguistics at Halle who, along with Karl Friedrich Geldner wrote the three-volume *Vedische Studien* (Stuttgart: W. Kohlhammer, 1889–1901).
83 Müller, *India, What Can It Teach Us?*, p. 140.
84 Müller, *India, What Can It Teach Us?*, p. 97.

85 Müller, *Chips from a German Workshop*, II: p. 40.
86 Müller, *India, What Can It Teach Us?*, p. 140.
87 Müller, *History of Ancient Sanskrit Literature*, pp. 510–12, 528, 559; see also Müller, *India, What Can It Teach Us?*, I: pp. 91–2; II: p. 132.
88 Müller, *Biographies of Words*, p. 127.
89 Müller, *Biographies of Words*, p. 154.
90 For a discussion of later nationalist (Indian and European) variations on this theme, see Figueira, *Aryans, Jews, Brahmins*.

CHAPTER EIGHT

'The Bible makes all nations one': biblical literacy and Khoesan national renewal in the Cape Colony

Jared McDonald

In London, on 27 June 1836, Andries Stoffels, a Gonaqua Khoekhoe from the Cape Colony, appeared before the House of Commons Select Committee on Aborigines in British Settlements. Convened at the behest of humanitarian MP, Thomas Fowell Buxton, the Committee investigated the impact of colonial settlement on indigenous peoples in Britain's expanding empire. Born in the Zuurveld near the Bushman's River some time between 1776 and 1786, Stoffels witnessed the Dutch conquest of his people's land in the eastern Cape. As a boy, he served on Boer *commandos* which attacked San *kraals*.[1] Between 1799 and 1802, he participated in the unsuccessful Khoe uprising against the Dutch settlers along the eastern Cape frontier, known as the Servants' Revolt.[2] In later years, Stoffels was described by a missionary as 'like Moses', in that 'he felt severely the degraded state of his countrymen as having lost their country, their property, and their liberty'.[3] Stoffels first encountered Protestant Christianity at Bethelsdorp, one of the earliest mission stations founded by the London Missionary Society (LMS) in the Cape Colony. At the helm of the mission at the time of Stoffel's arrival there in 1803 was the eccentric and controversial Dr Johannes van der Kemp, who, by espousing an egalitarian interpretation of the Gospel, undermined white settler ownership of Christianity, its symbols and perhaps most importantly, salvation.[4]

When asked by the Select Committee on Aborigines to describe the 'first thing' that van der Kemp taught those attending the mission, Stoffels replied, 'He taught us the Word of God.' According to Stoffels, van der Kemp also advised them to 'thank the English people for having sent ... the Word of God'.[5] James Read, van der Kemp's young apprentice at Bethelsdorp, explained that after his initial reluctance to listen and learn, Stoffels returned to the mission where 'his convictions were deepened by the Word of God'. Eventually, after a few years, 'light broke in upon his mind [and] he understood the way of salvation through a crucified Saviour'.[6] Thereafter, Stoffels became a committed promoter of Christianity, declaring the hope for national renewal it offered the battered remnants of his people. In describing the fate of the Gonaqua Khoe to the Select Committee in 1836, Stoffels commented that they had 'no water ... not a blade of grass ... no lands ... no wood'. The 'missionary and the Bible' was all that they had.[7] He continued, 'My nation is poor and degraded, but the Word of God is their stay and their hope ... The Bible makes all nations one. The Bible brings wild man and civilised together. The Bible is our light. The [Khoekhoe] nation was almost exterminated, but the Bible has brought the nations together, and here am I before you.'[8]

During the early nineteenth century, the public sphere in the Cape Colony was fraught with contesting views and rival opinions over notions of identity and belonging, and in particular, how such notions intersected with biblical literacy and interpretation. The nonconformist missionary enterprise, spearheaded in the Cape Colony by representatives of the LMS, disseminated biblical narratives which resonated with remnants of the region's indigenous population, the Khoesan. This is a convenient label commonly used to refer to the social conglomeration of the Cape's formerly independent pastoralists (Khoekhoe) and hunter-gatherers (San) which emerged during the late eighteenth and early nineteenth centuries. Though there was no such people as the Khoesan, the term has found traction in Cape scholarship as it alludes to the complex, mixed ancestries of the Cape's indigenous underclass, which was distinct from the Cape's slave population. The label is also free of the pejorative connotations of the colonial labels, Hottentots (Khoekhoe) and Bushmen (San). By the time of Britain's second occupation of the Cape Colony in 1806, many Khoesan had been incorporated into the colonial economy as forced labourers, with diminishing numbers eking out a precarious, semi-independent existence on the margins of colonial society.

The rapid growth in popularity of the Protestant, nonconformist missionary movement among Khoesan coincided with Britain's efforts to remould the Cape Colony into a territory which exhibited British characteristics. Cape society had already been structured according to a racial hierarchy, though race was not yet the sole determinant of belonging as it was to become from the 1840s and 1850s onwards (when the so-called barbarity of indigenous peoples became increasingly accepted in British attitudes towards the Empire).[9] Christian identity held important sway in the Cape Colony during the early nineteenth century and was an important marker of social status and inclusion. The early nineteenth-century Cape context presented possibilities for equality along religious lines for Khoesan, even as racial equality remained out of reach. Of course, even these possibilities were to be dashed by mid-century, when evangelical humanitarianism began to retreat from the colonial stage to be followed by a 'transition towards the strident racism of the age of high imperialism'.[10]

Mission Christianity, settler society and the colonial administration all emphasised 'respectability' when defining boundaries of status and belonging in the Cape Colony. Two of the most important markers of respectability were profession of the Christian faith and literacy, in addition to other markers such as sobriety, monogamy, regular compensated labour and European-style housing and clothing. Nonconformist missionaries stressed the need for Christian converts to become literate in order to substantiate missionaries' interpretations of Scripture in their own reading, and created an image of Protestant Christianity as a Bible-oriented religion among Khoesan. Biblical literacy (knowledge of idioms, narratives and tropes) held out the prospect of subverting and blurring social hierarchies for dispossessed and displaced Khoesan forcefully integrated into Cape society as a labouring underclass. With the Bible established as a significant cultural and political resource in a settler-colonial society wherein status was determined by religious identity as well as racial identity, literate Khoesan who had access to the sacred text could seek to claim a measure of social equality.

For Khoesan descended from distinct, pre-colonial ethnic lineages, biblical literacy offered a language through which a new Christian 'nation' could be imagined and articulated, and which could challenge settler-colonial hierarchies of power.[11] The following discussion explores how the Bible became a site of contestation in the struggle over the ownership of Protestant Christianity in the Cape Colony during the early nineteenth century. Khoesan acceptance of the Bible did not simply amount to submission to Western domination. Biblical literacy was not delivered to a passive audience, nor was its deployment unidirectional. Rather, Khoesan interpretations of Scripture positioned the Bible as a disruptive, anti-colonial text. This chapter argues that even though Protestant, nonconformist missionaries were instrumental in establishing the primacy of Christianity-as-text among Khoesan congregants, Khoesan appropriated biblical literacy in order to claim their own covenant with God. In doing so, Khoesan confirmed the Bible as a potent repository of symbolism and imagery to serve Khoesan national renewal and to challenge racially based notions of Christian identity. This was to have significant social and political ramifications during the early nineteenth-century colonial encounter in the Cape Colony.

THE BIBLE IN TRANSIT AND TRANSLATION

Khoesan social crisis and the arrival of the missionaries

In 1806, the second British occupation of the Cape Colony came into effect. This marked the beginning of an effort to transform the Cape Colony into a more clearly defined territory over which the British Crown could exercise legal jurisdiction. The British colonial authorities inherited a settler population descended largely from the early Dutch colonists. These settlers had established themselves as landed, farming communities throughout much of the south-western Cape and its hinterland. Settler advance into the Cape interior over the course of the previous century and a half, following the establishment of a trading port at Cape Town in 1652 by the *Verenigde Ooste-Indische Compagnie* (VOC), had been steady, but challenged by concerted resistance from the indigenous inhabitants. The Khoekhoe and San proved to be formidable enemies in the ensuing struggle over access to land and resources. The hunter-gatherers, or San, were more mobile than the pastoralist Khoekhoe, and retreated into the Cape interior, ahead of the colonial frontier. Khoekhoe independence had, for the most part, been eroded by 1803, following the end of the Khoekhoe uprising along the eastern Cape frontier in which Andries Stoffels had participated.

For Khoekhoe and San, the eighteenth century was a period of unrelenting social upheaval. Dispossessed of their land and cattle, Khoekhoe, along with some San, were incorporated into the agricultural and cattle-farming economy of the emerging settler society as a labouring underclass. On agrarian and cattle farms across the Cape Colony, Khoekhoe and San became servants to European masters. The master–servant relationship was shaped by the realities of a slave society. Slaves were first imported to the Cape in 1658, sourced from across the Indian Ocean rim. The VOC had decided not to enslave the Khoekhoe and San; however, the importation of slaves to the Cape was never of a sufficient scale to satisfy the labour demands of the wheat and wine industries of the south-western Cape. And as Dutch farmers ventured further into the interior, so the purchasing price of slaves rose. This shortage in the supply of slave labour in the Cape's frontier districts was filled by Khoesan servants. The predominant slave-owning mentality of the master class was a determining feature of master–Khoesan interactions on farmsteads across the Colony.[12] The right of the master to the submission and compliance of his slaves also extended to the 'free' Khoesan labourers in his service. Though never formally enslaved, nor officially bought and sold, Khoesan labour experiences were often akin to those of the slaves, alongside whom they worked and lived.

The distances between European settlement were narrowed over the course of the late eighteenth and early nineteenth centuries, limiting opportunities for an independent existence outside settler society and the settler economy. Some Khoesan chose a precarious existence on the physical margins of the Colony. Labelled vagrants by the colonial administration, theirs was an existence often based on livestock theft and eluding capture.[13] Other Khoesan made their way northwards, to the Gariep River and beyond, where they joined the ranks of the Oorlams and Griquas.[14] Many thousands, however, became members of a dispossessed underclass on which the settler economy depended as an alternative, or supplementary, source of labour to slaves. Their inferior social status was reinforced by the caustic tone of European representations of Khoekhoe and San as backward, uncivilised and lacking religion and cultural sophistication.

It was within this context that Protestant Christian missionaries first encountered the Khoesan. Systematic land and water alienation, accompanied by the brutal suppression of Khoesan resistance during the closing decades of the eighteenth century, meant that the missionaries happened upon a defeated, and in many ways devastated, people. Elizabeth Elbourne has argued that the social crisis in which the missionaries found the Khoesan meant that their efforts to persuade them of the merits of the new belief system they offered were made easier. Elbourne has contended that 'societies in a state of profound crisis – dissolution even – are far more prone to seek new explanations and meaning systems' than those which have maintained a sense of social and political cohesiveness and stability.[15] Elbourne's assessment has held out under scrutiny, certainly when considered in the light of the remarkable extent to which Khoesan within the Colony embraced missions, and subsequently, to varying degrees, Protestant Christianity.

Although the LMS was not the first European-based missionary society to establish missions in southern Africa, having been preceded by the Moravians, it would, nonetheless, become the most important in terms of its political influence both within and beyond the Colony. The Cape Colony was one of the LMS's earliest mission fields, along with the South Sea Islands. Four representatives arrived at Cape Town in 1799, four years after the Society had been founded. Their early missions to the Xhosa in the eastern Cape and the San in the northern Cape (both groups falling outside the official boundaries of the Cape Colony at the time and as such, maintaining a degree of independence) met with little success and these missions were soon abandoned. It would seem that the dispossessed, displaced Khoesan communities of the Cape Colony were more open to their ministrations and it was towards them that the LMS concentrated its efforts to disseminate the Gospel and to create Christian converts.

The establishment of mission stations throughout the Colony became the working template of the LMS, following the example of the Moravians, who had experienced much success with this approach.[16] While itinerant preaching remained an important aspect of the missionary's duties, mission stations were appealing for a community which had been dispossessed of its land, coerced into labour and subjected to oppressive colonial laws, such as the Caledon Code. Introduced by the Governor of the Cape in 1809, the Caledon Code, or 'Hottentot Code', required all Khoesan within the Colony to carry a pass indicating a fixed place of residence and employment. The Code established Khoesan as a legal category of labourers. Though distinct from the slaves in that they were not owned as property, the Khoesan were 'unfree' as they were subjected to legal restrictions which curtailed their mobility and their choice of where and when to work. Any Khoesan found without the required pass was deemed a vagrant and could be forced into labour. In this context, one of the few spaces of relative independence was the mission station. The mission station 'provided a place to leave stock and children, and served as a bastion against *de facto* enserfment'.[17]

The first mission station in the Cape Colony was founded by the Moravians at Baviaanskloof, subsequently named Genadendal, in the Overberg region, a few days journey by ox-wagon from Cape Town. Established in 1737 and abandoned in 1744 due to the hostility of the surrounding farmers and the opposition of the Dutch Reformed clergy, the short-lived first mission of Georg Schmidt set the disruptive tone for the mission project that was to recommence at the Cape in the 1790s. Schmidt taught his followers to read the Bible. He also baptised five Khoesan. These were highly subversive acts. Prior to Schmidt's arrival, the Khoekhoe and San had been regarded as beyond salvation, predestined to damnation. Profession of the Christian faith was understood to be a fundamental marker of white identity. Richard Elphick has noted that Schmidt's actions at Baviaanskloof were of powerful symbolic significance, disrupting Christianity's 'snug fit with the hierarchy of colonial society'.[18]

In 1792, nearly half a century after Schmidt's departure from the Cape, the Moravians renewed their mission at Baviaanskloof. Upon their arrival at the abandoned mission on 24 December that year, the new missionaries met an elderly Khoesan woman, said to be at least 80 years old at the time. Magdalena had been baptised by Schmidt and though almost blind and no longer able to read, she showed the missionaries the Dutch New Testament Schmidt had given her. It was neatly wrapped in two sheepskins and kept in a leather bag. A younger woman, who had been taught to read by another of Schmidt's converts, would regularly read the Scriptures to Magdalena. Asked to read a passage by the missionaries, the woman opened the book at the second chapter of the Gospel of Matthew and 'read the whole chapter very nicely'. That she chose to read a chapter about the birth of Jesus Christ on Christmas Eve was said to have moved the hearts of the missionaries.[19]

The subversive power of biblical literacy

Protestant Christianity is a Bible-oriented religion and the nonconformist missionaries who arrived at the Cape in the wake of the Moravians insisted on converts being literate. The ability to read the Scriptures was considered essential for converts to build individual relationships with God.[20] Protestantism, as a religion of text and practice, demanded that followers be able to read the Bible for themselves. The Comaroffs have noted that for nonconformists, literacy was associated with self-improvement and necessary for salvation. Evangelism and education were two sides of the same coin and literacy was essential for both.[21] Khoesan literacy represented more than just the ability to read. Being literate was a subversive act for *indigenes* in a colonial context where literacy was associated with respectability and status, and until the arrival of the missionaries, deemed the preserve of white settlers of social and political standing.[22] Until 1806, it was actually illegal to teach Khoesan to read and write. This highlights the powerful association between literacy and freedom that existed at the Cape at a time when the missionary movement had limited influence on colonial affairs.[23]

Biblical literacy had the potential to be even more subversive, as it threatened to upend the social hierarchy of the Cape Colony, which during the early nineteenth century was based on an assumed correlation between religious and racial identity. The dominant Calvinist doctrines of the VOC era meant that little effort had been made to evangelise and convert the Khoesan. White settlers referred to themselves as Christians and claimed a 'permanent monopoly' on Christianity.[24] In the eighteenth century, white superiority at the Cape came to be founded upon both race and religion, especially among Dutch communities on the Cape's frontiers (though it was only in the twentieth century that the idea of being a nation chosen by God would emerge more forcefully as a foundational element of Afrikaner nationalism).[25]

The Bible was an important medium by which foreign ways of thinking and believing were imposed on the Khoesan. Nonetheless, as a text open to multiple interpretations, the Bible also presented a means to challenge established authority, as well as the religious boundaries which underscored and reinforced the Cape's racial hierarchy. Jennifer Cooper has noted that the civilising mission embodied an inherent paradox. Missionaries may have 'built new systems of knowledge which informed and aided British imperial interests', yet at the same time, 'these new constructions made accessible to Africans avenues through which to enter the contest for power'.[26] Khoesan biblical literacy undermined settler control of the Scriptures and in doing so, provided access to the social status afforded to those who could read the most powerfully symbolic text in Cape colonial society. The social boundaries defined by religious identity were steadily eroded as growing numbers of Khoesan attended mission schools and learned to read the Scriptures.[27] In support of Elbourne, Elphick argues that in the light of the extensive social disintegration suffered by the Khoesan by the time the missionaries arrived, Christianity came to represent not only freedom from sin and guilt, but also freedom from social inferiority.[28]

Claims to social equality may have been momentary, but they were symbolically disruptive of the colonial order, especially in interpersonal exchanges between Khoesan and Boers. For example, three Khoesan Christians, while preaching to the labourers and slaves on a Boer farm, were challenged by the master to explain the singing and praying they were encouraging among his servants and slaves. Jacob Links, one of the Khoesan Christians, recognised the mocking tone in the delivery of the Boer's question. To this Jacob responded, 'many of the farmers say we ought to not have the gospel', but handing the Boer a Bible and turning to the Gospel of John, chapter three, enquired, 'Who are the persons that must be born again?' With the Boer claiming to be unable to read the passage for himself due to poor eyesight, Jacob Links declared, 'Jesus Christ says we are all sinners, and that we must be born again in the Spirit, or we cannot enter the kingdom of heaven.' At this point, Jan Links, another of the Khoesan Christians, weighed in, noting the Boer had once told him that Khoesan names did not appear in the book and the Gospel did not belong to them. Jacob Links remarked that the so-called Christians referred to the Khoesan as heathens. However, according to Scripture, 'Jesus came as light to lighten the Heidenen (Gentiles).' In response to the Boer's ignorance of Scripture, Hendrick Smit, the third member of the itinerant party, quoted 1 Corinthians 2:14, 'The man without the Spirit does not accept the things that come from the Spirit of God, for they are foolishness to him and he cannot understand them, because they are spiritually discerned.' Jacob Links then asked the Boer if he ever taught his slaves and servants 'anything of the gospel', to which the Boer is reported to have responded, 'No, certainly nothing at all, for were they taught, it would make them equally as wise as myself.'[29]

This encounter points towards the subversive power of biblical literacy when wielded by Khoesan Christians. Even if the Boer was illiterate, which is a reasonable assumption, Jacob, Jan and Hendrick were clearly better versed in Scripture. Their command of the Bible meant they were able to challenge the dominant representation of Khoesan as heathen beyond redemption.[30] In addition, they were so bold as to suggest that the Boer failed to understand 'the things of the Spirit of God'. This was not just a daring assertion, but a powerfully symbolic claim which struck at the heart of the colonial hierarchy. The weight of the slight may have been lost on the Boer, who offered little retort. Even so, the implication was that the three Khoesan men could claim a legitimate covenant with God, confirmed by Scripture and made possible by their ability to read and reference the Bible for themselves.

The Bible stood as a source of authority, and, in particular, the master's authority, on the settler farmstead. Its message was dispensed, or withheld, at the will of the master. For example, Diana, a Khoekhoe woman, reported that in her master's house, the Bible was never read in the presence of the servants and slaves. In a bid to hear some of the forbidden text, Diana would wash the feet of her master and his family while the reading was taking place. Eventually, her motive was discovered and she was barred from entering the room when the Bible was being read. Thereafter, Diana would listen by the door, aided by a gap near the threshold.[31] Literacy afforded access to this otherwise elusive source of authority, undermining the power of the master as gatekeeper. Not only could literate converts claim their own covenant with God, they could also claim increased social status and equality.[32]

The appeal of biblical literacy increased in step with the growth of the missionary movement at the Cape. Within a few years of its re-establishment in 1792, the Moravian mission at Genadendal had the second largest population of any settlement in the Colony after Cape Town. Following a slow, uncertain start among the San and Xhosa, the LMS began to encounter more success among the Khoesan. By the early nineteenth century, most Khoesan living in the Cape Colony were able (required) to speak Dutch, or its emerging local variant, Cape Dutch (the precursor to Afrikaans). For the most part, the European missionaries failed to learn the disappearing Khoesan languages. Johannes van der Kemp believed that Khoesan languages, and more broadly, African languages, were best suited to convey biblical messages and idioms, much like Robert Moffat and David Livingstone in subsequent years.

Van der Kemp is reported to have completed a catechism in a Khoesan language; likely, the most common Khoesan language spoken by the residents of Bethelsdorp, where he was the head missionary from 1803 until his death in 1811. Unfortunately, this translated catechism has been lost. Unlike many missionaries who were to follow him to the

Cape, van der Kemp deemed it necessary to have a sound knowledge of indigenous culture and vernacular, and to train up and send out indigenous evangelists as soon as possible.[33] As Elphick notes, van der Kemp was one of a few early Protestant missionaries who believed that 'African languages were the most appropriate instruments of evangelisation' and that 'African preachers were the most effective.'[34] This stood in stark contrast to the dominant, white settler claim to ownership of Christianity.

In addition to reading and writing, biblical teaching was also conveyed via prayers and hymn-singing.[35] Van der Kemp's egalitarian representation of the gospel positioned Khoesan as potential brothers and sisters in Christ, thus holding out the prospect of belonging to an ecumenical brotherhood in the Cape Colony and beyond. The transcendent tone of this interpretation had a clear influence on Andries Stoffels' understanding of Christian belonging, as indicated by his testimony to the Select Committee on Aborigines. The Khoesan having suffered extensive cultural and social disintegration, biblical imagery, themes and narratives offered them new, and often unintended, ways of responding to settler-colonialism. Inherent in the meaning-making encounter between the marginalised Khoesan, on the one hand, and the missionary project with its emphasis on biblical literacy on the other, were the religious, and therefore, political means by which Khoesan could challenge the legitimising tropes of the oppressive colonial system.

The Bible as repository for Khoesan national renewal

One of the Psalms Johannes van der Kemp taught his Khoesan followers to sing was Psalm 118, which in verses 6–8 asserts, 'The Lord is with me; I will not be afraid. What can man do unto me? The Lord is with me; he is my helper. I will look in triumph on my enemies. It is better to take refuge in the Lord than to trust in man.' This was one of the Psalms sung by Khoesan Christians in the church of the eastern frontier town of Graaff-Reinet in 1801, at the height of the Servants' Revolt. The white residents of Graaff-Reinet, along with Boers who had sought refuge in the town after having been forced to flee their farms along the eastern frontier, were alarmed by this intrusion into their religious domain. It was the first time Khoesan had been allowed to worship in the church and in response, the white congregants sang from Psalm 74, which in verse 4, reads, 'Your foes roared in the place where you met with us.' Verse 7 declares, 'They burned your sanctuary to the ground; they defiled the dwelling-place of your name'; while in verse 10, the psalmist asks, 'How long will the enemy mock you, O God? Will the foe revile your name forever?'

KHOESAN NATIONAL RENEWAL IN THE CAPE COLONY

By the 1820s, biblical literacy was widespread among Khoesan.[36] For those Khoesan who were not literate, and could not read the Scriptures for themselves, access to biblical narratives was facilitated by hymn-singing, prayers and exposure to biblical teachings at missions and as disseminated by itinerant missionaries, both Khoesan and European. During the 1820s and 1830s, the missionary movement at the Cape held considerable political influence. The superintendent of the LMS in southern Africa, John Philip, was well connected with prominent evangelical-humanitarian figures, such as Buxton. Taking full advantage of his political connections in London, Philip campaigned for the extension of civil liberties to the Khoesan, and in particular, for the repeal of the provisions of the Caledon Code.[37] His campaign was aided by the appointment of Richard Bourke as Governor of the Cape Colony in 1826. A humanitarian reformer, Bourke introduced the most significant piece of legislation for Khoesan during this period. Ordinance 50 of 1828 was endorsed by the House of Commons and confirmed by an Order of the King in Council in 1829, which meant that the law could not be repealed without House of Commons approval.

The Ordinance removed all legal requirements for Khoesan to enter service. Khoesan were no longer required to carry a pass proving their employment and residence. Ordinance 50 also placed all Khoesan on equal legal standing with the Cape's white inhabitants, that is, with other non-slave members of Cape society. The Ordinance emphasised personal liberty and was hailed by evangelical-humanitarians as a significant achievement in the campaign for Khoesan civil liberties.[38] The passage of Ordinance 50 was met with dismay by settler society and opposition to the measure was immediate and sustained. As the Cape acquired more of its own legislative powers during the 1830s and 1840s, so local lawmakers attempted to roll back the full extent of the Ordinance, wishing ultimately to repeal it. In 1842, a Masters and Servants Ordinance was passed by the Cape's Legislative Council, which diluted Ordinance 50. By 1856, a harsher Masters and Servants Act was enacted by the Cape's representative assembly which effectively dissolved the Ordinance.

The first attempt to undermine Ordinance 50 was made in 1834, the same year that the Cape's Legislative Council was constituted. Increased vagrancy, illegal squatting and crime were regarded as the consequences of the Ordinance among the Cape's Dutch and English settlers. Complaints about labour shortages were also reported.[39] Settler disapproval of Khoesan autonomy was communicated to the Governor and district commissioners in scores of petitions.[40] While there was little scope for an independent livelihood outside the settler economy even after Ordinance 50 came into effect, the Cape Government's provision of territory for Khoesan settlement on the eastern frontier of the Colony meant that some Khoesan had been able to acquire their own land. The Kat River Settlement was established in 1829, in the months following the passage of Ordinance 50. Intended to serve as a buffer zone between the Cape Colony and the Xhosa chieftaincies on the eastern frontier, the territory was settled in large part by Khoesan who had been residents at the Colony's largest LMS mission stations, such as Bethelsdorp, Theopolis and Hankey.[41] In 1834, when the Cape's newly established Legislative Council sought to reintroduce vagrancy legislation, directly infringing the principles and provisions of Ordinance 50, villages in the Kat River Settlement aligned with the LMS became sites of counter-protest and petitioning.[42] This was amid a climate of fear that Ordinance 50 would be repealed. The Khoesan petitions which were drafted in opposition to the Legislative Council's proposed vagrancy bill reveal the extent to which biblical literacy, and in turn, Christian identity, had come to influence and inspire Khoesan national renewal.

On 5 August 1834, a public meeting was held at Philipton, a village in the Kat River Settlement named in honour of the superintendent of the LMS in the Cape Colony, John Philip. The meeting had been convened in order for the Khoesan residents of the village to draft a petition voicing their protest against the proposed vagrancy bill which was to be sent to the Governor of the Cape for approval. This was one of several such meetings held in the Kat River Settlement, as well as at other mission stations in the Colony.[43] The ensuing agitation represents a moment of inclusive national renewal, for the body of petitioners was made up of individuals with diverse ethnic backgrounds. By 1834, Khoesan – commonly and erroneously referred to as 'Hottentots' in contemporary colonial parlance – continued to be a cobbled-together ethnic mosaic, including Khoekhoe and San, but also ex-slaves, with each category incorporating diverse ethnic collectives.[44]

In his submission to the Philipton meeting, Cubedo Oerson, a resident of Philippolis (a LMS mission station situated beyond the northern boundary of the Cape Colony, also named in honour of John Philip) commented that the Khoesan were 'a poor people', but that they had 'reason to thank God', for He had 'raised men to plead their cause'. Oerson added that 'if the Word of God had not come, the nation would have been extinct'. Continuing, Oerson noted that the Khoesan had been 'taught to read and write' and as a result, were able to 'defend themselves', showing 'firmness in preserving their rights' and doing so 'with humility and gentleness'. Esau Prins also addressed the gathering. The son of a Boer man and a Khoekhoe woman, Esau explained that he identified as Khoekhoe, noting however, that some had told him that he had 'Christian blood'. As far as he was concerned, he knew 'only of one blood that God [had] made'.

Another speaker, Cobus Ulbricht, urged those attending the meeting to 'acknowledge the Providence of God in directing the heart of the King of England, and his Council, for making a Law by which they [had] been delivered from servitude', thus placing them 'on an equal footing with other of His Majesty's subjects'. Mr Bergman, identified as a 'Bushman' in the meeting's minutes, remarked that though his heart was grieved by the proposed vagrancy law, he wanted to thank the Government for the ground he had been given at the Kat River Settlement. He also expressed his thanks to God 'for the Gospel', which he hoped would 'make all things right'. In closing, Mr Bergman commented that he had always seen 'pen and paper' with his master, but that he now saw pen and paper used by his friends. Andries Stoffels, whom we met earlier, also made an address at the gathering. He noted that it was the first time he had been given the opportunity 'to speak on behalf of his nation'. He declared his thanks to God, the King and his Council, and to the Governor for Ordinance 50, for with it, the Khoesan had for the first time 'tasted freedom'.[45]

An LMS missionary based at the eastern Cape mission of Theopolis remarked that the protest meetings held during the spring of discontent in 1834 signalled 'a new era in the history of the Colony'. By compiling and despatching petitions to the Governor, Khoesan had 'come forward for the first time in defence of their civil rights'.[46] It is apparent from these examples that Christianity shaped the language used to challenge the proposed vagrancy bill. As shown, biblical literacy provided Khoesan with the means to enter public debates and contests over power.[47] Knowledge of Scripture was a fundamental marker of Christian identity in a colonial context wherein the profession of the Christian faith afforded the professor social status and respectability, at least in principle, if not in effect. Biblical literacy offered the prospect of personal redemption and, together with ameliorative colonial legislation such as Ordinance 50, the possibility of national consolidation and renewal. This was demonstrated fittingly by those residents of the Kat River Settlement who kept copies of Ordinance 50 in their Bibles.[48] Though the Cape's Legislative Council endorsed the vagrancy bill in September 1834, it was prevented from becoming law by the Colonial Office, citing its inconsistency with the provisions of Ordinance 50.

'Fear God, honour the Queen'

At the time of its establishment in 1829, the Kat River Settlement was hailed as a 'civilising' project by the LMS. Many of the Settlement's original inhabitants were affiliated with LMS missionaries who supported Khoesan civil liberties. Considered radicals by polite settler society, these missionaries had been instrumental in cultivating a literate, biblically inspired political consciousness among Khoesan. But as was so often the experience with missionaries at the Cape, what their converts did with Christianity was beyond their control.[49] By the late 1840s, it was estimated that the Settlement was home to approximately 5,000 residents. Many in the Settlement were poor peasants, eking out a precarious existence on a volatile colonial frontier. Earlier frontier wars between the Cape Colony and the Xhosa chiefdoms had resulted in substantial losses of livestock and crops and had compromised the vision of a prosperous Khoesan Christian peasantry establishing itself in the Kat River valley.[50] Demand for land in the valley was high, especially among the region's white farmers, who looked with envy upon the fertile tract of territory reserved for Khoesan. In early 1851, the Settlement erupted into rebellion. Apart from the material factors which contributed to a general climate of discontent, Khoesan anxieties were compounded by rumours of the dire consequences that would follow the establishment of the Cape Colony's own elected representative assembly. The Kat River rebellion coincided with the Eighth Frontier War, also known as Mlanjeni's War, in recognition of the Xhosa prophet whose brand of millennarianism proved sufficiently influential among frontier Xhosa to provide a spark for war.

Christianity was deployed on both sides of the rebellion, by loyalists and rebels. The settler press was quick to condemn the meddling missionaries, in particular James Read (who began his missionary career as van der Kemp's assistant at Bethelsdorp), for stoking the rebellion's embers. That the rebels continued to profess and practise their faith in Christ was met with alarm by settler society. It was recorded that Kat River residents who were preparing to join the rebellion had been seen reading their Bibles and praying. Some were reported to have taken communion, all the while 'preparing to dedicate the morrow to rebellion and wayside murder', though these rumours were never proven.[51] Bibles were, however, found in rebel camps and in the baggage of rebels who had surrendered.[52] The Kat River rebels were accused of 'turning religion into rebellion and faith into faction'.[53] This further highlights how unreliable the Bible was for the imposition of Western ways of thinking and knowing. As a text with multiple, possible interpretations, it produced unpredictable and undesirable outcomes.

In an effort to persuade the rebels to reconsider the justification of their cause, James Read, along with several other missionaries, both Khoesan and European, as well as his half-Khoekhoe son, James Read junior, set out to a rebel camp on 9 January 1851. After imploring the rebels to desist from their 'wicked proceedings', Read delivered a sermon from the Beatitudes in the Gospel of Matthew, stressing verse 9 of chapter 5: 'Blessed are the peacemakers, for they shall be called the Sons of God.' In a clear indication of his belief in the bond between loyalty and Christianity, Read reminded those present of their deplorable and 'heathenish state' at the time he first arrived at the Cape in 1800. He insisted that they owed a 'debt of gratitude' to the 'English churches and nation' and that the 'Redeemer's cause ... [was being] tarnished by their revolting against the Government'.[54] Another missionary, Arie van Rooyen, had also turned to Scripture in a bid to dissuade potential rebels at a Sunday morning church service on 5 January. The central verse of his sermon was 1 Peter 2:17, 'Show proper respect to everyone; Love the brotherhood of believers, fear God, honour the King.' With Queen Victoria then on the throne, van Rooyen amended the verse accordingly.

Robert Ross has observed that the Kat River rebellion was a 'Christian movement', noting that the ideological basis of the uprising had a distinct 'Christian character'.[55] A subversive Christian thread is traceable from van der Kemp through the vagrancy agitation of 1834 to the Kat River rebellion. By 1851, the contradictions and disappointments of their liminal identity were glaring to Khoesan Christians.[56] A racially and religiously structured colonial society was an unlikely place to find scores of biblically literate, African Christians. The promises of the egalitarian message dispensed by van der Kemp, as well as by those radical missionaries who followed him, was always going to be difficult, if not impossible, to fulfil. No matter how far Khoesan imbibed respectable modes of living, as the nineteenth century progressed, so the possibilities for social equality based on religious identity were to diminish gradually. Racial boundaries of exclusion hardened from the 1840s onwards, placing social equality further and further beyond the reach of Khoesan Christians. Though palpable for a time, the promise of religious egalitarianism was to be dashed during the second half of the nineteenth century.

For missionary and humanitarian supporters of Khoesan rights, the Kat River rebellion represented an unfortunate conundrum: in their reading of Scripture, God was on the side of the oppressed, yet the oppressed were not supposed to rebel against the authority of the Crown. However, rebel grievances were due to unmet expectations on the part of Khoesan who considered themselves Christians entitled to equal treatment and respect. Some of the rebels indicated that they still valued Ordinance 50 and that since the time of its passage, twenty-three years earlier, they had become acquainted with colonial law and the Colony's press, thus acquiring political literacy in addition to biblical literacy.[57]

The original missionary intention had been for literacy to serve as the instrument of access to the Bible. This certainly happened, but literacy also afforded Khoesan access to public media and government notices and reports, increasing their awareness of colonial affairs and stoking political consciousness.

The Bible was a contested cultural resource in the charged climate of identity politics in the early nineteenth-century Cape Colony. The nonconformist missionary movement at the Cape was central to the dissemination of a Protestant Christian message which emphasised the importance of biblical literacy. Conversion demanded outward markers of the inner conviction. One of the most symbolically powerful markers of respectability was the acquisition of literacy. Assimilating to these imposed standards of respectability amounted to Khoesan performance of 'civilisation', but also afforded Khoesan social status and a language with which to challenge colonial subjugation and discrimination. This language was informed and legitimised by biblical references in a colonial context in which religious identity carried important symbolic weight and underpinned notions of white superiority. While Christian identity could be acquired via conversion, biblical literacy and the performance of respectability, social equality lay out of reach for Khoesan, especially as racial attitudes in British colonial territories hardened from the 1840s onwards.[58]

For Khoesan in the early nineteenth century, looking forward, biblical literacy promised to free them from social inferiority. Knowledge of the Word of God held out the prospect of redemption from oppression. The co-opting of this most powerful symbol of status extended the possibility of disrupting and subverting the colonial hierarchy. The deployment of biblical narratives had the potential to level the social playing field in contests for power and the Bible provided a vocabulary for challenging the colonial status quo; for talking back. In Khoesan readings of Scripture, if the meek were to inherit the earth, then it was possible to imagine a different social order.

Notes

1. A *commando* was an armed, mounted posse of Dutch farmers, often accompanied by Khoesan servants. A *kraal* was the basic social unit of San society, made up of small, mobile, extended-family foraging groups.
2. For a detailed account of the causes and consequences of the Servants' Revolt see Susan Newton-King and Vertrees C. Malherbe, *The Khoikhoi Rebellion in the Eastern Cape, 1799–1803* (Cape Town: Centre for African Studies, University of Cape Town, 1981).
3. Elizabeth Elbourne, 'Early Khoisan Uses of Mission Christianity', *Kronos: Journal of Cape History*, 19 (1992), 25.

KHOESAN NATIONAL RENEWAL IN THE CAPE COLONY

4   Ido H. Enklaar, *Life and Work of Dr. J. Th. Van der Kemp, 1747–1811: Missionary Pioneer and Protagonist of Racial Equality in South Africa* (Cape Town and Rotterdam: Balkema, 1988).
5   House of Commons Parliamentary Papers (hereafter, HCPP), 538 of 1836, 'Report from the Select Committee on Aborigines (British Settlements)', p. 583.
6   James Read and Josiah Bassett, *The Life of a Vagrant, or the Testimony of an Outcast* (London: Charles Gilpin, 1850), pp. 110–11.
7   HCPP, 538 of 1836, 'Report', p. 588.
8   Elbourne, 'Early Khoisan Uses', 26–7.
9   C. A. Bayly, 'The British and Indigenous Peoples, 1760–1860: Power, Perception and Identity', in Martin Daunton and Rick Halpern, eds, *Empire and Others: British Encounters with Indigenous Peoples, 1600–1850* (London: UCL Press, 1999), p. 33.
10 Andrew Bank, 'Losing Faith in the Civilising Mission: The Premature Decline of Humanitarian Liberalism at the Cape, 1840–60', in Daunton and Halpern, eds, *Empire and Others*, p. 364.
11 This discussion of Khoesan ownership of biblical text and imagery is informed by Richard Elphick, *The Equality of Believers: Protestant Missionaries and the Racial Politics of South Africa* (Charlottesville, VA: University of Virginia Press, 2012); Richard Gray, *Black Christians and White Missionaries* (New Haven, CT: Yale University Press, 1990); Leon De Kock, *Civilising Barbarians: Missionary Narrative and African Textual Response in Nineteenth-Century South Africa* (Johannesburg: Wits University Press, 1996); and Lamin Sanneh, *Translating the Message: The Missionary Impact on Culture* (Maryknoll, NY: Orbis Books, 1989).
12 Stanley Trapido, 'From Paternalism to Liberalism: The Cape Colony, 1800–1834', *International History Review*, 12 (1990), 79.
13 Nigel Penn, *Rogues, Rebels and Runaways: Eighteenth Century Cape Characters* (Cape Town: David Philip, 1999), pp. 147–9.
14 Martin Legassick, *The Politics of a South African Frontier: The Griqua, the Sotho-Tswana, and the Missionaries, 1780–1840* (Basle: Basler Afrika Bibliographien, 2010), pp. 50–60.
15 Elbourne, 'Early Khoisan Uses', 3.
16 Bernhard Kruger, *The Pear Tree Blossoms: The History of the Moravian Church in South Africa, 1737–1869* (Genadendal: Moravian Book Depot, 1966), pp. 76–80.
17 Elizabeth Elbourne and Robert Ross, 'Combating Spiritual and Social Bondage: Early Missions in the Cape Colony', in Richard Elphick and Rodney Davenport, eds, *Christianity in South Africa: A Political, Social and Cultural History* (Oxford and Cape Town: James Currey and David Philip, 1997), p. 36.
18 Elphick, *Equality of Believers*, p. 14.
19 H. C. Bredenkamp, A. B. L. Flegg and H. E. F. Pluddemann, trans., *The Genadendal Diaries: Diaries of the Herrnhut Missionaries H. Marsveld, D. Schwinn and J.C. Kuhnel*, 2 vols (Bellville: University of the Western Cape Institute for Historical Research, 1992), I: p. 61.
20 Gray, *Black Christians*, p. 95.
21 Jennifer Cooper, 'The Invasion of Personal Religious Experiences: London Missionary Society Missionaries, Imperialism, and the Written Word in Early 19th-Century Southern Africa', *Kleio*, 34 (2002), 49.
22 Robert Ross, *Status and Respectability in the Cape Colony, 1750–1870: A Tragedy of Manners* (Cambridge: Cambridge University Press, 1999), pp. 123–4.
23 Elizabeth Elbourne, 'A Question of Identity: Evangelical Culture and Khoisan Politics in the Early Nineteenth Century Eastern Cape', *Societies of Southern Africa in the Nineteenth and Twentieth Centuries*, 18 (1993), 19.
24 Leonard Guelke, 'Freehold Farmers and Frontier Settlers, 1657–1780', in Richard Elphick and Herman Giliomee, eds, *The Shaping of South African Society, 1652–1840* (Cape Town: Maskew Miller Longman, 1989), p. 97. See also for example John Barrow, *An Account of Travels into the Interior of South Africa in the Years 1797 and 1798*, 2 vols (New York: Johnson Reprint Corporation, 1968), I: p. 398.

25 Andre Du Toit, 'No Chosen People: The Myth of the Calvinist Origins of Afrikaner Nationalism and Racial Ideology', *American Historical Review*, 88 (1983), 923–5, and Elphick, *Equality of Believers*, pp. 248–9.
26 Cooper, 'Invasion of Personal Religious Experiences', 50.
27 Vertrees C. Malherbe, 'The Life and Times of Cupido Kakkerlak', *Journal of African History*, 20 (1979), 369.
28 Richard Elphick, 'Africans and the Christian Campaign in Southern Africa', in Howard R. Lamar and Leonard Thompson, eds, *The Frontier in History: North America and Southern Africa Compared* (New Haven, CT: Yale University Press, 1981), p. 298.
29 Barnabas Shaw, *Memorials of South Africa* (London: J. Mason, 1840), p. 117.
30 Elbourne, 'Early Khoisan Uses', 6.
31 Shaw, *Memorials*, p. 335.
32 Elizabeth Elbourne, *Blood Ground: Colonialism, Missions and the Contest for Christianity in the Cape Colony and Britain, 1799–1853* (Montreal and Kingston, Ont.: McGill-Queen's University Press, 2002), p. 193.
33 Elphick, *Equality of Believers*, p. 16.
34 Elphick, *Equality of Believers*, p. 17.
35 Janet Hodgson, 'A Battle for Sacred Power: Christian Beginnings among the Xhosa', in Richard Elphick and Rodney Davenport, eds, *Christianity in South Africa: A Political, Social and Cultural History* (Oxford and Cape Town: James Currey and David Philip, 1997), p. 70.
36 Elbourne, *Blood Ground*, p. 192.
37 Tim Keegan, *Dr Philip's Empire: One Man's Struggle for Justice in Nineteenth-Century South Africa* (Cape Town: Zebra Press, 2016), pp. 116–21.
38 Keegan, *Dr Philip's Empire*, p. 117.
39 Jared McDonald, 'Loyalism in the Cape Colony: Exploring the Khoesan Subject-citizen Space, c. 1828–1834', *New Contree*, 73 (2015), 16.
40 R. L. Watson, 'Slavery and Ideology: The South African Case', *International Journal of African Historical Studies*, 20, 1 (1987).
41 Robert Ross, *The Borders of Race in Colonial South Africa: The Kat River Settlement, 1829–1856* (New York: Cambridge University Press, 2014), pp. 87–9.
42 Elisabeth Elbourne, 'Freedom at Issue: Vagrancy Legislation and the Meaning of Freedom in Britain and the Cape Colony, 1799 to 1842', *Slavery and Abolition*, 15 (1994), 138.
43 Edna Bradlow, 'The Khoi and the Proposed Vagrancy Legislation of 1834', *Quarterly Bulletin of the South African Library*, 39 (1985), 99–103.
44 Elbourne, 'Freedom at Issue', 115.
45 Cape Archives Repository (hereafter CA), Accessions, 50, W.R. Morris Collection, 4, Report of Philipton Meeting, 5 August 1834.
46 School of Oriental and African Studies, Council for World Mission Archive, South Africa, Incoming Correspondence, 14A/2/B, George Barker, Theopolis, 6 October 1834.
47 See William H. Worger, 'Parsing God: Conversations about the Meanings of Words and Metaphors in Nineteenth Century Southern Africa', *Journal of African History*, 42 (2001), 417–19.
48 Ross, *Borders of Race*, p. 87.
49 For valuable comparative discussions, see Paul Landau, 'Religion and Christian Conversion in African History: A New Model', *Journal of Religious History*, 23 (1999), 10, and Stephen Volz, 'Written On Our Hearts: Tswana Christians and the "Word of God" in the Mid-Nineteenth Century', *Journal of Religion in Africa*, 38 (2008), 112–14.
50 Robert Ross, 'The Kat River Rebellion and Khoikhoi Nationalism: The Fate of an Ethnic Identification', *Kronos: Journal of Cape History*, 24 (1997), 99.
51 N. J. Merriman, *The Cape Journals of Archdeacon Merriman, 1844–1855* (Cape Town: Van Riebeeck Society, 1957), p. 155.

52 Noel Mostert, *Frontiers: The Epic of South Africa's Creation and the Tragedy of the Xhosa People* (London: Jonathan Cape, 1992), p. 1120.
53 N. J. Merriman, *The Kafir, the Hottentot, and the Frontier Farmer: Passages of a Missionary Life from the Journals of the Venerable Archdeacon Merriman* (London: George Bell, 1854), p. 117.
54 James Read, *The Kat River Settlement in 1851: Described in a Series of Letters Published in the 'South African Commercial Advertiser' by the Rev. James Read Junior* (Cape Town: A. S. Robertson, 1852), p. 26.
55 Ross, *Borders of Race*, p. 212.
56 Elbourne, *Blood Ground*, p. 64.
57 CA, Cape Colony Publications, 1/2/1/2, Communication to Governor Grey and Parliament from Rebel Hottentots, 27 March 1855.
58 Bank, 'Losing Faith', pp. 380–1.

CHAPTER NINE

Distinction and dispersal: the nineteenth-century roots of segregationist folk theology in the American South

Stephen R. Haynes

In March 1965 a new church was founded in Memphis, Tennessee. Although there was no shortage of churches in the city, it became necessary to launch a new congregation, because racial conflict had precipitated a split at the 3,500-member Second Presbyterian church when it became clear that hardline segregationists were no longer welcome there. The issue had been whether the church's Session – its board of lay leaders – should admit groups of black and white students who had come intending to worship on about a dozen occasions between March 1964 and March 1965. After months of internal and external efforts to get the Session to cease denying entrance to integrated groups of worshippers, the church's pastors publicly repudiated the Session's stance and the majority of the congregation voted to make the longest-serving Elders inactive for a period of three years. With their power under threat, the church's determined segregationists resigned their positions at Second Presbyterian and started their own church called – oxymoronically – Independent Presbyterian.

During the course of the conflict, members of Second Presbyterian learned that behind their Session's decision to bar integrated groups from worship was a policy, adopted in 1957, that committed the church to racial segregation in all its activities. That statement, like most mainline ecclesiastical attempts to defend segregation during the 1950s, was not theologically robust. It began, in fact, with the acknowledgement that since 'many learned and devout Christian men have debated pro and con the question of segregation being Scriptural ... this is a moot question'. In fact, the statement founded the necessity of racial separation not on a Bible proof text, but on the Cold War maxim that the main force behind integration was 'godless communism'.[1]

SEGREGATIONIST FOLK THEOLOGY IN THE AMERICAN SOUTH

When the Session's segregationist faction left Second Presbyterian in 1965 to found a new congregation, they were determined to create a strong theological foundation for racial homogeneity. Written into Independent Presbyterian's constitution was this attempt to establish once and for all the congregation's position on race:

> Believing that the scriptures teach that the separation of nations, people and groups will preserve the peace, purity and unity of the Church, it is, therefore, the will of this Church that its members and those visiting the Church, its worship services, and all its activities, shall be compatible with the congregation.[2]

With its avoidance of racially charged language, this article of the IPC constitution was less explicit than the policy adopted eight years previously at Second Presbyterian, which had condemned 'integrated meetings of the white and negro races in our local churches, camps and conferences, at all age levels'. However, by offering a 'scriptural' warrant for segregation the constitution accomplished something the authors of the 1957 segregation policy had not even dared to attempt. Those men had readily conceded there were no reliable proof texts in support of segregation. Eight years later, the men who founded the IPC defied the growing conviction among mainline Christians that segregation was 'unchristian'. Keenly aware that denominational and societal practices were fluid, they needed a solid foundation for maintaining the racial status quo, one that could withstand, or at least deflect, charges that segregation was discriminatory, immoral and unchristian. The founders of IPC located this foundation in 'the scriptures', which, they contended, teach 'the separation of nations, people and groups'.

This church document is notable for two reasons. First, it contradicts the scholarly consensus that Southern Christians had little confidence in the Bible as a basis for racial segregation. Second, its claim that the 'the scriptures teach ... separation' is just vague enough to suggest that the authors were alluding to an interpretive tradition they considered well-established. This leads to some intriguing questions: What part of the Bible did these men believe taught the 'separation of nations, peoples and groups'? And to what extent was this belief dependent on the nineteenth-century tradition of Bible exegesis that had been used to defend slavery and the perpetual separation and subjugation of Africans?

Religion and segregation in recent scholarship

Recent scholarship has tended to keep such questions from arising by emphasising that Christian support for segregation had little if anything in common with the biblical pro-slavery argument. This view is not unreasonable, but it is based on assumptions that need to be re-evaluated. The first assumption is that the biblical/theological arguments that dominated the works of pro-slavery authors had no practical application in the defence of segregation.[3] A second scholarly assumption is that segregationists were not committed to offering theological defences of segregation because they viewed it as a 'social issue' unrelated to the church's main mission of saving souls. On this view, claims that segregation was 'biblical', part of the created order, and in conformity with God's law ought to be understood as *ex post facto* rationalisations that emerged when Jim Crow came under attack from within the Christian community.[4] The third assumption underlying the supposed disconnect between pro-segregation arguments and pro-slavery thought is that the religious argument for segregation was considered weak by segregationists themselves because they constantly buttressed it with secular lines of thought.[5]

None of these assumptions, however, stands up to close scrutiny. First, as I will try to show, when we realise how malleable the interpretive traditions based in Genesis 9–11 were in the hands of nineteenth-century exegetes, the continuities between pro-slavery and prosegregation biblical arguments become evident. Second, the conviction of segregationists that enforced racial separation was a civil rather than a theological or moral issue was actually common among antebellum pro-slavery advocates as well, although this did not stop them from defending the South's peculiar institution. Third, the claim that religion was a weak link in the fence that defended segregation has been recently qualified by scholars who demonstrate that reluctance to claim biblical or theological warrants for segregation applied mainly to religious elites – that is, pastors and officials connected to the mainline denominations. Non-elites, they argue, especially laypeople and pastors of independent churches, developed a 'segregationist folk theology' that made ready use of whatever scraps of biblical and theological argument were close to hand.[6]

But what the case of Memphis's Independent Presbyterian Church suggests is that segregationist folk theology could be invoked in the mainline as well. Furthermore, as I will try to show, this 'folk theology' of divinely ordered separation, whether it was appealed to by seminary-educated suburban clergymen or self-schooled country pastors, had discernible roots in traditions of biblical interpretation developed in the nineteenth-century South. Once we have identified the dominant forms of this folk theology and its persistent themes, it will be possible to detect lines of continuity between the religious defences of slavery and segregation offered by Southern whites.

SEGREGATIONIST FOLK THEOLOGY IN THE AMERICAN SOUTH

Looking for parallels

In the introduction to *A Stone of Hope: Prophetic Religion and the Death of Jim Crow*, David L. Chappell summarises what has become a dominant view among scholars of the American South. 'Compared to the thorough, confident support that slave owners received from their leading theologians and other cultural authorities a century earlier,' Chappell writes, 'the segregationists look disorganised and superficial.'[7] It is true that, generally speaking, the sort of assured biblical and theological claims one associates with slavery apologists were often conspicuously absent among the Christian defenders of racial segregation. But Chappell's generalisation ignores the many *formal* parallels between the Christian pro-slavery and prosegregation arguments, including (1) the notion that slavery and segregation are 'natural' conditions in accord with the divine will; (2) the claim that while both systems are subject to abuse, it is not inherent in the systems themselves and believers are obliged to bring these racial arrangements up to a Christian standard;[8] (3) the affirmation that while Africans are ensouled human beings in need of salvation, the church *qua* church has no business meddling in the social arrangements that define their existence; (4) the assertion that under slavery and segregation blacks are safer, more civilised and more spiritually blessed than other people of African descent; (5) the contention that slavery and segregation are benevolent institutions that serve to prevent social chaos and insure blacks' survival by strengthening the bonds of mutual affection between the races;[9] (6) the belief that slave insurrections and resistance to segregation are the result of provocation by 'outside agitators'; (7) the argument that because slavery and segregation were 'instituted in the Old Testament and assumed in the New', there is no basis for declaring these institutions unchristian or incompatible with God's will;[10] and (8) the confident declaration that the forces behind abolition and integration are profoundly anti-God (described as 'infidelity' in the nineteenth century and everything from communism to plots by 'agents of Satan' in the twentieth).

More important, Chappell and other scholars have failed to recognise an important *substantive* link between the way nineteenth-century Southerners exploited the Bible and its invocation by advocates of segregation. This link is to be found in what I will call 'the distinction and dispersal tradition' that in antebellum America contributed to pro-slavery thought by racialising the descendants of Noah and viewing Noah's prophecy (Genesis 9), the Table of Nations (Genesis 10) and the Tower of Babel (Genesis 11) as parts of a continuous disclosure of God's will for all postdiluvian societies. The most obvious reflections of this tradition in the literature of support for segregation are tracts that recast the tale of Noah and his sons in Genesis 9:20-7 – which climaxes in Noah's exclamation, 'Cursed be Canaan! The lowest of slaves will he be to his brothers' – as having to do not with the imposition of slavery, but with the perpetual necessity of 'racial' separation.

An unusually confident and direct effort to apply Genesis 9 to American segregation appeared in 1959 in *The Christian Problem of Racial Segregation* by South Carolina Baptist Humphrey K. Ezell. Ezell contended that in Noah's curse, 'God has segregated the races. Shem and Japheth are to dwell in tents together; but a curse is placed upon Ham and his descendants, and they are to be servants to Shem and Japheth.' What is the connection between the prophecy of Ham's servitude and the necessity of racial separation? Ezell claims that 'since the descendants of Ham were to be servants unto them, it is not God's plan for the descendants of Shem and Japheth to intermarry with the descendants of Ham'.[11] Here the distinctions Noah draws between his sons' destinies entails a sort of 'segregation' that necessitates the prevention of intermarriage between Hamites and the descendants of Shem and Japheth.

Another attempt to apply the curse of Ham to segregation appeared in 1957 when Alabama attorney and Methodist layman Festus F. Windham published a 46-page tract entitled *A Bible Treatise on Segregation: An Analysis of Biblical References to Determine the True Relationship of the Races*.[12] Significantly, the majority of Windham's 'biblical references' are to Genesis; however, he does not begin with Genesis 9, but with Genesis 10 and 11 – that is, with 'the origin of nations immediately following the flood' in which, he notes, the 'unity of the race was destroyed because they undertook to build a city and a tower that would reach to heaven'. For this sin, Windham writes, God 'separated the descendants of Ham, Shem and Japheth ... and here began [their] segregation'.[13]

Only after describing this great act of distinction and dispersal does Windham turn back to Genesis 9 and Noah's response to 'the way Ham treated his father'. Windham connects these passages by noting that it was the dispersion of Ham's descendants that brought them to Africa, from which they 'emigrated ... as slaves of the Caucasian and other races'. Windham then combines the racialised themes in Genesis 9–11, arguing that the separation of Noah's sons is rooted in both creation and curse:

> In the distant past it was God's handiwork and intention to preserve inviolate the separation of the descendants of Ham and those of Japheth and Shem: Because of their sin, they must bear a mark different from that of the descendants of Shem and Japheth; they are always to be the

servants of others. It is this act of God in creation that brought about the necessary segregation of the races.¹⁴

Thus, segregation was intended by God from the beginning, and after being resisted at Babel was reimposed in the subsequent dispersion. The role of the interceding curse is to place a 'stamp' on Hamites that reinforces the separation of this inferior race by dooming it to serve others. The curse's function, then, is not to introduce segregation, but to reveal what blacks have been permanently segregated *for*. 'God segregated [the Negro] in Creation and he will remain so until the end of time', writes Windham. 'Any attempt, legal or otherwise, to integrate him with the white or any other race will not work because it is contrary to God's will and plan.'¹⁵

The minimal role played by Noah's curse in Windham's reading of Genesis 9–11 should alert us to the creative ways pro-segregation authors could apply 'Bible truths' from this section of Scripture to the question of God's plan for race relations. As we look for other examples of this sort of exegesis, key themes are likely to be the distinct people groups descending from Noah's sons, God's plan for dispersal of these groups and condemnation of attempts to resist.

The distinction and dispersal tradition and the biblical argument for segregation

With these clues in mind, let us peruse some primary texts by religious advocates of racial segregation to see if they reflect this broader tradition of distinction and dispersal that connects the sons of Noah, the Table of Nations and the Tower of Babel.

A good place to start is the widely circulated and oft-cited tract of G. T. Gillespie, a Presbyterian pastor and college president in Mississippi who was among the most prominent religious figures to articulate a theology for segregation in the years after *Brown v. Board of Education* (in which the US Supreme Court struck down 'separate but equal' schemes of public education). The first half of his infamous address to the Presbyterian Synod of Mississippi in 1954, subsequently published by the Association of Citizens' Councils of Winona, Mississippi as *A Christian View of Segregation*,¹⁶ advanced the view that the 'real issue' facing Southerners was the choice 'between the Anglo-Saxon ideal of racial integrity maintained by a consistent application of the principle of segregation and the Communist goal of amalgamation, implemented by the wiping out of all distinctions and the fostering of the most intimate contact between the races in all the relations of life'.¹⁷

Resisting the charges levelled by opponents of racial separation, Gillespie contended that segregation was not a function of 'race prejudice' and did not necessarily entail discrimination. On the contrary, Gillespie wrote, segregation tends to diminish friction and tension and prevent 'such intimacies as might lead to intermarriage and the amalgamation of the races'.[18] So far, these sorts of arguments, if one can call them that, represent standard white reactions to *Brown* among Southern whites. But in the second half of his address, Gillespie turns to the Bible in order to counter the claim, increasingly being heard from representatives of American Protestantism, that segregation is 'unchristian'.

Gillespie began with a concession that some scholars have interpreted as signalling a lack of confidence in the Bible's support for segregation, writing that 'the Bible contains no clear mandate for or against segregation as between the white and negro races'; crucially, however, he went on to say that Scripture does 'furnish considerable data from which valid inferences may be drawn in support of the *general principle of segregation as an important feature of the Divine purpose and Providence throughout the ages*'. Significantly, the bulk of the biblical passages from which Gillespie infers this 'general principle of segregation' are found in the primeval history of Genesis.[19]

The first is the story of Cain's mark in Genesis 4, to which Gillespie refers as 'the first separation'. The second example of the segregation principle in Genesis is seen in chapter 6, which according to Gillespie records 'the promiscuous intermarriage of the Sons of God, that is, the descendants of Seth, with the "Daughters of Men", who were apparently the descendants of Cain', a union that resulted in a 'complete breakdown of family life' and precipitated the flood. The third paradigm of segregation in Genesis involves the sons of Noah, about whom Gillespie offers the standard gloss that 'after the flood ... Shem, Ham and Japheth became the progenitors of three *distinct racial groups*, which were to repeople and overspread the earth'.[20] Gillespie then writes:

> This brief record [in Genesis 10, presumably], the accuracy of which has not been successfully disputed by the anthropologists and ethnologists, while affirming the unity of the race, also implies that an all-wise Providence has 'determined the bounds of their habitation'. Which same Providence by determining the climatic and other physical conditions under which many successive generations of the several racial groups should live, is thereby equally responsible for the *distinct racial characteristics* which seem to have become fixed in prehistoric times, and which are chiefly responsible for the *segregation of racial groups* across the centuries and in our time.[21]

Finally, Gillespie identifies the 'principle of segregation as an important feature of the Divine purpose' in the origin of linguistic differences narrated in Genesis 11, which he believes indicates that

> the Confusion of Tongues, which took place at Babel, with the consequent *scattering of the peoples* was an act of special Divine Providence to frustrate the mistaken efforts of godless men to assure the *permanent integration of the peoples of the earth*. Incidentally it indicates that the development of different languages was not merely natural or accidental, but served a Divine purpose, in becoming one of the most effective means of *preserving the separate existence of the several racial groups*.[22]

In this address we find a well-developed instance of the Genesis tradition of distinction and dispersal animating the Southern Christian imagination as political and religious challenges to segregation intensified after 1954. Absent are traditional elements of the 'curse of Ham' – Noah's drunkenness, the various responses of his sons, the details of his prophecy and the episode's legacy of sin and servitude. References to the post-diluvial events of Genesis 10 and 11 have now displaced the story of Noah's curse and determined how it is to be read, which is as a minor episode in a larger tale of post-diluvial distinction, dispersion, rebellion and re-dispersion.

To understand why the distinction and dispersal tradition has not received the attention it deserves in studies of Christian arguments for segregation, it is instructive to note how scholars have interpreted Gillespie's extended discussion of providence's role in creating 'distinct racial characteristics', 'segregat[ing] racial groups across the centuries and in our time' and 'scattering' the earth's peoples as a bulwark against their 'permanent integration'. Joseph Crespino summarises Gillespie's tract with the comment that it 'attempts to place the debate on segregation on political rather than religious grounds'.[23] David Chappell calls Gillespie's position 'hesitant and inconclusive as to its biblical bona fides' and concludes from his tract that 'even committed segregationists were unwilling to claim biblical sanction'.[24] Similarly, Randy J. Sparks expresses shock that Gillespie 'returns to the curse of Ham, one of the most enduring misinterpretations of the Bible'. Noting that Mississippi's defenders of slavery had employed this 'mischievous alleged curse' in the antebellum period, Sparks writes that 'seeing its reappearance so late in the twentieth century in defence of yet another form of racial discrimination is jarring'.[25]

Relying solely on these scholars' characterisations of Gillespie's tract, one would derive the mistaken impression that Gillespie not only invokes the curse of Ham but that this is the only part of Genesis with which he is concerned. In point of fact, however, Gillespie conspicuously ignores Genesis 9:20–7 and avoids any mention of a curse, slavery or subordination. Meanwhile, the forty or so lines of text Gillespie devotes to making the case that God's 'scattering of the peoples was an act of special Divine Providence' are ignored by these scholars. Apparently distracted by his reluctance to claim that the Bible *demands* segregation, these interpreters miss the way Gillespie uses Genesis 9–11 and other passages to convince Southern Christians that the 'general principle of segregation [is] an important feature of the Divine purpose and Providence throughout the ages'.

A younger colleague of Gillespie who served as Professor of Bible at Belhaven College during the 1950s was Morton H. Smith. In a *Southern Presbyterian Review* column written for church women in 1957, Smith emphasised many of the points touched on by Gillespie three years earlier, even citing some of the same biblical texts. After acknowledging 'the unity of mankind', Smith stressed the divine preference for diversity revealed in the story of the Tower in Genesis 11:

> There in Genesis 11 we find the history of man's attempt to rebel against *God's command to disperse* and replenish the earth by remaining together as a unified people. There we see that it is *God himself who scattered the people*, enforcing this by the confusing of tongues ... This may not be the origin of the races, but it certainly is the *divine separation of people into different groups*.[26]

From this and related Bible passages, Smith distilled a lesson for the present-day:

> [I]t is certain that in the combined accounts of the genealogies of the sons of Noah and the dispersion at the Tower of Babel we find *God's direct action of separation of different elements of the human race into different groups*. On the basis of this fact, it would seem that the principle of separation of peoples or of segregation is not necessarily wrong *per se*. In fact, it seems clearly to be God's order of things, in order to see that man fulfills his God appointed tasks on earth.[27]

Smith cites other texts, but Genesis 9–11 is the centre of gravity in his biblical argument for segregation. This becomes clear when he repeats, in a discussion of racial intermarriage, that 'Babel was an attempt to [amalgamate the races]' to which God responded by 'scattering man'. Who are we', Smith asks, 'to fly in the fact of God's revealed will?'

Unlike most other twentieth-century segregationists, however, Smith provided the source for his version of the distinction and dispersal tradition by quoting at length from Benjamin M. Palmer (1818–1902), an antebellum expositor of Ham's curse who in the 1870s was beginning to apply the Bible's primeval history to the relationship of the races in the postbellum South. Smith commended the view that, as Palmer put it, 'the declared policy of the Divine Administration from the days of Noah until now' is that 'it is indispensable that the purity of race be preserved':

> The sacred writings clearly teach that, to prevent the amazing wickedness which brought upon the earth the purgation of the Deluge, God saw fit to *break the human family into sections*. He *separated them by destroying the unity of speech; then by the actual dispersion*, appointing the bounds of their habitation, to which they were conducted by the mysterious guidance of his will.[28]

'The first pronounced insurrection against [God's] supremacy', Palmer claimed in 1872, was Nimrod's rebellion at Babel.[29]

The Southern Presbyterian Journal

Because Gillespie and Smith were Southern Presbyterians, their writings no doubt had a special appeal for the men who established Memphis's IPC on a segregated basis in 1965. But they were certainly not the only leaders in this denomination to utilise Genesis 9–11 in prosegregation arguments. In fact, if we peruse the pages of *The Southern Presbyterian Journal* (after 1959, *The Presbyterian Journal*, and abbreviated here as *SPJ*), which between 1942 and 1973 was the organ of choice for Southern Presbyterians concerned about nascent liberalism in their denomination, we find repeated references to the distinction and dispersal tradition relative to segregation.

Between the mid-1940s and late 1950s the *SPJ* regularly ran articles and editorials that defended segregation, at times with direct reference to the distinction and dispersion tradition. The first direct application to race relations appeared in March 1944 in an editorial response to the 'Annual Race Relations Message' of the Federal Council of Churches (FCC) by the founder of the journal, L. Nelson Bell. One looks in vain at this FCC statement, Bell noted, for recognition of the fact that separating 'friendly race relations' from 'unrestricted social equality' is 'a line which must not be crossed'. This 'God-ordained racial line', Bell went on, 'was established by God when he made men of different races'. 'Why God saw fit to make some men white and some men black may go back to Genesis 9', Bell observed.[30]

In December 1946 the *SPJ* included an article by B. W. Crouch, a Presbyterian elder from South Carolina, titled 'Dr. Palmer on Racial Barriers'. As Morton Smith would do a decade later, Crouch developed an argument for segregation based in the views of the nineteenth-century divine Benjamin M. Palmer, whom the author claimed was 'among the profound thinkers of a former generation'. According to Crouch, Palmer recognised that blacks and whites 'must be separate and free from social intermingling, and neither allowed to cross the bounds set both as taught by history and in God's word'. Crouch cited the same 1872 address Morton Smith would commend to *SPJ* readers in 1957, in which Palmer argued on biblical grounds that 'the human family, originally one, has been divided into certain large groups for the purpose of being kept historically distinct'. 'How different and sensible is the philosophy of this great Divine', Crouch wrote, from that of those who wish to pull down God-established barriers between the races.[31]

In March 1948 the *SPJ* published an article by the Mississippian J. David Simpson with the rather declarative title 'Non-Segregation Means Eventual Inter-marriage'. Arguing that segregation is 'definitely Scriptural', Simpson relied mainly on two passages: Acts 17:26, where Paul tells his Athenian audience that God has determined 'the bounds of [human] habitation'; and Genesis 11, of which Simpson asks rhetorically: 'What do you think the "Tower of Babel" confusion story in the Scriptures meant if it did not mean that even the races should for the most part establish even their territorial boundary lines for their habitation, as well as racial?' A Bible study published in the *SPJ* the same year affirmed that 'the real division of different groups of men came at Babel'. Segregation might be necessary, according to the study, in order to control the 'hatred, suspicions and cultural differences' stemming from the confusion with which God punished the rebellious people involved in building the Tower.[32]

J. E. Flow, the author of a 1951 *SPJ* editorial titled 'Is Segregation Unchristian?' supported his assertion that segregation is 'in harmony with the plan and purpose of the Almighty Himself' by invoking the distinction and dispersal tradition. Distinction was evident to Flow in the 'stubborn fact' that there are 'three most distinct races of men distinguished by the colour of their faces, the yellow man, the black man, and the white man'. Dispersal, of course, stems from the judgement at Babel: 'When the people began to build the tower of Babel, in the land of Shinar,' Flow wrote, 'God interfered and confused their language so that they could no longer understand each other's speech and were forced to scatter out in different directions.' Flow concluded that it made no sense to argue that segregation is unchristian if the separation of peoples was initiated by God after the flood.[33]

In late 1956, J. V. N. Talmage, a veteran Presbyterian missionary in Korea, began to contribute pieces to the *SPJ* that cited archaeological and geological evidence to support the historicity of the Bible's primeval history. In one of these, entitled 'The Tower of Babel', Talmage sought to pinpoint the historical moment of 'the great dispersion' after the flood. According to the author, the Tower story 'disapproves the ideas that some men have of a one-world government under the control of a few, by showing that racial and language barriers were set up by divine intervention in order to preserve local freedom'. According to Talmage, 'the division and dispersion begun [at Babel] have led to the diversified world we know today'.[34]

In February 1957 Presbyterian Women's Circle study aids published in the *SPJ* included an instalment on 'Nationalism versus Internationalism' by Carl W. MacMurray. 'Why did God divide mankind into separate nations?' MacMurray asked. For regular readers of the *SPJ*, the answer was not in the least surprising: 'In Genesis 11:6–8 we learn that mankind at Babel was united in apostasy, and when God saw there was nothing by which they would be "restrained" in their vain imaginations, He confused their language, disrupted their unity, and scattered them abroad.' According to MacMurray, this passage clearly indicates 'that the division of mankind resulting in separate nations was a judgment of God designed in mercy to "restrain" human society in its evil course'.[35]

In June 1957 the *SPJ* included a reworked version of G. T. Gillespie's 1954 address entitled 'A Southern Christian Looks at the Race Problem'. In this article Gillespie began a contracted section on segregation in the Bible with the story of the Tower: 'God, himself, thwarted the *first man-made plan of integration* by the confusion of tongues at the Tower of Babel, and scattered the peoples abroad upon the face of the whole earth.' Gillespie went on to claim that divine providence was 'directly responsible for the linguistic differences and other factors which have served to keep the peoples of the earth segregated into tribal, national or racial groups, from prehistoric times down to our day'.[36]

Outside the mainstream

How widespread was this distinction and dispersal tradition in scriptural arguments for maintaining segregation? Did it appear beyond the bounds of mainstream Protestantism? On the 'fringes of the segregationist movement', as Chappell puts it, were pastors like the Texas Baptist Carey Daniel, who developed an 'obsessive reading of Scripture' which cast segregation as a major theme of holy writ. Fringe figure or not, Daniel's debt to the distinction and dispersal tradition is abundantly clear, particularly in his embellishment of the legend of Nimrod that had evolved over the centuries and had been pressed into racist service in the nineteenth-century South.[37]

Like Festus Windham, Daniel found evidence of a divine blueprint for separation in creation itself, as well as in the tripartite division of humankind after the flood, in which God 'assigned three parts of the earth (proportionate with their future numbers) to the three sons of Noah and their families'.[38] In Daniel's view, the Bible 'repeatedly forbids the co-mingling of the children of Shem, Ham and Japheth', a prohibition egregiously violated in the building of the Tower of Babel. Daniel cast Nimrod the tower-builder as 'a twofold rebel, a double-dyed anarchist' who resisted both God's plan of salvation and God's scheme of racial segregation, the latter by leading people to defy God's command to 'scatter and separate from one another racially'.[39]

In 1956 another Baptist, New Yorker Kenneth R. Kinney, presented a biblical argument for segregation in *The Baptist Bulletin* that precisely recapitulated the distinction and dispersal tradition as it had come to be applied to racial segregation.[40] Kinney proclaimed his 'firm conviction that *God* ordained, for the period of man's life on earth, the segregation (which term is the equivalent of the familiar Biblical term "separation") of the three lines which descended from the sons of Noah'.[41] Kinney emphasised that one of these three segregated groups – the Hamitic –possessed 'a spirit of rebellion' manifest in Hamite occupation of the Semites' inheritance in the land of Shinar. 'The judgment of Babel' resulted from resistance to God's decree that Noah's descendants separate and disperse according to plan. The solution for Hamite rebellion, according to Kinney, resonates with the political language of his day. It is

> for them to return to the proper observation of God's order; thus to develop their own culture. Thus, we believe, to return to the principle of *separate* but *equal* cultures ... [It] would seem that as it was the Hamitic family of old which rebelled against God's 'order', so their descendants are doing today, aided and abetted by spurious liberals whose bleeding hearts are likely more concerned about *votes* than about the people involved.[42]

According to Kinney, since God intended that the three groups stemming from Noah's sons should maintain familial and national identity, intermarriage between 'Japhetic (European), Shemitic (Oriental) and Hamitic (African) groups' ought to be forbidden.

Dake's Annotated Reference Bible, first published in 1963 by the Georgia Pentecostal Finis Jennings Dake, developed the theme of divinely ordered dispersion in a short article on 'Separation in Scripture':

> God made 'all nations of men' from 'one blood'; but [Acts 17:27] also speaks of 'the bounds of their habitation'. In spite of a common ancestry, from Adam first and later Noah, it was God's will for man to scatter over the earth, to 'be fruitful and multiply' (Gen. 1:28; 8:17; 9:1). Man's failure to obey caused God to confuse his language (Gen. 11:1–9) and to

physically separate the nations by dividing the earth into continents (Gen. 10:25). Both physically and spiritually, separation has been a consistent theme for God's people.[43]

The centrality of the distinction and dispersal tradition in the arguments of Christian spokesmen as diverse as Gillespie, Smith, Daniel, Kinney and Dake indicates the tradition's central role in the broader Christian defence of segregation. Its roots in the nineteenth century compel us to revisit the question of the relationship between twentieth-century readings of the Bible by segregationists and racialised readings minted before and after the Civil War.

Slavery and segregation revisited

There is some evidence for direct literary influence between pro-slavery arguments regarding Ham's curse and segregationist folk theology. But the key thematic links with the nineteenth century are to be found in readings of Genesis 9–11 that emphasised the unique characters and destinies of Noah's sons, the refusal of Ham's descendants to accept their allotment in God's scheme of land distribution, and God's enforced separation of peoples after the rebellion at Babel.

Before the Civil War, the notion that Hamites had rebelled against God-ordained dispersion was well established in popular interpretations of Genesis that emphasised Noah's curse. Frederick Dalcho, Thomas Smyth and Josiah Priest were among the pro-slavery authors who perpetuated the charge that the sons of Ham had usurped land allotted to other descendants of Noah. According to Priest's *Slavery as it Relates to the Negro or African Race* (1843), the adaptation of men and animals to their proper location is 'a grand law of God in nature' that was violated with impunity by the descendants of Ham. Among Priest's contributions to nineteenth-century American biblical interpretation was to develop a racialised portrait of Ham's grandson Nimrod that personified rebellion against Noah's (and God's) rule.[44]

Another antebellum source in which the theme of Hamite rebellion figures largely is Jerome Holgate's 1860 novel *Noachidae: or, Noah, and His Descendants*.[45] In this 350-page fictionalised retelling of Genesis 6–11, the major villain is the negro Orion (Nimrod), who strenuously resists the dispersion of Noah's descendants after the flood. When Nimrod's followers arrive on the Plain of Shinar, they encounter Semites from the family of Asshur to whom Noah has assigned this region. In refusing to acknowledge Noah's role as God's vicegerent in the post-diluvian world, Nimrod embodies Hamite contempt for the divinely appointed ordering of society.

In the period between 1865 and 1910 the interpretive tradition of Hamite rebellion was kept alive by authors such as Buckner H. Payne, who under the pen name 'Ariel' wrote *The Negro: What Is His Ethnological Status?* in 1867. 'Ariel's' surmise that blacks were actually pre-Adamite creatures who survived the flood by boarding the Ark with other 'beasts of the field' forced him to relinquish the identification of Africans with cursed sons of Ham. But he preserved the theme of Hamite rebellion in his claim that Nimrod's accomplices in tower building were 'mostly negroes' who resisted being 'scattered over the earth'. It was precisely 'to prevent this concentration of power and numbers', according to 'Ariel', that God confounded their language, broke them into bands ... and scattered or dispersed them over the earth'.[46]

Previous reference has been made to Benjamin M. Palmer, who between the 1850s and his death in 1902 studiously applied Genesis 9–11 to the shifting realities of America's racial landscape. As the appeals to Palmer's 1872 lecture by Presbyterian segregationists B. W. Crouch and Morton H. Smith attest, Palmer's segregationist reading of Genesis remained well known in the middle of the twentieth century. As we have seen, Crouch and Smith found particular relevance in Palmer's claim that in order to avoid the necessity of another flood God had limited postdiluvial wickedness by 'break[ing] the human family into sections'. The first 'insurrection' against this plan was Nimrod's scheme of consolidation, which Palmer regarded as the first of many evil schemes to force distinct human groups together.[47]

In 1887 Palmer again utilised Genesis as a basis for maintaining separation when he argued against an overture of reunion with Northern Presbyterians. In reminding Southern Presbyterians that 'the race problem' constituted 'an insuperable barrier' to reunification, Palmer appealed again to Genesis, claiming that 'God has divided the human race into several distinct groups, for the sake of keeping them apart'. Having promised Noah that the world would not again be destroyed by flood, God restrained human wickedness by breaking 'the unity of human speech' and scattering the tower builders 'upon the face of all the earth'.[48] Facing a rising tide of pro-reunion sentiment, Palmer stood fast on Scriptural ground he had occupied since the 1850s, alleging that the postdiluvian dispensation in human history is regulated by a divine law of separation. When this law is violated, according to Palmer, condemnation is inevitable, as 'all the attempts to restore the original unity of the race by the amalgamation of these severed parts' are destined for divine judgement.[49]

A third postbellum writer who attempted to maintain the relevance of Genesis 9–11 for American race relations was J. W. Sandell, a Confederate veteran who was extolling the virtues of the Old South as late as 1907. In *The United States in Scripture,* Sandell reiterated the efficacy of Noah's curse, though four decades after the Emancipation Proclamation he was obliged to view it in terms of ungovernability rather than servitude.[50] Sandell found the legend of Nimrod and the tower eminently serviceable as a biblical rationale for racial segregation. God's response to the Tower of Babel proves that 'it is an outrage upon nature to undertake to force the extremes of the races to equality with each other'.[51]

In the first half of the twentieth century, when segregation and racial hierarchy were largely uncontested, the principle of separation purportedly taught in Genesis was kept alive in popular biblical commentaries and preaching aids. While ignoring the question of Ham and Nimrod's racial identity, these works reiterated aspects of the interpretive tradition that would be foundational for the eventual recycling of the distinction and dispersal tradition by segregationists: (1) Genesis 9–11 sets out the principles upon which our world is founded; (2) God willed that after the flood Noah's descendants should disperse and repopulate the world; (3) those who resisted this dispersion were very likely led by Nimrod, whose name means 'let us rebel'; (4) the emblems of this post-diluvian defiance were the Hamite usurpation of Semitic land and the building of the Tower of Babel; and (5) God thwarted the rebellion at Babel and dispersed the builders according to the original divine scheme.

That white Bible readers continued to find in Genesis 9–11 a useful resource for interpreting social and political movements into the middle of the twentieth century is reflected in Harry Lacey's *God and the Nations* (1947). In condemning the trend towards post-war internationalism, Lacey advanced the familiar argument that following the Deluge God prepared each land, 'with a view toward separating the sons of Adam'. God's decision to divide the human race 'rather than communising it', according to Lacey, contained a clear lesson for post-war America. Current attempts to unify humankind 'will be as anti-God in [their] object and prove as disastrous in [their] end as original Babel was'.[52]

Conclusion

Scholars have been correct to note that the weakness of the segregationist case was revealed when some well-known religious advocates of segregation failed to mention the Bible in their publications, when some who did displayed little confidence or passion, and when leading conservatives such as L. Nelson Bell pointedly admitted that 'there is no biblical or legal justification for segregation'.[53] But these observations should not blind us to the fact that a consistent theme among the religious figures who *did* use the Bible to defend the practice of racial segregation was the distinction and dispersal tradition centred in the Bible's primeval history, a tradition that had been central to American attempts at reinforcing what, beginning in the antebellum era, were believed to be God-ordained lines of separation. Only when we appreciate the life and shape of his tradition can we make sense of mid-twentieth-century claims that 'the scriptures teach' that institutional and society harmony requires 'the separation of nations, people and groups'.

Notes

1. Minutes of the Session of Second Presbyterian Church, Memphis, Tennessee, 7 October 1957, p. 3.
2. Constitution of Independent Presbyterian Church, Memphis, Tennessee, Article III, paragraph 2.
3. As David Chappell writes, 'the Bible, which had so much slavery in it, offered so little objective support for post-emancipation racism'. See David L. Chappell, *A Stone of Hope: Prophetic Religion and the Death of Jim Crow* (Chapel Hill, NC: University of North Carolina Press, 2005), p. 112.
4. 'Like the southern divines writing about slavery,' concludes Paul Harvey, 'religious thinkers often began by assuming that segregation was a civil institution. Yet the logic of their arguments ultimately led them to uphold race as inherently godly and biblical.' Paul Harvey, *Freedom's Coming: Religious Culture and the Shaping of the South from the Civil War to the Civil Rights Era* (Chapel Hill, NC: University of North Carolina Press, 2005), p. 232.
5. Harvey, *Freedom's Coming*, p. 230; Joseph Crespino, *In Search of Another Country: Mississippi and the Conservative Counterrevolution* (Princeton, NJ: Princeton University Press, 2007), pp. 284–5, n.24; Chappell, *A Stone of Hope*, pp. 105–30.
6. This phrase was coined by Paul Harvey. See *Freedom's Coming*, pp. 229–45. See also Carolyn Dupont, *Mississippi Praying: Southern White Evangelicals and the Civil Rights Movement, 1945–1975* (New York: New York University Press, 2013).
7. Chappell, *Stone of Hope*, p. 6.
8. As G. T. Gillespie put it in 1957: 'The evils and injustices which have arisen under the system of segregation have been purely incidental, and have been due to any fallacy in the principle of segregation, but to the weaknesses and perversities of individual members of both races.' See 'A Southern Christian Looks at the Race Problem', *Southern Presbyterian Journal*, 5 June 1957, p. 9.
9. As Humphrey Ezell wrote in 1959, 'Racial segregation will aid in the prosperity, the happiness, and the divine blessings of both the White and Negro races.' See Humphrey K. Ezell, *The Christian Problem of Racial Segregation* (New York: Greenwich Book Publishers, 1959), p. 26.
10. G. T. Gillespie makes this claim to solidify his 'biblical' argument for segregation: 'Since the practice of segregation was instituted among the Hebrew people by divine authority, and enforced by stern theocratic sanctions for many centuries, and since Christ and the Apostles demonstrated that the principles of charity and Christian brotherhood could be made operative in all the relations of life without involving revolutionary changes in the social, economic or political order, there is certainly no valid ground for the charge that segregation is inherently wrong, contrary to the will of God, and essentially un-Christian.' See 'Southern Christian', p. 11.
11. Ezell, *Christian Problem*, p. 14.
12. Festus F. Windham, *A Bible Treatise on Segregation* (New York: William-Frederick Press, 1957).
13. Windham, *Bible Treatise*, p. 7.
14. Windham, *Bible Treatise*, p. 9.

15 Windham, *Bible Treatise*, p. 13. In other places, Windham suggests that segregation is in fact rooted in the curse: 'With Adam sin came into the world and with Ham segregation and servitude for his descendants' (p. 19).
16 G. T. Gillespie, *A Christian View of Segregation* (Winona, MS: Association of Citizens' Councils, 1954): see Digital Collection, University Libraries, University of Southern Mississippi, http://digilib.usm.edu/cdm/ref/collection/manu/id/1880. Gillespie's address was also republished in the *Southern Presbyterian Journal*, 5 June 1957 and the *Natchez Times*, 22 November 1954.
17 Gillespie, *Christian View of Segregation*, pp. 2, 3.
18 Gillespie, *Christian View of Segregation*, pp. 3, 8.
19 Gillespie, *Christian View of Segregation*, p. 8; emphasis added.
20 Gillespie, *Christian View of Segregation*, pp. 8, 9; emphasis added.
21 Gillespie, *Christian View of Segregation*, p. 9; emphasis added.
22 Gillespie, *Christian View of Segregation*, p. 9; emphasis added.
23 Crespino, *In Search of Another Country*, p. 68.
24 Chappell, *Stone of Hope*, pp. 110, 112. Inexplicably, Chappell mentions Gillespie's extended interpretation of Genesis only to note the Mississippian's reliance on 'the curse laid on Noah's son Ham after the Flood,' commenting that he 'could not do much with it'.
25 Randy J. Sparks, *Religion in Mississippi* (Jackson, MS: University Press of Mississippi, 2001), p. 229.
26 Smith, 'Bible Study for Circle Bible Leadership on "Jesus and Citizenship," Lesson 8. Brotherhood and Race', *Southern Presbyterian Journal*, 7 July 1957, p. 18; emphasis added.
27 Smith, 'Bible Study for Circle Bible Leadership', p. 19; emphasis added.
28 Benjamin M. Palmer, *The Present Crisis and its Issues, An Address Delivered before the Literary Societies of Washington and Lee University, Lexington, Va., 27th June, 1872* (Baltimore, MD: John Murphy and Co., 1872), pp. 18–19; emphasis added.
29 Palmer, *Present Crisis*, p. 19.
30 L. Nelson Bell, 'Race Relations – Whither?', *Southern Presbyterian Journal*, March 1944, pp. 4–5. Another application of Genesis 9–11 to racial matters appeared in the same journal a few months later: [W. G. Foster, ed.], 'Third Sunday: The White Problem', *Southern Presbyterian Journal*, October 1944, pp. 22–3.
31 B. W. Crouch, 'Dr. Palmer on Racial Barriers', *Southern Presbyterian Journal*, 2 December 1946, pp. 5–6.
32 J. David Simpson, 'Non-Segregation Means Eventual Inter-Marriage', *Southern Presbyterian Journal*, 15 March 1948, pp. 6–7; W. G. Foster, 'Young People's Department', *Southern Presbyterian Journal*, 1 July 1948, pp. 14–15.
33 J. E. Flow, 'Is Segregation Unchristian?', *Southern Presbyterian Journal*, 29 August 1951, pp. 4–5.
34 J. V. N. Talmage, 'The Tower of Babel', *Southern Presbyterian Journal*, 21 November 1956, pp. 5–6.
35 Carl W. MacMurray, 'Helps for Circle Bible Study for March', *Southern Presbyterian Journal*, 13 February 1957, p. 11.
36 See G. T. Gillespie, 'A Southern Christian Looks at the Race Problem', *Southern Presbyterian Journal*, 5 June 1957, pp. 7–12; p. 11; original emphasis.
37 Carey Daniel, 'Segregation's Archenemy: Hiss' United Nations, Or, Let's Get the U.S. Out of the U.N.', in Daniel, *God the Original Segregationist and Seven other Segregation Sermons* (n.p, n.d.), pp. 53–4.
38 Daniel, 'Segregation's Archenemy', p. 17.
39 Daniel, 'Segregation's Archenemy', p. 17.
40 Kenneth R. Kinney, 'The Segregation Issue', *Baptist Bulletin* (October 1956), 9–10.
41 Kinney, 'Segregation Issue', 9.
42 Kinney, 'Segregation Issue', 9.
43 *Dake's Annotated Reference Bible* (Lawrenceville, GA: Dake Bible Sales, 1991), pp. 9, 159.

44 Josiah Priest, *Slavery as it Relates to the Negro or African Race* (1843; New York: Arno Press, 1977), p. 39.
45 Jerome B. Holgate, *Noachidae: Or, Noah and his Descendants* (Buffalo, NY: Breed, Butler and Co., 1860), p. 25. See also pp. 90–1, 143, 147.
46 [Buckner H. Payne], *The Negro: What Is His Ethnological Status?* (Cincinnati, OH: n.p., 1867), p. 32.
47 Palmer, *Present Crisis*, p. 19.
48 Thomas Carey Johnson, *The Life and Letters of Benjamin Morgan Palmer* (Richmond, VA: Presbyterian Committee of Publication, 1906), p. 472.
49 Johnson, *Benjamin Morgan Palmer*, pp. 472–3.
50 J. W. Sandell, *The United States in Scripture: The Union against the States; God in Government* (n.p.: Tucker Printing House, 1907), pp. 41, 44.
51 Sandell, *United States in Scripture*, p. 48.
52 Harry Lacey, *God and the Nations* (New York: Loizeaux Brothers, 1947), pp. 23, 26.
53 Chappell, *Stone of Hope*, pp. 115, 117, 126, 250, n.20.

CHAPTER TEN

Afterword/afterlife: identity, genealogy, legacy

David N. Livingstone

It might be thought something of a curiosity that in Andrew Dickson White's *History of the Warfare of Science with Theology in Christendom* – in many ways the Urtext of the conflict thesis on the relations between science and religion – one of the exhibits in his catalogue of scientific martyrdom is a figure who resorted to the Hebrew Bible to map the dispersal of the sons of Noah across the face of the earth. In his 1878 *Adamites and Preadamites* and, at much greater length two years later in *Preadamites: or A Popular Discussion Concerning the Remote Representatives of the Human Species and the Relation to the Biblical Adam*, Alexander Winchell (1824–91) devoted his energies to that very task.[1] Briefly reconsidering Winchell's intriguing case will bring to the fore some of the major threads that are woven through *Chosen Peoples*, and provide a lens by which to further inspect links between the Bible, identity and genealogy, and their lingering legacy.

In considering the whole question of early human migration, Winchell, variously a professor of geology, physics, engineering and palaeontology who taught at the Universities of Michigan, Syracuse and Vanderbilt, besides serving as State Geologist for Michigan, announced that 'the first requisite is to trace the geographical dispersion of the descendants of Noah'. 'The oldest document available for information on this subject is the Book of Genesis', he went on; 'and, aside from any claim to inspiration, its statements respecting the immediate posterity of Noah have been found so closely accordant with the observed facts, that ethnologists are content to adopt its information as a starting point'.[2] In his telling, the white race was composed of 'three family types', and he was pleased to report that the scientific consensus concerning 'the dispersion of these three families accords with the biblical account of the dispersion of the posterity of the three sons of Noah', designating them 'Hamites, Semites and Japhetites', respectively.[3] For

Winchell there was no incompatibility between scriptural chronology and the deliverances of modern science. Indeed he was at pains to point out that his own biblical findings were fully in accord with leading men of science. 'Do not think me laying corner stones,' he declared; 'they have been laid by Moses; they have been laid by [Jean-François] Champollion, and [Karl Richard] Lepsius, and Sir William Jones, and the Rawlinsons, and [Émile] Haug, and Max Müller, and George Smith; they have been laid by philologists and archaeologists and ethnologists; by zoologists and geologists, and by interpreters of our sacred histories'.[4] So confident indeed was Winchell in the reliability of scriptural genealogy that he concluded his *Adamites and Preadamites* with a patriarchal chronology in tabular form specifying, with conspicuous precision, the number of years from Adam to the flood (7737), from the flood to the birth of Abraham (2763) and from 'Adam to the present year' (14378).[5]

Winchell's extended 1880 account dwelt in much more detail on the migration patterns of the Hamites, Semites and Japhetites, and was augmented by a cartographic portrayal of the 'Dispersions of the Noachites' and a complex 'Chart of the Progressive Dispersion of Mankind' across the face of the earth – a task which drew on a wide range of contemporary geographical and anthropological scholarship. Convinced that the latest research had 'ascertained with considerable certainty the regions in which most of the peoples were located whose names are mentioned in the tenth chapter of Genesis', Winchell systematically worked his way through the various places and names mentioned in the Pentateuchal text and their precise locations.[6] For instance, Sabtah, derived from the third son of Cush, was 'generally understood to have been located in eastern Arabia, on the Persian Gulf, or on the contiguous shore of the Indian Ocean', while 'Nimrod settled, beyond all dispute, in the plain of Shinar, which answered to Mesopotamia and the bordering country'.[7] By painstakingly scrutinising name after name, Winchell could conclude that 'not only ... was the primitive civilisation of Egypt Hamitic, but also that of Barbary, as well as that of Phoenicia, Judea, Syria, Chaldea, Assyria, Babylonia, Susiana and Himyaritic (or eastern and part of southern) Arabia'; that the 'Semites have always been confined within narrow geographical limits – 'a parallelogram sixteen hundred miles long, from the parallel of Aleppo to the south of Arabia'; and that 'the Japhetites or Indo-Europeans – called also Aryans' separated into a range of families – Javanic, Kimmerian, Thracian and Ligurian among them – and swept through Europe.[8]

Plainly, taking the Hebrew Bible's chronology with great seriousness was not at all incompatible with scientific endeavour. As the editors of this collection remark in their introduction, 'Even amid spreading secularism and the development of professionalised science, scriptural notions of lineage, descent and inheritance continued to inform not just popular understandings of race, nation and character but the conceptual scaffolding surrounding them.' In Winchell's case, his charting of Noahite cartography was marshalled in the cause of showing that humans had existed prior to Adam. This was intended, at once, to preserve the integrity of biblical chronology, and yet to allow for a much longer genealogy of the human species that pre-dated the Genesis record. It was, moreover, compatible with evolutionary theory, and on that account Winchell was dismissed from his post at Vanderbilt University in 1878 and wound up in White's heroic gallery of those who had been martyred in the centuries-long warfare between science and theology. As White put it:

> his relations to this Southern institution were destined to be brief. That his lectures at the Vanderbilt University were learned, attractive, and stimulating, even his enemies were forced to admit; but he was soon found to believe that there had been men earlier than the period assigned to Adam, and even that all the human race are not descended from Adam. His desire was to reconcile science and Scripture, and he was now treated by a Methodist Episcopal Bishop in Tennessee just as, two centuries before, La Peyrère had been treated, for a similar effort by a Roman Catholic vicar-general in Belgium ... It was evident, at last, that a defence must be made, and a local organ of the sect, which under the editorship of a fellow-professor had always treated Dr. Winchell's views with the luminous inaccuracy which usually characterises a professor's ideas of a rival's teachings, assumed the task.[9]

If White lionised the Vanderbilt victim as a champion of true science in its long struggle against the dark forces of dogma, his was certainly not the last word on Winchell's reputational legacy. For Winchell's afterlife has been anything but heroic. In March 2013, the University of Michigan, where Winchell had served as a professor of physics and engineering from 1854 to 1872, removed his name from one of the university's halls of residence for promoting 'bigoted ideas'.[10] As its President, Mark Schisslel, explained, 'The decision to change the name of a building or house within our residence hall is not one we take lightly.' The reason was that 'by both contemporary standards and even in the context of Winchell's day, his most notable work – the 1880 book titled, *Preadamites, or a Demonstration of the Existence of Men before Adam* – was unambiguously racist and out of step with the University's own aspirations in those times'. 'Winchell's book continues to be used in support of white supremacy', Schlissel went on. 'His name does not merit, nor does it belong, as the name of one of our houses in a University of Michigan residence hall.'[11]

If the virulent scientific racism that Winchell displayed in his writings eventually resulted in the erasure of his name from the University of Michigan's architectural complex, the legacy of his racial ideology has indeed continued to thrive in the writings of those who peddle a dark theology of race hatred.[12] Chief among these is the Kingdom Identity or Christian Identity movement which, rooted to one degree or another in nineteenth-century British Israelism, continues to preach an ethnic gospel of white supremacy which denigrates non-white races as sub-human and opposes interracial marriage.[13] In 1967, for example, supporters reprinted 'the salient points' of Charles Carroll's outrageous 1900 text, *The Negro a Beast*, under the title *In the Image of God*. Here Winchell's authority was called upon in scientific support of black inferiority and staged for a mid-twentieth-century audience.[14] And much more recently, in a work published at some point after 1995, Everett Ramsey, pastor of Faith Baptist Church in Louisville, Nebraska, was still calling on Winchell's testimony in support of his claim that racial difference is 'more than skin deep'. The concluding pages sought to incite readers by attributing a range of ghastly ailments to race-mixing, by stirring up followers to resist all efforts at multiculturalism and by condemning blood transfusions and organ transplants. 'I believe that unless we stop promoting the mixing of the races at all levels', he announced, 'we will reap a whirlwind of infections, diseases, deformities and brain damage to our selves and our children down to the third generation and further'.[15]

The circumstances of Winchell's life and afterlife may be seen as emblematic in the context of *Chosen Peoples*, inasmuch as they speak to a number of themes that snake their way through this collection of essays on the Bible, race and empire in the long nineteenth century. Primarily, matters of identity and genealogy which pervade Winchell's ethno-biblical science, and its enduring legacy, resonate with many of the topics that the authors in this volume have chosen for interrogation.

Identity

Winchell's passion to separate out pre-Adamite and Adamite stock was born of a deep yearning to secure the distinctive identity of the white race. The chapters here confirm just how significant the Bible has been in the manufacturing and moulding of various identities. Senses of imperial, racial and national identity were frequently grounded in scriptural texts that spoke of a chosen people, an elect race, a holy nation, a sacred lineage and the like. But biblical identity-formation certainly did not always take place in predictable ways. As the editors make clear in their introduction: 'the Bible could at once bolster nationalist and imperial causes and at the same time confront them with uncomfortable counter-narratives. Slaves and their owners, abolitionists and anti-abolitionists alike all returned repeatedly to the proof-texts that justified their views.' John Coffey, for example, shows how the slave rising in the Demerara sugar colony in British Guiana drew inspiration from biblical narratives of liberation, and how the slaves found in Scripture resources to forge a new collective identity. As Coffey writes: 'Scripture had long been cited to reinforce the hierarchical domination of white masters over black slaves, but with the conversion and baptism of the enslaved, it became harder to justify such domination by reference to the Israelites' enslavement of heathens.' The 'distinctive interpretative community' that came into being around Bethel Chapel 'arrived at a more militant reading of Scripture' as it identified itself with the oppressed Hebrew slaves in Egypt.

In similar vein Jared MacDonald's narrative of the deep connections between biblical literacy and Khoesan national renewal in the Cape Colony reveals how, under the influence of missionary endeavour, 'an egalitarian interpretation of the Gospel undermined white settler ownership of Christianity, its symbols and perhaps most importantly, salvation'. Democratising soteriology had immediate political significance. Because espousing Christian faith was long regarded as a signifier for white identity, nonconformist missionaries committed to universally spreading the gospel effectively disrupted the social hierarchy of colonial society. Even the capacity to read the biblical text itself became a means by which the Khoesan 'could seek to claim a measure of social equality' and delivered 'a language through which a new, Christian "nation" could be imagined and articulated, and which could challenge settler-colonial hierarchies of power'.

In Russia, as Stephen Batalden shows, the Russian Bible Society's new approach to bible translation with its use of modern idioms and an interconfessional perspective was itself a challenge to the Russian Empire as a confessional state. This had the effect of subverting the presumption, as Batalden puts it, that the 'state was both the protector and ultimate arbiter of religious and confessional practice'.

In other contexts, of course, as the editors explain, 'teaching people to read using the Bible was undoubtedly part of the inculcation of "civilisation", loyalty and "British values" among local elites'. Elsewhere, they note: 'Across America, Africa, the Middle East and Asia, scriptural stories, scenes and phrases provided ideological ammunition for liberation and nationalist movements.' In different arenas, it is clear, biblical hermeneutics and translation practices were mobilised in different ways in cultivating particular senses of identity.

Genealogy

For Alexander Winchell questions about identity were intimately interwoven with matters of genealogy. Lines of descent were critical to the task of securing and stabilising identities. In Winchell's case this took the form of conjoining Noahite lineage with anthropometric science. For others, linguistic archaeology dominated. Whether human languages were of monogenetic or polygenetic origin exercised the minds of numerous students of philology. The use of the labels Hamitic, Japhetic and Semitic to designate lines of linguistic ancestry discloses how intimately connected the early science of language was with biblical thought-forms.

Matters of genealogy loom large in this collection, not least in connection with language. The editors, for example, point to the profound impact the 'discovery of Aryan or Indo-European linguistics' had on the understanding of race, and on 'consequent readings of the Bible as a product of a "Semitic race"'. Thus Hilary Carey dwells on language in her depiction of the missionary-linguist John Fraser who claimed 'that he had demonstrated beyond doubt the existence of linguistic and ethnic connections between the Aborigines of Australia and the Dravidians of southern India'. Fraser was a staunch advocate of linguistic monogenism and was convinced that he had unearthed indubitable ethno-linguistic evidence that aboriginal Australians were of Hamitic descent. Perhaps not surprisingly, as a firm believer that all languages had a common origin, Fraser was 'a consistent and humane advocate for the Aboriginal people of Australia, being opposed to any suggestion that they were not human or had evolved separately to other peoples'.

Linguistic genealogy also surfaces in Dorothy Figueira's account of a range of post-Enlightenment thinkers who turned to the 'Vedic past in an attempt to find a utopia outside Europe and as an alternative tradition to that of the Bible'. For Max Müller, for example, the quest to track the 'first germs of the language, religion and mythology' of Europe to Aryan roots was intrinsic to the project of refurbishing his own cultural tradition. As he put it: 'We are by nature Aryan, Indo-European, not Semitic: our spiritual kith and kin are to be found in India, Persia, Greece, Italy, Germany; not in Mesopotamia, Egypt, or Palestine.'

But perhaps most conspicuously the genealogical impulse has frequently manifested itself in the passion to claim descent from the Lost Tribes of Israel. In Chapter 4, Brian Murray concentrates on the

AFTERWORD/AFTERLIFE

Anglo-Saxon rendition of this mythology in the shape of British Israelism. Here he pursues the ramifications of the idea that the British were linguistically and racially the descendants of the ten Lost Tribes, an ethno-theology that 'emerged from a specifically late-Victorian confluence of khaki conservatism and evangelicalism'. In particular he focuses on the Irish dimensions of the subject and on its denigration of the Catholic Irish. Here, he remarks, by 'viewing modern politics through the lens of biblical empires, the British colonisation of Ireland was literally rendered as a recapitulation of Israel's conquest of Canaan'. This meant that any continuing resistance from the 'Celtic Canaanites' was simply 'because the Chosen People had, from antiquity to present, been far too humane in their treatment of their providently enshrined enemies'. Indeed on occasion, calls for extermination took precedence over evangelism. For these British Israelites, genealogy licensed eradication.

Finding Britain in the Bible, as it were, could also manifest itself in other ways, as Gareth Atkins's chapter on Britain's maritime empire reveals (Chapter 3). Atkins examines various efforts by English clergy to find prophetic utterances in Scripture that found their fulfilment in British overseas exploits. Among these was a strain of thinking that identified Tarshish, depicted as a place of great wealth, and its ships as restoring exiles to the land of Israel, as referring prophetically to maritime England. This was an exercise in reading Britain's seafaring destiny providentially and providing an identity that could be tracked back at least to the eighth century BCE.

Those for whom genealogy and identity were umbilically connected continued to find sustenance in the way the generations that structure the book of Genesis provided the basis for the table of the nations descended from the sons of Noah. Not surprisingly, for many nineteenth-century Bible readers, ancestry, pedigree and lineage continued to loom large in projects to justify particular senses of racial, cultural and national identity.

Legacy

Charting the use of the Bible in establishing the identity and genealogy of racial groups is no exercise in the mere cataloguing of historical oddities. As Winchell's afterlife plainly demonstrates, words and reputations survive their owners and take on a life of their own. Whether acclaimed by supremacists or castigated by modern university managers, his legacy lingers on in different arenas. In many ways attending to the post-history of texts and status is an exercise in engaging what has been called the history of the present.

The authors in this collection are well aware of the aftermath of the ideas and movements they have scrutinised. Again and again, *Chosen Peoples* advertises the lingering shadows of earlier ethno-biblical manoeuvres. Stephen Haynes's scrutiny of the nineteenth-century roots of what he calls 'segregationist folk theology' during the 1960s is a case in point. Having established just how flexible interpretations of the Genesis account of Noah and his sons could be, he illustrates 'the continuities between pro-slavery and pro-segregation biblical arguments'. Whatever the rhetorical differences between pro-slavery champions and their latter-day segregationist successors, Haynes identifies key thematic continuities in how slaveholders interpreted the destiny of the Noahite family that persisted into the middle of the twentieth century, in particular 'the refusal of Ham's descendants to accept their allotment in God's scheme of land distribution, and God's enforced separation of peoples after the rebellion at Babel'.

As several authors also make clear, the widespread longing on the part of different groups to claim descent from the Lost Tribes of Israel continues to have resonances into our own day. Carey, for example, reminds us that 'many Pacific people still accept the legitimacy of the theory of the lost tribes', adding that 'the most highly developed version of this mythic history focused on the Maori of New Zealand'. These scriptural notions, she concludes, 'resurfaced as recently as the 1987 coup, when claims for biblical ancestry were used to support arguments for political and racial ascendancy by Fijian leaders over Indian and other ethnic emigrants'. Similarly Gareth Atkins pauses to note that '[g]iven that parts of the internet are populated with people still convinced that Britain (or America) really is Tarshish, that subculture continues to resonate with some even today'. And Murray, conscious that the 'legacies of British Israelism are complex and diverse' and that 'the movement has spawned distinct offshoots in different regions of the English-speaking world', reminds us that some of 'the last strongholds of British-Israel identity' are to be found 'among the extremist fringes of white Protestant communities in South Africa and Northern Ireland, groups with covenantal settler identities that have been forged against a background of racial and sectarian conflict'. In the latter case an Ulster loyalist group operating under the name Tara, and with strong roots in British-Israelism and links with paramilitary organisations, peddled its own brand of fierce anti-Catholicism during the 1960s and 1970s.[16]

The legacies of Bible translation have also continued to resonate down to the present day. As Heather Sharkey observes, the British and Foreign Bible Society's Arabic translations had the political potential to inform Arab national identity in a range of ways. Choices about whether to use vernacular or elite forms of Arabic were contentious and had lasting consequences. During the 1960s, publishing Arabic portions of the Bible in what it called 'Sudanese' and 'Algerian' versions attracted the charge that the Society was engaged in promoting particular senses of identity for particular Arab communities. Consequently, as she points out, 'Mid-to late twentieth-century Arab nationalists denounced the Bible society's territorially focused colloquial Arabic printing as part of a larger British imperial scheme ... to divide Arab peoples into smaller bounded lands in order to weaken, control or reconfigure them.' By insisting on 'a plurality of Arabics' the Society – intentionally or unintentionally – may have created among Arabic speakers a greater awareness of 'regional barriers to communication and therefore communion across the region, while fortifying conceptions of communities built within narrower state borders, among Egyptians, Algerians and the like'.

In similar vein, Batalden observes that the 'issue of an appropriate medium or sacred language for modern Russian religious culture, enjoined in the battle over Russian biblical translation, has continued to be a focus of interest to the present'. In contemporary Ukraine, he points out, 'modern biblical translation, with its appeal to national languages, became embroiled in the conflict between empire and nation. In that conflict the modern Bible not only helped to fashion the nation, but subtly challenged the imperial claims and the authority of the confessional state.'

In all these cases it is clear that how the Bible was handled in the nineteenth century has had long-lasting consequences. Its legacy, in one way or another, continues to shape communities and identities in sometimes predictable, sometimes unanticipated, ways.

Chosen Peoples richly portrays the roles the Bible played in the making and maintenance of senses of ethnic and national identity during the long nineteenth century. Sometimes this impulse expressed itself in efforts to find ethno-national roots in biblical patrilineages. On other occasions it was bound up with the consequences of the language choices that Bible translators made in different settings. In yet other situations the rereading of narratives like the Exodus could serve as a site of resistance and stimulate subversive and liberationist senses of group identity. In all of these, the Bible acted as a resource on which readers could draw to understand themselves, their sense of nationhood and their place in the world. So powerful was this vocabulary that even in our own more secular age, the Bible still can provide tropes that our culture calls upon in coming to terms with its own sense of itself.

In the world of molecular genetics, the impulse to find human identity in genealogy has been deep and lasting, and from time to time biblical vocabulary has been called upon to express its latest findings. When it was announced that research on mitochondrial DNA – which is only inherited from mothers and remains unchanged in transmission from generation to generation save for chance mutations – could be used to trace the matrilineal lineages of living people back to a common ancestor,[17] the front cover of *Newsweek* welcomed the finding with the headline 'The Search for Adam and Eve'.[18] So-called 'Mitochondrial Eve' had appeared on humanity's genetic stage.[19] Soon the search was on for her male counterpart, and 'Y-chromosome Adam' – humanity's most recent paternal common ancestor – presently arrived on the scene. In turn the idea that 'the diverse mitochondrial DNA sequences found in modern humans coalesce to one ancestral sequence, the "mitochondrial Eve" or "mother of us all"', prompted some geneticists to advance the 'Noah's Ark' hypothesis which proposed that the transition from archaic to modern Homo Sapiens 'was associated with a very narrow bottleneck, consisting of only two or very few individuals who are the ancestors of all modern mankind'.[20] Even if only as a source of rich metaphor, the Genesis narrative continues to cast its shadow over the genealogical project of tracing the genetic story and thus the identity of our own species.

Notes

1 I have discussed Winchell in *Adam's Ancestors: Race, Religion and the Politics of Human Origins* (Baltimore, MD: Johns Hopkins University Press, 2008).
2 Alexander Winchell, *Adamites and Preadamites: or A Popular Discussion Concerning the Remote Representatives of the Human Species and the Relation to the Biblical Adam* (Syracuse, NY: John T. Roberts, 1878), pp. 7–8.
3 Winchell, *Adamites*, p. 8.
4 Winchell, *Adamites*, p. 26.
5 Winchell, *Adamites*, p. 52.
6 Alexander Winchell, *Preadamites; or a Demonstration of the Existence of Men before Adam; Together with a Study of their Condition, Antiquity Racial Affinities, and Progressive Dispersion over the Earth* (Chicago, IL: S. C. Griggs, 1880), p. 16.
7 Winchell, *Preadamites*, pp. 18, 19.
8 Winchell, *Preadamites*, pp. 23, 37, 43.
9 Andrew Dickson White, *A History of the Warfare of Science with Theology in Christendom*, 2 vols (New York: Appleton, 1896), I: pp. 313–14.
10 Scott Jaschik, 'Ending Honors for Racists', *Inside Higher Ed*, 30 March 2018, accessed 23 January 2019, https://www.insidehighered.com/news/2018/03/30/university-michigan-removes-honors-late-president-and-professor-racist-legacies?width=775&height=500&iframe=true.
11 See 'U-M Will Remove Little, Winchell Names from Campus Facilities', *Vice President for Communications: Michigan News*, University of Michigan, 29 March 2018, accessed 23 January 2019, https://news.umich.edu/u-m-will-remove-little-winchell-names-from-campus-facilities/.
12 Colin Kidd, *The Forging of Races: Race and Scripture in the Protestant Atlantic World, 1600–2000* (Cambridge: Cambridge University Press, 2006).

13 See Michael Barkun, *Religion and the Racist Right: The Origins of the Christian Identity Movement* (Chapel Hill, NC: University of North Carolina Press, rev. ed., 1997); Robert S. Robbins and Jerrold N. Post, *Political Paranoia: The Psychopolitics of Hatred* (New Haven, CT: Yale University Press, 1997), Ch. 7.
14 *In the Image of God* [1967] (Merrimac, MA: Destiny Publishers, 1984).
15 Everett Ramsey, *Racial Difference: More that Skin Deep* (Harrison, AZ: Kingdom Identity Ministries, n.d.), p. 75.
16 Chris Moore, *The Kincora Scandal: Political Cover-Up and Intrigue in Northern Ireland* (Dublin: Marino Press, 1996); Steve Bruce, *The Red Hand* (Oxford: Oxford University Press, 1992).
17 Rebecca L. Cann and Allan C. Wilson, 'The Recent African Genesis of Humans', *Scientific American*, 13.2 (2003), 54–61; p. 58. This article, updated, was originally published in the April 1992 edition of the *Scientific American*.
18 John Tierney, Lynda Wright, and Karen Springen, 'The Search for Adam and Eve,' *Newsweek*, 11 January 1988, 46–52; p. 46.
19 Rebecca L. Cann, 'In Search of Eve', *The Sciences*, 27 (1987), 30–7.
20 Francisco J. Ayala, Anaías Escalante, Colm O'Huigin and Jan Klein, 'Molecular Genetics of Speciation and Human Origins', in Walter M. Fitch and Francisco J. Ayala (eds), *Tempo and Mode In Evolution: Genetics and Paleontology 50 Years After Simpson* (Washington, DC: National Academy Press, 1995), p. 203.

SELECT BIBLIOGRAPHY

Akenson, Donald. *God's Peoples: Covenant and Land in South Africa, Israel, and Ulster.* Ithaca, NY: Cornell University Press, 1992.

Anderson, Benedict. *Imagined Communities: Reflections on the Origin and Spread of Nationalism.* London: Verso, 1983.

App, Urs. *The Birth of Orientalism.* Philadelphia, PA: University of Pennsylvania Press, 2010.

Atkins, Gareth. *Converting Britannia: Evangelicals and British Public Life, c. 1770–1840.* Woodbridge: Boydell and Brewer, 2019.

Bar-Yosef, Eitan. *The Holy Land in English Culture, 1799–1917.* Oxford: Oxford University Press, 2005.

Barkun, Michael. *Religion and the Racist Right: The Origins of the Christian Identity Movement.* Chapel Hill, NC: University of North Carolina Press, 1997.

Batalden, Stephen K. *Russian Bible Wars: Modern Scriptural Translation and Cultural Authority.* Cambridge: Cambridge University Press, 2013.

Batalden, Stephen K., Kathleen Cann and John Dean (eds). *Sowing the Word: The Cultural Impact of the British and Foreign Bible Society, 1804–2004.* Sheffield: Sheffield Phoenix, 2004.

Bayly, C. A. *The Birth of the Modern World, 1780–1914.* Oxford: Blackwell, 2004.

Becker, Judith (ed.). *European Missions in Contact Zones: Transformation through Interaction in a (Post-)Colonial World.* Göttingen: Vandenhoeck and Ruprecht, 2015.

Bell, Duncan. *The Idea of Greater Britain: Empire and the Future of World Order, 1860–1900.* Princeton, NJ: Princeton University Press, 2007.

Belich, James. *Replenishing the Earth: The Settler Revolution and the Rise of the Angloworld.* Oxford: Oxford University Press, 2009.

Benes, Tuska. *In Babel's Shadow: Philology and the Nation in Nineteenth-Century Germany.* Detroit, MI: Wayne State University Press, 2008.

Bhabha, Homi K. *Nation and Narration.* New York: Routledge, 1990.

Boehmer, Elleke. *Empire, the National, and the Postcolonial, 1890–1920: Resistance in Interaction.* Oxford: Oxford University Press, 2002.

Brantlinger, Patrick. *Rule of Darkness: British Literature and Imperialism, 1830–1914.* Ithaca, NY: Cornell University Press, 1990.

Brantlinger, Patrick. *Dark Vanishings: Discourse on the Extinction of Primitive Races, 1800–1930.* Ithaca, NY: Cornell University Press, 2003.

Brett, Mark. *Decolonizing God: The Bible in the Tides of Empire.* Sheffield: Sheffield Phoenix, 2008.

Brown, Stewart J., and Timothy Tackett (eds). *The Cambridge History of Christianity, Volume VII: Enlightenment, Reawakening and Revolution, 1660–1815.* Cambridge: Cambridge University Press, 2006.

Burton, Antoinette and Isabel Hofmeyr (eds). *Ten Books that Shaped the British Empire: Creating an Imperial Commons.* Durham, NC: Duke University Press, 2014.

SELECT BIBLIOGRAPHY

Byrd, James P. *Sacred Scripture, Sacred War: The Bible and the American Revolution*. New York; Oxford University Press, 2013.

Cabrita, Joel. *Text and Authority in the South African Nazaretha Church*. Cambridge: Cambridge University Press, 2014.

Callahan, Allen Dwight. *The Talking Book: African Americans and the Bible*. New Haven, CT: Yale University Press, 2006.

Canton, William. *The History of the British and Foreign Bible Society*, 5 vols. London: John Murray, 1904–10.

Cantor, Geoffrey. *Religion and the Great Exhibition of 1851*. Oxford: Oxford University Press, 2011.

Carey, Hilary M. (ed.). *Empires of Religion*. Basingstoke: Palgrave Macmillan, 2008.

Carey, Hilary M. *God's Empire: Religion and Colonialism in the British World, c.1801–1908*. Cambridge: Cambridge University Press, 2011.

Chidester, David. *Empire of Religion: Imperialism and Comparative Religion*. Chicago, IL: University of Chicago Press, 2014.

Coffey, John. *Exodus and Liberation: Deliverance Politics from John Calvin to Martin Luther King Jr*. Oxford: Oxford University Press, 2013.

Cox, Jeffrey. *The British Missionary Enterprise Since 1700*. New York: Routledge, 2008.

Craton, Michael. *Testing the Chains: Resistance to Slavery in the British West Indies*. Ithaca, NY: Cornell University Press, 1982.

Daniell, David. *The Bible in English: Its History and Influence*. New Haven, CT: Yale University Press, 2003.

Daunton, Martin and Rick Halpern (eds). *Empire and Others: British Encounters with Indigenous Peoples, 1600–1850*. London: UCL Press, 1999.

Davis, David Brion. *Inhuman Bondage: The Rise and Fall of New World Slavery*. New York: Oxford University Press, 2006.

De Kock, Leon. *Civilising Barbarians: Missionary Narrative and African Textual Response in Nineteenth-Century South Africa*. Johannesburg: Wits University Press, 1996.

Doğan, Mehmet Ali and Heather J. Sharkey (eds). *American Missionaries and the Middle East: Foundational Encounters*. Salt Lake City, UT: University of Utah Press, 2011.

Elbourne, Elizabeth. *Blood Ground: Colonialism, Missions and the Contest for Christianity in the Cape Colony and Britain, 1799–1853*. Montreal and Kingston, Ontario: McGill-Queen's University Press, 2002.

Elphick, Richard. *The Equality of Believers: Protestant Missionaries and the Racial Politics of South Africa*. Charlottesville: University of Virginia Press, 2012.

Etherington, Norman (ed.). *Missions and Empire*. Oxford: Oxford University Press, 2005.

Fabian, Johannes. *Time and the Other: How Anthropology Makes Its Object*. New York: Columbia University Press, 1983.

Fabian, Johannes. *Language and Colonial Power: The Appropriation of Swahili in the Former Belgian Congo, 1880–1938*. Cambridge: Cambridge University Press, 1986.

SELECT BIBLIOGRAPHY

Fea, John. *The Bible Cause: A History of the American Bible Society*. Oxford: Oxford University Press, 2016.

Figueira, Dorothy. *Aryans, Jews, Brahmins: Theorizing Authority through Myths of Identity*. Albany, NY: State University of New York Press, 2002.

Gange, David and Michael Ledger-Lomas (eds). *Cities of God: The Bible and Archaeology in Nineteenth-Century Britain*. Cambridge: Cambridge University Press, 2013.

Gilley, Sheridan and Brian Stanley (eds.) *The Cambridge History of Christianity, Volume VIII: World Christianities, c. 1815–c. 1914*. Cambridge: Cambridge University Press, 2006.

Gilmour, Rachael. *Grammars of Colonialism: Representing Languages in Colonial South Africa*. Basingstoke: Palgrave Macmillan, 2006.

Gilroy, Paul. *The Black Atlantic: Modernity and Double Consciousness*. London: Verso, 1993.

Glasson, Travis. *Mastering Christianity: Missionary Anglicanism and Slavery in the Atlantic World*. New York: Oxford University Press, 2012.

Glaude, Eddie S. *Exodus! Religion, Race, and Nation in Early Nineteenth-Century Black America*. Chicago, IL: Chicago University Press, 2000.

Gray, Richard. *Black Christians and White Missionaries*. New Haven, CT: Yale University Press, 1990.

Green, Abigail and Vincent Viaene (eds). *Religious Internationals in the Modern Age: Globalization and Faith Communities since 1750*. Basingstoke: Palgrave Macmillan, 2012.

Gregory, Jeremy (ed.). *The Oxford History of Anglicanism, Volume II: Establishment and Empire, 1662–1829*. Oxford: Oxford University Press, 2017.

Gutjahr, Paul. *An American Bible: The History of the Good Book in the United States*. Stanford, CA: Stanford University Press, 1996.

Hall, Catherine (ed.). *Cultures of Empire: Colonisers in Britain and the Empire in the Nineteenth and Twentieth Centuries*. Manchester: Manchester University Press, 2000.

Hall, Catherine. *Civilising Subjects: Metropole and Colony in the English Imagination, 1830–1867*. Cambridge: Polity Press, 2002.

Hardwick, Joseph. *An Anglican British World: The Church of England and the Expansion of the Settler Empire, c. 1790–1860*. Manchester: Manchester University Press, 2014.

Harries, Patrick and David Maxwell (eds). *The Spiritual in the Secular: Missionaries and Knowledge About Africa*. Grand Rapids, MI: Eerdmans, 2012.

Hastings, Adrian. *The Construction of Nationhood: Ethnicity, Religion and Nationalism*. Cambridge: Cambridge University Press, 1997.

Haynes, Stephen R. *Noah's Curse: The Biblical Justification of American Slavery*. New York: Oxford University Press, 2002.

Heschel, Susannah. *Abraham Geiger and the Jewish Jesus*. Chicago, IL: Chicago University Press, 1998.

Heschel, Susannah. *The Aryan Jesus: Christianity, Nazis and the Bible*. Princeton, NJ: Princeton University Press, 2007.

Hobsbawm, Eric. *Nations and Nationalism since 1780: Programme, Myth, Reality*. Cambridge: Cambridge University Press, 1990.

SELECT BIBLIOGRAPHY

Hofmeyr, Isabel. *The Portable Bunyan: A Transnational History of the Pilgrim's Progress*. Princeton, NJ: Princeton University Press, 2004.

Howsam, Leslie. *Cheap Bibles: Nineteenth-Century Publishing and the British and Foreign Bible Society*. Cambridge: Cambridge University Press, 1991.

Hutchison, William R. *Errand to the World: American Protestant Thought and Foreign Missions*. Chicago, IL: University of Chicago Press, 1987.

Israel, Hephzibah. *Religious Transactions in Colonial South India: Language, Translation and the Making of Protestant Identity*. Basingstoke: Palgrave Macmillan, 2011.

Kidd, Colin. *British Identities before Nationalism: Ethnicity and Nationhood in the Atlantic World, 1600–1800*. Cambridge: Cambridge University Press, 1999.

Kidd, Colin. *The Forging of Races: Race and Scripture in the Protestant Atlantic World, 1600–2000*. Cambridge: Cambridge University Press, 2006.

Larsen, Timothy. *A People of One Book: The Bible and the Victorians*. Oxford: Oxford University Press, 2011.

Larsen, Timothy. *The Slain God: Anthropologists and the Christian Faith*. Oxford: Oxford University Press, 2014.

Larsen, Timothy and Michael Ledger-Lomas (eds). *The Oxford History of Protestant Dissenting Traditions, Volume III: The Nineteenth Century*. Oxford: Oxford University Press, 2017.

Lewis, Donald M. *The Origins of Christian Zionism*. Cambridge: Cambridge University Press, 2009.

Livingstone, David N. *Adam's Ancestors: Race, Religion and the Politics of Human Origins*. Baltimore, MD: Johns Hopkins University Press, 2011.

Ledger-Lomas, Michael, and Scott Mandelbrote (eds.) *Dissent and the Bible in Britain, c.1650–1950*. Oxford: Oxford University Press, 2013.

Lorimer, Douglas. *Science, Race Relations and Resistance: Britain, 1870–1914*. Manchester: Manchester University Press, 2013.

Makdisi, Ussama. *Artillery of Heaven: American Missionaries and the Failed Conversion of the Middle East*. Ithaca, NY: Cornell University Press, 2008.

Marchand, Suzanne. *German Orientalism in the Age of Empire: Religion, Race and Scholarship*. New York: Cambridge University Press, 2005.

McClintock, Anne. *Imperial Leather: Race, Gender, and Sexuality in the Colonial Contest*. London: Routledge, 1995.

Miller, Randall, Harry Stout, and Charles Wilson (eds.). *Religion and the American Civil War*. New York: Oxford University Press, 1998.

Mosse, George. *Toward the Final Solution: A History of European Racism*. New York: Howard Fertig, 1978.

Moxnes, Halvor. *Jesus and the Rise of Nationalism: A New Quest for the Nineteenth Century Historical Jesus*. London: I. B. Tauris, 2011.

Noll, Mark. *In the Beginning was the Word: The Bible in American Public Life, 1492–1783*. New York: Oxford University Press, 2016.

Olender, Maurice. *The Languages of Paradise: Race, Religion, and Philology in the Nineteenth Century*. Cambridge, MA: Harvard University Press, 1992.

Oshatz, Molly. *Slavery and Sin: The Fight against Slavery and the Rise of Liberal Protestantism*. New York: Oxford University Press, 2012.

SELECT BIBLIOGRAPHY

Parfitt, Tudor. *The Lost Tribes of Israel: The History of a Myth*. London: Phoenix, 2003.

Parfitt, Tudor. *Black Jews in Africa and the Americas*. Cambridge, MA: Harvard University Press, 2013.

Pennington, Brian. *Was Hinduism Invented? Britons, Indians and Colonial Construction of Religion*. Oxford: Oxford University Press, 2005.

Pestana, Carla. *Protestant Empire: Religion & the Making of the British Atlantic World*. Philadelphia, PA: University of Pennsylvania Press, 2009.

Poliakov, Léon. *The Aryan Myth: A History of Racist and Nationalist Ideas in Europe*, trans. E. Howard. London: Chatto and Heinemann for Sussex University Press, 1974.

Porter, Andrew. *Religion versus Empire? British Protestant Missionaries and Overseas Expansion, 1700–1914*. Manchester: Manchester University Press, 2004.

Porter, Bernard. *The Absent-Minded Imperialists: Empire, Society, and Culture in Britain*. Oxford: Oxford University Press, 2004.

Powery, Emerson B. and Rodney S. Sadler Jr., *The Genesis of Liberation: Biblical Interpretation in the Antebellum Narratives of the Enslaved*. Louisville, KY: Westminster John Knox Press, 2016.

Prior, Michael. *The Bible and Colonialism: A Moral Critique*. Sheffield: Sheffield Academic Press, 1997.

Pugach, Sara. *Africa in Translation: A History of Colonial Linguistics in Germany and Beyond, 1814–1945*. Ann Arbor, MI: University of Michigan Press, 2012.

Rafael, Vicente. *Contracting Colonialism: Translation and Christian Conversion in Tagalog Society under Early Spanish Rule*. Ithaca, NY: Cornell University Press, 1998.

Rutz, Michael A. *The British Zion: Congregationalism, Politics and Empire, 1790–1850*. Waco, TX: Baylor University Press, 2011.

Said, Edward. *Orientalism*. New York: Pantheon Books, 1978.

Samson, Jane. *Race and Redemption: British Missionaries Encounter Pacific Peoples, 1797–1920*. Grand Rapids, MI: Eerdmans, 2017.

Sanneh, Lamin. *Translating the Message: The Missionary Impact on Culture*. Ossining, NY: Orbis, 1989.

Sanneh, Lamin and Michael McClymond (eds). *The Wiley-Blackwell Companion to World Christianity*. Hoboken, NJ: Wiley-Blackwell, 2016.

Segovia, Fernando F. and Stephen Moore (eds). *Postcolonial Biblical Criticism: Interdisciplinary Intersections*. London: T.&T. Clark, 2005.

Segovia, Fernando F. and R. S. Sugirtharajah (eds). *A Postcolonial Commentary on the New Testament Writings*. London: T.&T. Clark, 2007.

Shalev, Zur. *Sacred Words and Worlds: Geography, Religion, and Scholarship, 1550–1700*. Leiden: Brill, 2012.

Sharkey, Heather J. *American Evangelicals in Egypt: Missionary Encounters in an Age of Empire*. Princeton, NJ: Princeton University Press, 2008.

Sharkey, Heather J. (ed.). *Cultural Conversions: Unexpected Consequences of Christian Missions in the Middle East, Africa, and South Asia*. Syracuse, NY: Syracuse University Press, 2013.

SELECT BIBLIOGRAPHY

Sheehan, Jonathan. *The Enlightenment Bible: Translation, Scholarship, Culture.* Princeton, NJ: Princeton University Press, 2005.

Smalley, William. *Translation as Mission: Bible Translation in the Modern Missionary Movement.* Macon, GA: Mercer University Press, 1991.

Smith, Anthony D. *Chosen Peoples: Sacred Sources of National Identity.* Oxford: Oxford University Press, 2003.

Stanley, Brian. *The Bible and the Flag: Protestant Mission and British Imperialism in the Nineteenth and Twentieth Centuries.* Leicester: Apollos, 1990.

Stanley, Brian (ed.). *Missions, Nationalism and the End of Empire.* Grand Rapids, MI: Eerdmans, 2004.

Stanley, Brian (ed.). *The World Missionary Conference, Edinburgh 1910.* Grand Rapids, MI: Eerdmans, 2009.

Stine, Philip (ed.). *Bible Translation and the Spread of the Church: The Last Two Hundred Years.* Leiden: E. J. Brill, 1990.

Stocking, George. *Victorian Anthropology.* New York: Free Press, 1987.

Strong, Rowan. *Anglicanism and the British Empire, c. 1700–1850.* Oxford: Oxford University Press, 2007.

Strong, Rowan. *Victorian Christianity and Emigrant Voyages to British Colonies, c. 1840–c. 1914.* Oxford: Oxford University Press, 2017.

Strong, Rowan (ed.). *The Oxford History of Anglicanism, Volume III: Partisan Anglicanism and its Global Expansion, 1829–c.1914.* Oxford: Oxford University Press, 2017.

Sugirtharajah, R. S. *The Bible and Empire: Postcolonial Explorations.* Cambridge: Cambridge University Press, 2005.

Sugirtharajah, R. S. *Troublesome Texts: The Bible in Colonial and Contemporary Culture.* Sheffield: Sheffield Phoenix Press, 2008.

Tadmor, Naomi. *The Social Universe of the English Bible.* Cambridge: Cambridge University Press, 2010.

Todorov, Tzvetan. *On Human Diversity: Nationalism, Racism, and Exoticism in French Thought,* trans. Catherine Porter. Cambridge, MA: Harvard University Press, 1993.

Turner, James. *Philology: The Forgotten Origins of the Modern Humanities.* Princeton, NJ: Princeton University Press, 2014.

Wheeler, Michael. *The Old Enemies: Catholic and Protestant in Nineteenth-Century English Culture.* Cambridge: Cambridge University Press, 2009.

Whitford, David Mark. *The Curse of Ham in the Early Modern Era.* Farnham: Ashgate, 2009.

Wimbush, Vincent. *White Men's Magic: Scripturalization as Slavery.* New York: Oxford University Press, 2012.

Young, Robert J. C. *Colonial Desire: Hybridity in Theory, Culture and Race.* New York: Routledge, 1995.

Young, Robert J. C. *The Idea of English Ethnicity.* Oxford: Blackwell, 2008.

Zwartjes, Otto and Even Hovdhaugen (eds). *Missionary Linguistics.* Amsterdam: John Benjamins, 2004.

INDEX

Aborigines 11, 16, 19, 55–69, 99, 167, 176, 210
Abraham 36, 89, 154, 155, 206
Acts of the Apostles 35, 55, 68, 80, 196, 198
Adam 1, 2, 14, 15, 152, 198, 201, 205–8, 214
  pre-Adamites 14, 104, 200, 205–8
Africa 2, 9, 10, 13, 14, 37, 47, 61, 65, 67, 82, 91, 97, 157, 187, 189–90, 198–200, 209
  see also Egypt; Sudan
  North Africa 111–24
  Southern Africa 8, 11, 56, 58, 104, 167–82, 212
  West Africa 97
African Americans 15–16, 31, 186–202
Afrikaner 104, 173
  see also Boers
Aldred, Ebenezer 78
Alexander I (Tsar) 130–2
Alexander II (Tsar) 5, 132–3, 135–6, 144, 146
Alexander the Great 77
Alexander, Michael Solomon 79
Algeria 121–4
Ali, Abdullah Yusuf 113
Allenby, Edmund 83
Allen, J. H. 91, 99, 102, 104
America see Canada, United States, South America
American Board of Commissioners for Foreign Missions 4, 7
American Civil War 46, 49, 199
American Revolution 8, 31, 115
Amfiteatrov, Fyodor Georgievich 133, 135, 147
Anderson, Benedict 2, 3, 123
Anglicans 5, 11, 16, 39, 45, 46, 74, 79, 82, 92, 114, 118, 120

Anglo-Asante War 97
Anglo-Saxons 15, 17, 18, 19, 63, 81, 89–91, 93, 94, 98, 104, 157, 162, 191, 210–11
anthropology 10, 15, 16, 57, 61, 63, 64, 66–7, 159, 192, 206, 210
Anthropological Society 58
anti-colonial 12, 13, 112, 169
anti-Semitism 17–18, 93, 97, 137, 141–6, 162–3
  see also racism
Anti-Slavery Society 46–7
apartheid 104
  see also racism, segregation
apocalypse 44, 74, 79
  see also millennium; Revelation
Arabic (language) 12, 13, 19, 67, 111–24, 134, 139, 212–13
  Judaeo-Arabic 121, 123
Arakcheev, Aleksei 132
archaeology 3, 6, 13, 16, 81–2, 84, 88, 89, 94, 101–2, 196, 206, 210
Ark, Noah's 68, 200, 214
Ark of the Covenant 101–2
Armageddon 74, 78
Arnold, Matthew 82–3, 84
Arnold, Thomas 74
Aryan 16–17, 56–61, 66–8, 151–63, 206, 210
  see also Indo-European
Asir, Yusuf al- 117
Assyria 16, 65, 206
  see also Syria
Atlantic Ocean 3, 4, 8, 56, 77, 90
  Atlantic World 3, 4, 56
  transatlantic 99, 119
Austin, W. S. 39, 45, 47
Australasia 16, 62, 91
  see also Oceania

[222]

INDEX

Australasian Society for the Advancement of Science (AAAS) 62
Australia 11, 16, 19, 55–69, 99, 210

Babel 68, 189–91, 193–9, 201, 212
Babylon 1, 19, 55–69, 78, 82, 84, 157, 206
Ballantyne, James 10
Bannister, John 81
Bantu 160
Baptists 10, 31, 33, 36, 114, 190, 197–8, 208
Baptist Missionary Society 4, 64
Barbados 42, 44, 48
Basu, Ramram 10
Bates, Daisy 61
Belarus 135
Belgium 207
Bell, L. Nelson 195, 201
Bethel Chapel (Demerara) 29–39, 44, 47
Bhabha, Homi 2
Bhagavad Gita 12
Bible Societies 5, 7, 13
   American Bible Society 13, 111–12, 114–20
   British and Foreign Bible Society 5–8, 13, 41, 46, 79, 111–24, 130–1, 140, 212–13
   German Bible Society 5
   Prussian Bible Society 5
   Russian Bible Society 129–32, 136
Biblical scholarship and criticism 3, 6, 11, 16, 17, 67, 74, 77, 81–4, 95, 146
Bicheno, James 78
Bickersteth, Edward 78, 79
Bird, Edward Wheler 98
Bleek, William 56, 58
blood libel 141–6
   see also anti-Semitism
Bochart, Samuel 77, 95
Boers 104, 167, 174–6, 178
   see also Afrikaner
Bogue, David 33, 44
Bogue, Jane 33
Book of Common Prayer 76
Bopp, Franz 56–7

Bourke, Richard 177
Brexit 104
Briscoe, Gustavus Villiers 102
Britain 3–8, 10–13, 18–19, 29–33, 43–9, 56, 63, 65, 73–84, 88–105, 111–24, 130–1, 140, 167–8, 170, 174, 182, 208, 209–11, 212–13
   see also Anglo-Saxons; Ireland; Scotland; Wales
Brothers, Richard 93, 97
Brougham, Henry 46–7
Browne, Archibald 43, 45, 46, 49
Brown v. Board of Education 191–2
Brutus of Troy 89
Buddhism 8
Buddicom, Robert 46
Bunyan, John 22n46, 113
Bustani, Butrus al- 117, 122
Buxton, Thomas Fowell 29, 34, 45, 167, 177

Cain 15, 192
Calvinism 4, 173
Caldwell, Robert 57, 58
Canaan 1, 8, 36, 39, 41, 43, 44, 65, 98–100, 105, 190, 211
Canada 62, 115
Canning, George 34
Cape Colony 56, 167–82, 209
Carey, William 10–11, 64, 65
Caribbean 3, 4, 29–49
   see also Demerara; Jamaica; Surinam
Carroll, Charles 208
catechism 37, 41, 175
Catholicism 4, 5, 7, 12, 78, 81, 90, 92, 94–6, 98–9, 116, 117, 119, 121, 132, 153, 207, 211, 212
Caucasian 93, 190
Celts 15, 18, 62, 63, 90, 94–6, 98–102, 156, 157, 159, 211
Chamberlain, Walter 73–5, 77, 84
Champollion, Jean-François 206
China 2, 4, 14
Church Missionary Society 4, 118, 121
Civil War, American 46, 49, 199
Civil War, English 44
Clarke, Adam 78

[223]

INDEX

Clough, Arthur Hugh 83
Cold War 186
Colenso, William 67, 74
Colossians (Paul's epistle) 115
communism 186, 189, 191
Congregationalism 3, 33, 40, 44
Congress of Vienna 132
Constantine the Great 142
Conybeare, W. J. 74
Cook, James 4, 56, 65, 66
Cook, Thomas 116
Cooper, Anthony Ashley 79
Coptic 67, 116, 121
Corinthians (Paul's epistles) 174
Creuzer, Friedrich 154–5
Cromwell, Oliver 44, 47
Cropper, James 46
Crouch, B. W. 195–6, 200
Cuninghame, William 79
Cush 60, 61, 206

Dake, Finis Jennings 198–9
Dalcho, Frederick 199
Dal', Vladimir Ivanovich 142
Daniel, Carey 197–8
Daniel (prophet) 74–5
Darwin, Charles 14, 16, 63, 67, 117
David (biblical king) 43, 44, 89, 93, 97, 101
decolonisation 122
Defoe, Daniel 76, 117
Deism 153
Devil 34, 152
  see also Satan
De Wette, W. M. L 81
Demerara 19, 29–49, 209
Dilke, Charles 18, 91
Dissenters see nonconformists
Douglass, Frederick 15
Dravidians 55–61, 63, 68, 160, 210
Drozdov, Mikhaylovich 132–3, 135
Duff, the (ship) 66
Duperron, Anquetil 154
Durnovo, N. S. 142–3
Dutch 7, 114, 117, 167, 170, 172, 173, 175, 177

Eden 16
Edward I (England) 88–9

Egypt 1, 8, 14, 15, 30, 36, 38, 39, 41, 43, 44, 48, 60–2, 78, 88, 94, 97, 100, 104, 112, 114, 116, 118, 120–1, 124, 157, 206, 209, 210, 213
Eliot, George 83
Elliott, Edward Bishop 74, 79
Enlightenment 2, 5, 64, 66, 90, 95, 151, 161, 210
  Jewish 136–41
Enoch 152
Eochaid see Ollom Fotla
Ephesians (Paul's epistle) 35, 36, 37
evangelicalism 4, 5–7, 11, 32, 33, 44, 46, 49, 74, 75, 78–81, 83, 92, 98, 104, 112, 115, 116, 121, 124, 169, 177, 211
evangelism see Gospels, missionaries
Eve 1, 214
evolution 14, 63–4, 67, 117, 207
  see also Darwin, Charles
Exhibitions 6, 11, 55
Exodus 8, 12, 15, 18, 31–2, 35, 38–9, 40–2, 44, 48, 104, 213
Ezekiel 47, 73, 74, 78
Ezell, Humphrey K. 190

Faber, G. S. 78
Fanon, Frantz 3
Farrukh, 'Umar 123
Fedotov, Georgii 134
Fenians 98, 99, 100
Fiji 12, 61, 67, 212
Finland 131
First Nations see Native Americans
Fison, Lorimer 61, 63
flood (Genesis) 15, 68, 189, 190, 192–3, 195, 196–201, 206
Florovsky, Georges 134
Flow, J. E. 196
France 5, 10, 17, 18, 57, 73, 77, 78, 93, 95, 112, 116
  French language 6, 123
Francis I (Austria) 5
Fraser, John 11, 16, 55–69, 210
Frazer, J.G. 16
Frederick II (the Great) 153
Frederick William III (Prussia) 5

INDEX

French Revolution 77, 93
Fort William College 10
Frere, James Hatley 78
Freud, Sigmund 16

Gabelentz, Hans Conon von der 57
Gairdner, W. H. T. 118–19
Gandhi, M.K. 12
Gaon, Saadia 139
Geldner, Karl Friedrich 160
Gellner, Ernest 2
genetics 213–14
Genesis (biblical book) 1, 11, 14–15, 31, 35, 36, 37, 45, 59–60, 65, 88–9, 111, 153, 188–201, 205–7, 211–12, 214
Germany 5, 7, 13, 18, 57, 81, 114, 137, 138, 142, 146, 156–7, 159, 161, 210
  German language 6, 139, 144, 155
  missionaries 5, 114, 116
Giers, Aleksander Karlovich 143–4
Gillespie, G. T. 191–5, 197, 199
Gladstone, Jack 30, 35, 39–44, 47–9
Gladstone, John 30, 46, 47
Gladstone, William Ewart 98
Glover, John Hawley 97
Glover, Frederick 96–8
Gog and Magog 74, 152
Gonne, Maud 101–2
Gordon, Iona 140, 152
Görres, Joseph 154–5
Gospels 10, 15, 36, 37, 43, 46, 167, 171, 174, 176, 179, 209
  John 35, 111, 114–15, 174
  Luke 36, 56, 121
  Mark 117
  Matthew 35, 38, 173, 181
Gothic 59, 94
Great Exhibition 6
Greece 1, 17, 94, 82, 94, 95, 115, 152, 156, 157, 159, 161, 210
  Greek (language) 42, 59, 113, 117, 131, 133, 151
Grey, George 56, 58
Griffith, Arthur 101
Guyana *see* Demerara

Haggard, H. Rider 83
Ham 15, 16, 37, 45, 58, 60–1, 65–7, 91, 190–4, 198–201, 205, 206, 210, 212
Hamilton, John 38, 40
Hanan, Denis 101
Hanoverians 31, 97
Hankey, William 33, 47
Hardy, Thomas 83
Haskalah 136–41
Haug, Émile 206
Hebrew 59, 66, 67, 78, 79, 81, 82, 113, 117, 121, 131, 134, 138–41, 143, 146, 158
Hegel, G. F. H. 162
Henry VIII 113
Herder, Johann Gottfried 153–5
Heyrick, Elizabeth 48
Hinduism 8, 10, 11, 12, 19, 57, 151–63
Hine, Edward 97–9, 102
Hobsbawm, Eric 2
Hobson, J. A. 2
Holgate, Jerome 199
Holy Alliance 5–6
Holy Land 16
  see also Canaan; Israel; Palestine
Holy Synod (Russia) 129–36, 138–40
Horne, George 77
Horsley, Samuel 78
Horton, Wilmot 47
House of Commons (UK) 44, 46, 167, 177
Humboldt, Wilhelm von 57
Hyde, Douglas 102
hymns 32, 41, 43, 91, 176, 177

India 2, 4, 7, 10, 12, 55, 57–62, 67, 68, 81, 82, 98, 112, 151–63, 210, 212
  Indian Mutiny (1857) 11
  Indian Ocean 170, 206
Indo-European 16–17, 57, 151, 155, 157, 206, 210
  see also Aryan
Inuit 117
Iran *see* Persia
Ireland 11, 63, 88–105, 121, 211, 212
Isaiah 73–4, 77–9, 82–4

[225]

INDEX

Isaac 89, 91, 94
Islam 10, 19, 65, 78, 113–14, 116–24, 130, 134, 136
Israel 1, 9, 16, 19, 30, 31, 32, 40–5, 48, 76–8, 81–2, 90, 93–4, 97–101, 123, 154, 209
  British Israel 18, 88–105, 208, 210–11
  Lost tribes of 12, 64–5, 66–8, 73–4, 81, 89, 93, 95, 97, 210, 211, 212
  'New Israel' 5, 76
Italy 95, 157, 210

Jacob 65, 88–9, 95
Japheth 17, 62, 91, 190, 192, 198, 205, 206, 210
Jamaica 31, 33
James, John Angell 33
Jeremiads 19, 74
Jeremiah 74, 88–90, 96–8, 100–5
Jerusalem 1, 34, 47, 79, 82, 83, 84, 89, 97
Jim Crow laws 188, 189
John the Baptist 36
Jonah 77
Jones, Mary 111
Jones, William 206
Joshua (biblical book) 3, 8, 31–2, 35, 41–3
Judaism 7, 10, 12, 18, 30, 43–4, 64, 65, 77–8, 79, 81, 93–4, 97, 100–2, 116, 120–4, 152–5, 157–9, 162–3, 209
  Jewish Enlightenment 136–41
  in Russia 129–30, 134, 136–46
  see also Hebrew
Judges (biblical book) 35

Kaggia, Bildad 12
Kant, Immanuel 157
Keith, Alexander 79
Kett, Henry 78
Khalidi, Mustafa 123
Khoesan 58, 167–82, 209
Khvol'son, Daniil Avraamovich 137, 139–46
King James Bible 8, 41–2, 77, 96
Kings (biblical book) 35, 77

Kinney, Kenneth R. 198–9
Kipling, Rudyard 18, 84, 91
Knibb, William 33
Knox, Robert 14–15, 18
Kokovtsev, Pavel Konstantinovich 146
Koran 111, 113–4, 117, 118, 120, 122, 124, 134
Kostomarov, N. I. 145
Kush 60, 61, 206

Lacey, Harry 201
Lancaster, Joseph 131
Lebanon 117
Lee, Samuel 81
Lepsius, Karl Richard 206
Lesson, A. B. 57
Levanda, Lev 140
Levison, Vasilii 141, 143–5
Lewis, George Cornewall 82
liberation 2, 11, 12, 15–16, 47, 144, 209, 213
Links, Jan 174–5
Links, Jacob 174–5
Lithuanian 59
Liutostanskii, Ippolit 145
Livingstone, David (missionary) 175
London 4, 5, 11, 46, 58, 93, 111, 117, 118, 119, 120, 122, 167, 177
London Missionary Society (LMS) 4, 30, 32–3, 36, 38, 39, 40, 45, 47, 66, 167, 168, 171–2, 175, 177, 178–80
Louis XVI 77
Lutheranism 4, 5, 15, 79, 142
Luther Bible 8

Macaulay, Zachary 46
Macaulay, Thomas Babington 25n105, 47
MacDonald, Daniel 63, 64, 66
MacMurray, Carl W. 197
Maghreb 112, 116, 123
Malay 59, 61, 63, 66
Malta 7
Mandel'shtam, Leon 138–40
Mant, Richard 80
Maori 65–7, 99, 212

[226]

INDEX

Maronite 116, 117
Marx, Karl 162
Maslov, Mikhail 141
Masoretic text 131
Mathew, John 63, 64
Mau Mau 12
Mediterranean 18, 73, 81, 94, 116
Melanesia 59, 61, 66
Melville, Herman 77
Mendelssohn, Moses 137, 139
Mesopotamia 68, 157, 210
Methodism 8, 14, 36, 42, 44, 78, 91, 104, 114, 120, 122, 190, 207
    see also Wesleyan
Meyer, A. B. 57
Middle East 2, 7, 10, 73, 78, 82, 112, 115–20
Milesians 88, 90, 94–5, 101
millenarianism 4, 5, 104, 180
millennium 67, 74–5
    see also apocalypse; millenarianism Revelation
Minton, Samuel 75
missionaries 2, 3–13, 16, 19, 30–45, 78, 80, 81, 100–1, 105, 210
    in Demerara (Guyana) 29–49
    in Australasia 56–69
    in the Arab World 111–24
    in Cape Colony (South Africa) 167–82, 209
    in Korea 196
    missionary societies 4, 30, 32–3, 40, 64, 66, 167
        see also individual entries
    World Missionary Conference 118
modernity 1, 2, 6, 17, 138
Moffat, Robert 175
Mohawk 111, 114–15
monotheism 95, 153–4, 155, 158, 161–2
Moore, George 102
Moravians 171–3, 175
Mormonism 8, 15
Morocco 120, 121
Morris, Alfred 100–1
Moses 8, 32, 41, 42, 48, 88, 167, 206
Müller, Friedrich Max 57, 58, 68, 81, 151, 155–63, 206, 210
Müller, Wilhelm 161

Murray, John (colonial governor) 29, 34

Napoleon III 73
Napoleon Bonaparte 78, 93, 130, 132
nationalism 1–3, 5, 17, 19, 31, 88, 90, 129, 137, 153, 163, 197, 198, 208–9, 211
    Arab 112, 123–4, 212–13
    Irish 101–2
    Jewish 137, 141
        see also Zionism
    Khoesan 167–82
    Ukraine 134, 146–7, 213
Native Americans 4, 65, 99, 115, 116–17, 157
    Mohawk 111, 114–15
Nazareth 36
Nazaretha Church 8
Nazism 17
Nebuchadnezzar 77, 89
Nelson, Horatio 78
New South Wales 55, 60–3
Newton, John 76
New York 111, 115, 118, 119, 139
New Zealand 25n105, 56, 65–8, 212
Nicholas I (Tsar) 131, 132, 143, 144
Nimrod 195, 197–8, 199–201, 206
Nineveh 19, 84, 92
Noah 2, 15, 65–8, 189–202, 205, 207, 210, 211, 212, 214
    see also Ham; Japeth; Shem
nonconformists 11, 33, 36, 38, 168–9, 173, 182, 209
    see also individual denominations
Norov, Avraam Sergeevich 144
Norton, John 114–15
Numbers (biblical book) 99

Oceania 56
    see also Australasia
O'Connor, Feargus 96
O'Connor, Roger 96
O'Conor, Charles 95–6
Oerson, Cubedo 178
O'Halloran, Sylvester 95–6
Ollivant, Alfred 80
Ollom Fotla 89–90, 95–8, 100–1

[227]

INDEX

Orientalism 17, 94, 137, 140, 146, 151
Orthodox Christianity
  Greek 7, 15, 65, 67, 116
  Russian 5, 7, 9, 129–47, 213
  Ukrainian 134–5, 146–7
Ottoman Empire 7, 73, 79, 112

Pacific 16, 60–9, 98, 212
Palestine 11, 89, 93, 116, 157, 210
  see also Israel, Holy Land
Palmer, Benjamin M. 194–6, 200
Papua New Guinea 56, 59, 63, 64
Parham, Charles Fox 104
Parliament 29, 32, 46, 47
  see also House of Commons
Paul (apostle) 35, 81, 196
  epistles 35, 36, 37, 42, 44, 45, 115, 174
Pavskii, Gerasim 141, 143–6
Payne, Buckner H. 200
Peel, Robert 79
Pentateuch 35, 74, 136, 138–9, 140, 206
Pentecostalism 6, 102, 104, 198
Persia 5, 61, 94, 120, 154, 156–7, 210
  Persian Gulf 62, 206
Peter (epistles) 35, 36, 37, 38, 45, 181
Pharaoh 8, 32, 38, 41, 43, 48, 88, 97, 104
Philip, John 177, 178
Philippines 12
philology 3, 13, 16–17, 55–7, 60, 63, 67, 73, 81, 82, 90, 94–7, 142, 151, 154, 160, 206, 210
Phoenicians 81, 82, 90, 94–6, 99, 206
Pickthall, Marmaduke (Muhammad) 113
Pischel, Richard 160
Pius VI 78
Plato 157
polygenesis 14, 15, 104, 210
Polynesia 59, 61, 62, 63, 66
Polynesian Society 61, 62
Polytheism 95, 153–4, 161, 162, 163
postcolonial 3, 11, 12, 13, 64, 112, 123

Presbyterianism 60, 63, 64, 66, 114, 118, 186–7, 188, 191, 194, 195–7, 200
  Independent Presbyterian Church (Tennessee) 186–7, 195
Priest, Josiah 199
Prins, Esau 178–9
Promised Land see Canaan
prophecy 15, 18, 19, 31, 34, 36, 46, 73–84, 88–94, 96, 97, 100–4, 136, 155, 156, 180, 189, 190, 193, 211
proselytise see Missionaries
Protestantism 1, 4–9, 11, 31, 56, 73–84, 89, 92, 98, 100, 104, 111–22, 167–73, 176, 182, 192, 197, 212
  see also Anglicans; Lutheranism; nonconformists; *individual denominations*
Psalms 31, 35, 43, 77, 176
Pusey, E. B. 81
Putin, Vladimir 147

Quakers 48, 131
Quamina 30, 32, 35, 38–41, 43, 49
Qur'an 111, 113–14, 117, 118, 120, 122, 124, 134

race science 1, 14–18, 90–1, 93, 159, 208, 210
racism 4, 13–19, 64, 93, 99, 169, 186–202, 208
  segregation 19, 104, 186–202, 212
  see also anti-Semitism; apartheid; white supremacy
Ramsey, Everett 208
Rawlinson, George 206
Rawlinson, Henry 206
Read, James 167, 180–1
Reformed Church of America 121
Renan, Ernest 17
Revelation 34, 36, 74, 78, 79
Risley, Herbert Hope 159
Ritter, Karl 155
Roehl, Karl 13
Roman Catholicism see Catholicism

[228]

INDEX

Roman Empire 82, 84, 94, 157, 159
Romans (Paul's epistle) 36, 37, 42, 44, 45
Romanticism 151, 153–5, 160–2
Rome 78, 84, 94
Rousseau, Jean-Jacques 160
Royal Society of Antiquaries of Ireland 101
Royal Society of New South Wales 61, 62, 63
Ruskin, John 76
Russia 5, 7, 9, 12, 19, 73, 129–47, 209, 213
Ruth 35

Said, Edward 17
Samuel 35
San *see* Khoesan
Sandell, J.W. 200–1
Sanskrit 10, 16, 57, 59, 66, 67, 151, 155, 157–8, 162
   see also Vedas
Saratov Affair 141–6
   see also blood libel
Satan 189
   see also Devil
Saul 44
Sayce, Archibald 16
Schmidt, Georg 172
scientific racism *see* race science
Scotland 43, 45, 60, 74, 88–9, 114
Scythian 57–8, 96, 115
Seeley, J. R. 18, 91
Semitic languages 17, 57, 58, 59, 61, 95, 158, 160, 210
   see also Arabic; Hebrew; Judaism
Septuagint 133
Serfdom 141, 172
Shaftesbury (7th Earl) 79
Sharpe, Sam 31
Shem 65, 91, 93, 190, 192, 198
   see also Judaism
Sherstobitov, Feofan 141
Shinar 196, 198, 199, 206
Shteinberg, Yehoshua 140
Sidonskii, Fedor 143
Simpson, J. David 196

slavery 3, 4, 5, 8, 13, 15–16, 29–49, 76, 113, 159, 168, 170–1, 172, 174, 175, 177, 178, 187–90, 193–4, 199–201, 209, 212
   abolition 3, 5, 15, 29, 32, 33, 34, 36, 42, 44–9, 76, 189, 209
   emancipation 16, 29, 33, 48–9, 76, 211
   pro-slavery arguments 3, 44–6, 49, 188–9, 199, 212
Slavonic 9, 130–5, 146–7
Slonimskii, D. 140
Smith, Eli 117
Smit, Hendrick 174–5
Smith, George 206
Smith, John (missionary) 3, 29–49
Smith, Joseph 15
Smith, Morton H. 194–6, 199, 200
Smith, Percy 122
Smith, Sidney 78
Smith, Sydney 46
Smith, William 82, 84
Smyth, Thomas 199
Solomon 77, 81, 82, 83, 88
South America 4, 11, 29–49, 116–17, 124
Spanish Empire 4, 12, 76
Spanish (language) 6, 67
Spain 4, 6, 77, 82, 89, 94, 101
Spencer, Walter Baldwin 63
Spengler, Oswald 162
Stanley, A. P. 88–9
Stephen, James 48
St Lucia 39, 49
Stoffels, Andries 167–8, 170, 176, 179
Strabo 77
Sudan 112, 120, 121, 123, 213
Suez Canal 116
Sumner, C. R. 80
Surinam 113
Swahili 13
Sweden 114, 116, 121
Syria 79, 115, 116, 117, 120, 206
   see also Assyria

Table of Nations 37, 189, 191, 211
Talboys, Thomas 36–7
Talmage, J. V. N. 196–7

[229]

INDEX

Talmud 137, 138
Tamil 57, 62, 82, 112
Tarshish 19, 73, 77–84, 211, 212
Taylor, Richard 66
Tennent, James Edward 82
Teuton 18, 155, 157, 161
  see also Germany
Thomason, James 10
Threlkeld, Lancelot 55, 56, 59, 62–3
Timothy (Paul's epistles) 42
Torah see Pentateuch
Totten, Charles 98, 102
translation 3, 4, 7–13, 15, 19, 31, 55, 83, 209, 213
  Arabic Bibles 111–24
  Russian Bibles 129–47, 209, 213
Trump, Donald 104
Tunisia 121, 123, 124
Turanian 57–8, 61, 157, 160
Twisleton, Edward 82
Tylor, Edward Burnett 66
Tyndale, William 113
Tyonenhokarawen 114
Tyre 19, 76–7, 80, 83, 84, 92

Ukraine 129, 135, 146–7, 213
Ulbricht, Cobus 179
Unitarian 78
United States 6, 8, 13, 15–16, 19, 31, 45, 49, 61, 65, 84, 91–2, 98–9, 102–4, 111–22, 124, 157, 186–202, 205–8, 212
universalism 4, 9, 10, 14, 83, 153, 155, 157, 162, 209
Uvarov, Sergei 138

van der Kemp, Johannes 167, 175–6, 180, 181
Van Dyck, Cornelius 117–22
van Rooyen, Arie 181

Vedas 16, 17, 61, 151–63
  Rig Veda 155–6, 158, 160, 162
  Upanishads 154
Velishkoe Affair 142, 144
  see also blood libel
vernacular 3, 7–8, 119–22, 124, 176, 212
Victoria (Queen) 11, 18, 84, 181
Voltaire 151–3, 162

Wales 111
Watts, Isaac 37, 41
Wedgwood, Ralph 78
Wellhausen, Julius 81
Wesleyan 61, 63
Wesley, Charles 43
Wesley, John 43
West Indies see Caribbean
Whewell, William 80
White, Andrew Dickson 205, 207
white supremacy 2, 15, 104, 207–8, 211
Wilberforce, William 33, 46–7, 48–9
William III (England) 76
Wilson, John 93–4, 97
Winchell, Alexander 14, 205–11
Windham, Festus F. 190–1, 197
World Columbian Exposition 11, 55
World Council of Churches 118
Wray, John 33, 36, 44

Xhosa 113, 171, 175, 178, 180

Yanukovych, Viktor 147
Yaziji, Nasif al- 117
Yeats, W. B. 102
Young, Brigham 15

Zedekiah 81, 89, 90, 97, 98
Zionism 79, 138
  see also nationalism, Jewish
Zwemer, Samuel 114, 121–2

EU authorised representative for GPSR:
Easy Access System Europe, Mustamäe tee 50,
10621 Tallinn, Estonia
gpsr.requests@easproject.com

www.ingramcontent.com/pod-product-compliance
Lightning Source LLC
Chambersburg PA
CBHW071408300426
44114CB00016B/2223